MW00888537

The Complete Air Fryer Cookbook for Beginners

A Comprehensive Guide to 2000+ Days of Easy and Flavorful Recipes to Delight Your Taste Buds, Making Healthy Eating Fun and Simple

Charles Clayborn

Table of Contents

INTRODUCTION

Welcome to the wonderful world of air frying! Whether you're a seasoned home cook looking to expand your culinary repertoire or a kitchen novice eager to explore the endless possibilities of this innovative appliance, this cookbook is your gateway to delicious, healthy, and convenient meals. Air fryers have revolutionized the way we cook by offering a versatile, efficient, and healthier alternative to traditional frying methods. In this introduction, we'll delve into the benefits of air frying, the basics of how an air fryer works, and what you can expect from this cookbook.

The Magic and Benefits of Air Frying

Air fryers have taken the culinary world by storm, and it's easy to see why. These compact and powerful appliances use hot air circulation to cook food to crispy perfection with little to no oil. This means you can enjoy all your favorite fried foods—like French fries, chicken wings, and mozzarella sticks—without the guilt associated with traditional deep frying.

One of the most significant advantages of air frying is the potential for healthier meals. Traditional frying methods require submerging food in hot oil, which not only adds a significant amount of fat and calories but can also produce harmful compounds when oils are heated to high temperatures. Air fryers, on the other hand, require only a fraction of the oil,

if any, resulting in dishes that are lower in fat and calories without compromising on taste and texture.

The appeal of air fryers extends beyond just health benefits. They are incredibly versatile, capable of cooking a wide range of dishes from appetizers and side dishes to main courses and even desserts. With an air fryer, you can bake, roast, grill, and of course, fry. This versatility makes it an indispensable tool in any kitchen.

Air fryers are designed for convenience. They heat up quickly and cook food faster than conventional ovens, making them ideal for busy weeknights when you need to get dinner on the table in a hurry. The compact size of an air fryer also means it takes up less space on your countertop and is easier to clean than traditional deep fryers or ovens.

How Air Fryers Work

To fully appreciate the magic of air frying, it's helpful to understand how these appliances work. Air fryers use a powerful fan to circulate hot air around the food at high speeds. This rapid circulation of hot air creates a crispy layer on the outside of the food while locking in moisture and flavor on the inside. The result is food that has the same deliciously crispy texture as fried food but with significantly less oil.

Most air fryers come with a basket or tray where the food is placed. This allows the hot air to circulate freely around the food, ensuring even cooking. Some models also come with additional accessories, such as baking pans, grilling racks, and skewers, which further enhance their versatility.

Exploring This Cookbook

This cookbook is designed to be your ultimate guide to air frying. Whether you're new to air frying or looking to expand your culinary skills, you'll find a wealth of recipes that cater to all tastes and skill levels. Here's what you can expect:

Diverse and Delicious Recipes

We've curated a collection of recipes that showcase the versatility of the air fryer. From classic comfort foods to innovative new dishes, there's something for everyone. You'll find recipes for every meal of the day, including breakfast, lunch, dinner, snacks, and desserts.

Each recipe in this cookbook comes with detailed, step-by-step instructions that are easy to follow. We understand that not everyone is a seasoned chef, so we've made sure to include tips and tricks to help you achieve perfect results every time.

For those who are health-conscious, we've included nutritional information for each recipe. This allows you to make informed choices about what you're eating and tailor your meals to meet your dietary needs.

In addition to recipes, this cookbook is packed with tips and tricks to help you get the most out of your air fryer. From cleaning and maintenance tips to advice on how to achieve the perfect level of crispiness, we've got you covered.

Conclusion: Experiment and Enjoy

Finally, we encourage you to experiment and have fun with your air fryer. Don't be afraid to try new things and make adjustments to suit your taste.

The beauty of air frying is its flexibility, so let your creativity shine in the kitchen.

Air frying represents a modern approach to cooking that combines convenience, health benefits, and delicious results. This cookbook is your companion on this culinary journey, offering a wealth of recipes and tips to help you make the most of your air fryer. Whether you're looking to prepare quick weeknight dinners, impress guests with gourmet dishes, or enjoy guilt-free versions of your favorite fried foods, this book has something for you. So, plug in your air fryer, gather your ingredients, and get ready to explore a whole new world of cooking. Happy air frying!

Chapter 1

Breakfasts

All-in-One Toast

Prep time: 10 minutes | Cook time: 10 minutes | Serves 1

- 1 strip bacon, diced
- 1 slice 1-inch thick bread
- 1 egg
- Salt and freshly ground black pepper, to taste
- ¼ cup grated Colby cheese

1. Preheat the air fryer to 400°F (204°C). 2. Air fry the bacon for 3 minutes, shaking the basket once or twice while it cooks. Remove the bacon to a paper towel lined plate and set aside. 3. Use a sharp paring knife to score a large circle in the middle of the slice of bread, cutting halfway through, but not all the way through to the cutting board. Press down on the circle in the center of the bread slice to create an indentation. 4. Transfer the slice of bread, hole side up, to the air fryer basket. Crack the egg into the center of the bread, and season with salt and pepper. 5. Adjust the air fryer temperature to 380°F (193°C) and air fry for 5 minutes. Sprinkle the grated cheese around the edges of the bread, leaving the center of the yolk uncovered, and top with the cooked bacon. Press the cheese and bacon into the bread lightly to help anchor it to the bread and prevent it from blowing around in the air fryer. 6. Air fry for one or two more minutes, just to melt the cheese and finish cooking the egg. Serve immediately.

Berry Muffins

Prep time: 15 minutes | Cook time: 12 to 17 minutes | Makes 8 muffins

- 1⅓ cups plus 1 tablespoon all-purpose flour, divided
- ¼ cup granulated sugar
- 2 tablespoons light brown sugar
- 2 teaspoons baking powder
- 2 eggs
- ⅔ cup whole milk
- ⅓ cup safflower oil
- 1 cup mixed fresh berries

1. In a medium bowl, stir together 1⅓ cups of flour, the granulated sugar, brown sugar, and baking powder until mixed well. 2. In a small bowl, whisk the eggs, milk, and oil until combined. Stir the egg mixture into the dry ingredients just until combined. 3. In another small bowl, toss the mixed berries with the remaining 1 tablespoon of flour until coated. Gently stir the berries into the batter. 4. Double up 16 foil muffin cups to make 8 cups. 5. Insert the crisper plate into the basket and the basket into the unit. Preheat the unit by selecting BAKE, setting the temperature to 315°F (157°C), and setting the time to 3 minutes. Select START/STOP to begin. 6. Once the unit is preheated, place 4 cups into the basket and fill each three-quarters full with the batter. 7. Select BAKE, set the temperature to 315°F (157°C), and set the time for 17 minutes. Select START/STOP to begin. 8. After about 12 minutes, check the muffins. If they spring back when lightly touched with your finger, they are done. If not, resume cooking. 9. When the cooking is done, transfer the muffins to a wire rack to cool. 10. Repeat steps 6,

7, and 8 with the remaining muffin cups and batter. 11. Let the muffins cool for 10 minutes before serving.

Savory Sweet Potato Hash

Prep time: 15 minutes | Cook time: 18 minutes | Serves 6

- 2 medium sweet potatoes, peeled and cut into 1-inch cubes
- ½ green bell pepper, diced
- ½ red onion, diced
- 4 ounces (113 g) baby bella mushrooms, diced
- 2 tablespoons olive oil
- 1 garlic clove, minced
- ½ teaspoon salt
- ½ teaspoon black pepper
- ½ tablespoon chopped fresh rosemary

1. Preheat the air fryer to 380°F (193°C). 2. In a large bowl, toss all ingredients together until the vegetables are well coated and seasonings distributed. 3. Pour the vegetables into the air fryer basket, making sure they are in a single even layer. (If using a smaller air fryer, you may need to do this in two batches.) 4. Roast for 9 minutes, then toss or flip the vegetables. Roast for 9 minutes more. 5. Transfer to a serving bowl or individual plates and enjoy.

Gold Avocado

Prep time: 5 minutes | Cook time: 6 minutes | Serves 4

- 2 large avocados, sliced
- ¼ teaspoon paprika
- Salt and ground black pepper, to taste
- ½ cup flour
- 2 eggs, beaten
- 1 cup bread crumbs

1. Preheat the air fryer to 400°F (204°C). 2. Sprinkle paprika, salt and pepper on the slices of avocado. 3. Lightly coat the avocados with flour. Dredge them in the eggs, before covering with bread crumbs. 4. Transfer to the air fryer and air fry for 6 minutes. 5. Serve warm.

Parmesan Sausage Egg Muffins

Prep time: 5 minutes | Cook time: 20 minutes | Serves 4

- 6 ounces (170 g) Italian sausage, sliced
- 6 eggs
- ⅛ cup heavy cream
- Salt and ground black pepper, to taste
- 3 ounces (85 g) Parmesan cheese, grated

1. Preheat the air fryer to 350°F (177°C). Grease a muffin pan. 2. Put the sliced sausage in the muffin pan. 3. Beat the eggs with the cream in a bowl and season with salt and pepper. 4. Pour half of the mixture over the sausages in the pan. 5. Sprinkle with cheese and the remaining egg mixture. 6. Bake in the preheated air fryer for 20 minutes or until set. 7. Serve immediately.

Canadian Bacon Muffin Sandwiches

Prep time: 5 minutes | Cook time: 8 minutes | Serves 4

- 4 English muffins, split
- 8 slices Canadian bacon
- 4 slices cheese
- Cooking spray

1. Preheat the air fryer to 370°F (188°C). 2. Make the sandwiches: Top each of 4 muffin halves with 2 slices of Canadian bacon, 1 slice of cheese, and finish with the remaining muffin half. 3. Put the sandwiches in the air fryer basket and spritz the tops with cooking spray. 4. Bake for 4 minutes. Flip the sandwiches and bake for another 4 minutes. 5. Divide the sandwiches among four plates and serve warm.

Fried Chicken Wings with Waffles

Prep time: 10 minutes | Cook time: 30 minutes | Serves 4

- 8 whole chicken wings
- 1 teaspoon garlic powder
- Chicken seasoning, for preparing the chicken
- Freshly ground black pepper, to taste
- ½ cup all-purpose flour
- Cooking oil spray
- 8 frozen waffles
- Pure maple syrup, for serving (optional)

1. In a medium bowl, combine the chicken and garlic powder and season with chicken seasoning and pepper. Toss to coat. 2. Transfer the chicken to a resealable plastic bag and add the flour. Seal the bag and shake it to coat the chicken thoroughly. 3. Insert the crisper plate into the basket and the basket into the unit. Preheat the unit by selecting AIR FRY, setting the temperature to 400°F (204°C), and setting the time to 3 minutes. Select START/STOP to begin. 4. Once the unit is preheated, spray the crisper plate with cooking oil. Using tongs, transfer the chicken from the bag to the basket. It is okay to stack the chicken wings on top of each other. Spray them with cooking oil. 5. Select AIR FRY, set the temperature to 400°F (204°C), and set the time to 20 minutes. Select START/STOP to begin. 6. After 5 minutes, remove the basket and shake the wings. Reinsert the basket to resume cooking. Remove and shake the basket every 5 minutes until the chicken is fully cooked. 7. When the cooking is complete, remove the cooked chicken from the basket; cover to keep warm. 8. Rinse the basket and crisper plate with warm water. Insert them back into the unit. 9. Select AIR FRY, set the temperature to 360°F (182°C), and set the time to 3 minutes. Select START/STOP to begin. 10. Once the unit is preheated, spray the crisper plate with cooking spray. Working in batches, place the frozen waffles into the basket. Do not stack them. Spray the waffles with cooking oil. 11. Select AIR FRY, set the temperature to 360°F (182°C), and set the time to 6 minutes. Select START/STOP to begin. 12. When the cooking is complete, repeat steps 10 and 11 with the remaining waffles. 13. Serve the waffles with the chicken and a touch of maple syrup, if desired.

Cheesy Cauliflower "Hash Browns"

Prep time: 30 minutes | Cook time: 24 minutes | Makes 6 hash browns

- 2 ounces (57 g) 100% cheese crisps
- 1 (12-ounce / 340-g) steamer bag cauliflower, cooked according to
- package instructions
- 1 large egg
- ½ cup shredded sharp Cheddar cheese
- ½ teaspoon salt

1. Let cooked cauliflower cool 10 minutes. 2. Place cheese crisps into food processor and pulse on low 30 seconds until crisps are finely ground. 3. Using a kitchen towel, wring out excess moisture from cauliflower and place into food processor. 4. Add egg to food processor and sprinkle with Cheddar and salt. Pulse five times until mixture is mostly smooth. 5. Cut two pieces of parchment to fit air fryer basket. Separate mixture into six even scoops and place three on each piece of ungreased parchment, keeping at least 2 inch of space between each scoop. Press each into a hash brown shape, about ¼ inch thick. 6. Place one batch on parchment into air fryer basket. Adjust the temperature to 375°F (191°C) and air fry for 12 minutes, turning hash browns halfway through cooking. Hash browns will be golden brown when done. Repeat with second batch. 7. Allow 5 minutes to cool. Serve warm.

Oat Bran Muffins

Prep time: 10 minutes | Cook time: 10 to 12 minutes per batch | Makes 8 muffins

- ⅔ cup oat bran
- ½ cup flour
- ¼ cup brown sugar
- 1 teaspoon baking powder
- ½ teaspoon baking soda
- ⅛ teaspoon salt
- ½ cup buttermilk
- 1 egg
- 2 tablespoons canola oil
- ½ cup chopped dates, raisins, or dried cranberries
- 24 paper muffin cups
- Cooking spray

1. Preheat the air fryer to 330°F (166°C). 2. In a large bowl, combine the oat bran, flour, brown sugar, baking powder, baking soda, and salt. 3. In a small bowl, beat together the buttermilk, egg, and oil. 4. Pour buttermilk mixture into bowl with dry ingredients and stir just until moistened. Do not beat. 5. Gently stir in dried fruit. 6. Use triple baking cups to help muffins hold shape during baking. Spray them with cooking spray, place 4 sets of cups in air fryer basket at a time, and fill each one ¾ full of batter. 7. Cook for 10 to 12 minutes, until top springs back when lightly touched and toothpick inserted in center comes out clean. 8. Repeat for remaining muffins.

Cheddar Eggs

Prep time: 5 minutes | Cook time: 15 minutes | Serves 2

- 4 large eggs
- 2 tablespoons unsalted butter, melted
- ½ cup shredded sharp Cheddar cheese

1. Crack eggs into a round baking dish and whisk. Place dish into the air fryer basket. 2. Adjust the temperature to 400ºF (204ºC) and set the timer for 10 minutes. 3. After 5 minutes, stir the eggs and add the butter and cheese. Let cook 3 more minutes and stir again. 4. Allow eggs to finish cooking an additional 2 minutes or remove if they are to your desired liking. 5. Use a fork to fluff. Serve warm.

Spinach and Bacon Roll-ups

Prep time: 5 minutes | Cook time: 8 to 9 minutes | Serves 4

- 4 flour tortillas (6- or 7-inch size)
- 4 slices Swiss cheese
- 1 cup baby spinach leaves
- 4 slices turkey bacon
- Special Equipment:
- 4 toothpicks, soak in water for at least 30 minutes

1. Preheat the air fryer to 390ºF (199ºC). 2. On a clean work surface, top each tortilla with one slice of cheese and ¼ cup of spinach, then tightly roll them up. 3. Wrap each tortilla with a strip of turkey bacon and secure with a toothpick. 4. Arrange the roll-ups in the air fryer basket, leaving space between each roll-up. 5. Air fry for 4 minutes. Flip the roll-ups with tongs and rearrange them for more even cooking. Air fry for another 4 to 5 minutes until the bacon is crisp. 6. Rest for 5 minutes and remove the toothpicks before serving.

Peppered Maple Bacon Knots

Prep time: 5 minutes | Cook time: 7 to 8 minutes | Serves 6

- 1 pound (454 g) maple smoked center-cut bacon
- ¼ cup maple syrup
- ¼ cup brown sugar
- Coarsely cracked black peppercorns, to taste

1. Preheat the air fryer to 390ºF (199ºC). 2. On a clean work surface, tie each bacon strip in a loose knot. 3. Stir together the maple syrup and brown sugar in a bowl. Generously brush this mixture over the bacon knots. 4. Working in batches, arrange the bacon knots in the air fryer basket. Sprinkle with the coarsely cracked black peppercorns. 5. Air fry for 5 minutes. Flip the bacon knots and continue cooking for 2 to 3 minutes more, or until the bacon is crisp. 6. Remove from the basket to a paper towel-lined plate. Repeat with the remaining bacon knots. 7. Let the bacon knots cool for a few minutes and serve warm.

Breakfast Sausage and Cauliflower

Prep time: 5 minutes | Cook time: 45 minutes | Serves 4

- 1 pound (454 g) sausage, cooked and crumbled
- 2 cups heavy whipping cream
- 1 head cauliflower, chopped
- 1 cup grated Cheddar cheese, plus more for topping
- 8 eggs, beaten
- Salt and ground black pepper, to taste

1. Preheat the air fryer to 350ºF (177ºC). 2. In a large bowl, mix the sausage, heavy whipping cream, chopped cauliflower, cheese and eggs. Sprinkle with salt and ground black pepper. 3. Pour the mixture into a greased casserole dish. Bake in the preheated air fryer for 45 minutes or until firm. 4. Top with more Cheddar cheese and serve.

Sausage Egg Cup

Prep time: 10 minutes | Cook time: 15 minutes | Serves 6

- 12 ounces (340 g) ground pork breakfast sausage
- 6 large eggs
- ½ teaspoon salt
- ¼ teaspoon ground black pepper
- ½ teaspoon crushed red pepper flakes

1. Place sausage in six 4-inch ramekins (about 2 ounces / 57 g per ramekin) greased with cooking oil. Press sausage down to cover bottom and about ½-inch up the sides of ramekins. Crack one egg into each ramekin and sprinkle evenly with salt, black pepper, and red pepper flakes. 2. Place ramekins into air fryer basket. Adjust the temperature to 350ºF (177ºC) and set the timer for 15 minutes. Egg cups will be done when sausage is fully cooked to at least 145ºF (63ºC) and the egg is firm. Serve warm.

Pita and Pepperoni Pizza

Prep time: 10 minutes | Cook time: 6 minutes | Serves 1

- 1 teaspoon olive oil
- 1 tablespoon pizza sauce
- 1 pita bread
- 6 pepperoni slices
- ¼ cup grated Mozzarella cheese
- ¼ teaspoon garlic powder
- ¼ teaspoon dried oregano

1. Preheat the air fryer to 350ºF (177ºC). Grease the air fryer basket with olive oil. 2. Spread the pizza sauce on top of the pita bread. Put the pepperoni slices over the sauce, followed by the Mozzarella cheese. 3. Season with garlic powder and oregano. 4. Put the pita pizza inside the air fryer and place a trivet on top. 5. Bake in the preheated air fryer for 6 minutes and serve.

Spinach and Swiss Frittata with Mushrooms

Prep time: 10 minutes | Cook time: 20 minutes | Serves 4

- Olive oil cooking spray
- 8 large eggs
- ½ teaspoon salt
- ½ teaspoon black pepper
- 1 garlic clove, minced
- 2 cups fresh baby spinach
- 4 ounces (113 g) baby bella
- mushrooms, sliced
- 1 shallot, diced
- ½ cup shredded Swiss cheese, divided
- Hot sauce, for serving (optional)

1. Preheat the air fryer to 360°F(182°C). Lightly coat the inside of a 6-inch round cake pan with olive oil cooking spray. 2. In a large bowl, beat the eggs, salt, pepper, and garlic for 1 to 2 minutes, or until well combined. 3. Fold in the spinach, mushrooms, shallot, and ¼ cup of the Swiss cheese. 4. Pour the egg mixture into the prepared cake pan, and sprinkle the remaining ¼ cup of Swiss over the top. 5. Place into the air fryer and bake for 18 to 20 minutes, or until the eggs are set in the center. 6. Remove from the air fryer and allow to cool for 5 minutes. Drizzle with hot sauce (if using) before serving.

Vegetable Frittata

Prep time: 10 minutes | Cook time: 19 minutes | Serves 1 to 2

- ½ red or green bell pepper, cut into ½-inch chunks
- 4 button mushrooms, sliced
- ½ cup diced zucchini
- ½ teaspoon chopped fresh oregano or thyme
- 1 teaspoon olive oil
- 3 eggs, beaten
- ½ cup grated Cheddar cheese
- Salt and freshly ground black pepper, to taste
- 1 teaspoon butter
- 1 teaspoon chopped fresh parsley

1. Preheat the air fryer to 400°F (204°C). 2. Toss the peppers, mushrooms, zucchini and oregano with the olive oil and air fry for 6 minutes, shaking the basket once or twice during the cooking process to redistribute the ingredients. 3. While the vegetables are cooking, beat the eggs well in a bowl, stir in the Cheddar cheese and season with salt and freshly ground black pepper. Add the air-fried vegetables to this bowl when they have finished cooking. 4. Place a cake pan into the air fryer basket with the butter using an aluminum sling to lower the pan into the basket. Air fry for 1 minute at 380ºF (193ºC) to melt the butter. Remove the cake pan and rotate the pan to distribute the butter and grease the pan. Pour the egg mixture into the cake pan and return the pan to the air fryer, using the aluminum sling. 5. Air fry at 380ºF (193ºC) for 12 minutes, or until the frittata has puffed up and is lightly browned. Let the frittata sit in the air fryer for 5 minutes to cool to an edible temperature and set up. Remove the cake pan from the air fryer, sprinkle with parsley and serve immediately.

Whole Wheat Blueberry Muffins

Prep time: 10 minutes | Cook time: 15 minutes | Serves 6

- Olive oil cooking spray
- ½ cup unsweetened applesauce
- ¼ cup raw honey
- ½ cup nonfat plain Greek yogurt
- 1 teaspoon vanilla extract
- 1 large egg
- 1½ cups plus 1 tablespoon whole wheat flour, divided
- ½ teaspoon baking soda
- ½ teaspoon baking powder
- ½ teaspoon salt
- ½ cup blueberries, fresh or frozen

1. Preheat the air fryer to 360°F(182°C). Lightly coat the inside of six silicone muffin cups or a six-cup muffin tin with olive oil cooking spray. 2. In a large bowl, combine the applesauce, honey, yogurt, vanilla, and egg and mix until smooth. 3. Sift in 1½ cups of the flour, the baking soda, baking powder, and salt into the wet mixture, then stir until just combined. 4. In a small bowl, toss the blueberries with the remaining 1 tablespoon flour, then fold the mixture into the muffin batter. 5. Divide the mixture evenly among the prepared muffin cups and place into the basket of the air fryer. Bake for 12 to 15 minutes, or until golden brown on top and a toothpick inserted into the middle of one of the muffins comes out clean. 6. Allow to cool for 5 minutes before serving.

Hearty Blueberry Oatmeal

Prep time: 10 minutes | Cook time: 25 minutes | Serves 6

- 1½ cups quick oats
- 1¼ teaspoons ground cinnamon, divided
- ½ teaspoon baking powder
- Pinch salt
- 1 cup unsweetened vanilla almond milk
- ¼ cup honey
- 1 teaspoon vanilla extract
- 1 egg, beaten
- 2 cups blueberries
- Olive oil
- 1½ teaspoons sugar, divided
- 6 tablespoons low-fat whipped topping (optional)

1. In a large bowl, mix together the oats, 1 teaspoon of cinnamon, baking powder, and salt. 2. In a medium bowl, whisk together the almond milk, honey, vanilla, and egg. 3. Pour the liquid ingredients into the oats mixture and stir to combine. Fold in the blueberries. 4. Lightly spray a baking pan with oil. 5. Add half the blueberry mixture to the pan. 6. Sprinkle ⅛ teaspoon of cinnamon and ½ teaspoon sugar over the top. 7. Cover the pan with aluminum foil and place gently in the air fryer basket. 8. Air fry at 360ºF (182ºC) for 20 minutes. Remove the foil and air fry for an additional 5 minutes. Transfer the mixture to a shallow bowl. 9. Repeat with the remaining blueberry mixture, ½ teaspoon of sugar, and ⅛ teaspoon of cinnamon. 10. To serve, spoon into bowls and top with whipped topping.

French Toast Sticks

Prep time: 10 minutes | Cook time: 9 minutes | Serves 4

- Oil, for spraying
- 6 large eggs
- 1⅓ cups milk
- 2 teaspoons vanilla extract
- 1 teaspoon ground
- cinnamon
- 8 slices bread, cut into thirds
- Syrup of choice, for serving

1. Preheat the air fryer to 370ºF (188ºC). Line the air fryer basket with parchment and spray lightly with oil. 2. In a shallow bowl, whisk the eggs, milk, vanilla, and cinnamon. 3. Dunk one piece of bread in the egg mixture, making sure to coat both sides. Work quickly so the bread doesn't get soggy. Immediately transfer the bread to the prepared basket. 4. Repeat with the remaining bread, making sure the pieces don't touch each other. You may need to work in batches, depending on the size of your air fryer. 5. Air fry for 5 minutes, flip, and cook for another 3 to 4 minutes, until browned and crispy. 6. Serve immediately with your favorite syrup.

Onion Omelet

Prep time: 10 minutes | Cook time: 12 minutes | Serves 2

- 3 eggs
- Salt and ground black pepper, to taste
- ½ teaspoons soy sauce
- 1 large onion, chopped
- 2 tablespoons grated Cheddar cheese
- Cooking spray

1. Preheat the air fryer to 355ºF (179ºC). 2. In a bowl, whisk together the eggs, salt, pepper, and soy sauce. 3. Spritz a small pan with cooking spray. Spread the chopped onion across the bottom of the pan, then transfer the pan to the air fryer. 4. Bake in the preheated air fryer for 6 minutes or until the onion is translucent. 5. Add the egg mixture on top of the onions to coat well. Add the cheese on top, then continue baking for another 6 minutes. 6. Allow to cool before serving.

Strawberry Toast

Prep time: 10 minutes | Cook time: 8 minutes | Makes 4 toasts

- 4 slices bread, ½-inch thick
- Butter-flavored cooking spray
- 1 cup sliced strawberries
- 1 teaspoon sugar

1. Spray one side of each bread slice with butter-flavored cooking spray. Lay slices sprayed side down. 2. Divide the strawberries among the bread slices. 3. Sprinkle evenly with the sugar and place in the air fryer basket in a single layer. 4. Air fry at 390ºF (199ºC) for 8 minutes. The bottom should look brown and crisp and the top should look glazed.

Egg in a Hole

Prep time: 5 minutes | Cook time: 5 minutes | Serves 1

- 1 slice bread
- 1 teaspoon butter, softened
- 1 egg
- Salt and pepper, to taste
- 1 tablespoon shredded Cheddar cheese
- 2 teaspoons diced ham

1. Preheat the air fryer to 330ºF (166ºC). Place a baking dish in the air fryer basket. 2. On a flat work surface, cut a hole in the center of the bread slice with a 2½-inch-diameter biscuit cutter. 3. Spread the butter evenly on each side of the bread slice and transfer to the baking dish. 4. Crack the egg into the hole and season as desired with salt and pepper. Scatter the shredded cheese and diced ham on top. 5. Bake in the preheated air fryer for 5 minutes until the bread is lightly browned and the egg is cooked to your preference. 6. Remove from the basket and serve hot.

Bourbon Vanilla French Toast

Prep time: 15 minutes | Cook time: 6 minutes | Serves 4

- 2 large eggs
- 2 tablespoons water
- ⅔ cup whole or 2% milk
- 1 tablespoon butter, melted
- 2 tablespoons bourbon
- 1 teaspoon vanilla extract
- 8 (1-inch-thick) French bread slices
- Cooking spray

1. Preheat the air fryer to 320ºF (160ºC). Line the air fryer basket with parchment paper and spray it with cooking spray. 2. Beat the eggs with the water in a shallow bowl until combined. Add the milk, melted butter, bourbon, and vanilla and stir to mix well. 3. Dredge 4 slices of bread in the batter, turning to coat both sides evenly. Transfer the bread slices onto the parchment paper. 4. Bake for 6 minutes until nicely browned. Flip the slices halfway through the cooking time. 5. Remove from the basket to a plate and repeat with the remaining 4 slices of bread. 6. Serve warm.

Oat and Chia Porridge

Prep time: 10 minutes | Cook time: 5 minutes | Serves 4

- 2 tablespoons peanut butter
- 4 tablespoons honey
- 1 tablespoon butter, melted
- 4 cups milk
- 2 cups oats
- 1 cup chia seeds

1. Preheat the air fryer to 390ºF (199ºC). 2. Put the peanut butter, honey, butter, and milk in a bowl and stir to mix. Add the oats and chia seeds and stir. 3. Transfer the mixture to a bowl and bake in the air fryer for 5 minutes. Give another stir before serving.

Breakfast Calzone

Prep time: 15 minutes | Cook time: 15 minutes | Serves 4

- 1½ cups shredded Mozzarella cheese
- ½ cup blanched finely ground almond flour
- 1 ounce (28 g) full-fat cream cheese
- 1 large whole egg
- 4 large eggs, scrambled
- ½ pound (227 g) cooked breakfast sausage, crumbled
- 8 tablespoons shredded mild Cheddar cheese

1. In a large microwave-safe bowl, add Mozzarella, almond flour, and cream cheese. Microwave for 1 minute. Stir until the mixture is smooth and forms a ball. Add the egg and stir until dough forms. 2. Place dough between two sheets of parchment and roll out to ¼-inch thickness. Cut the dough into four rectangles. 3. Mix scrambled eggs and cooked sausage together in a large bowl. Divide the mixture evenly among each piece of dough, placing it on the lower half of the rectangle. Sprinkle each with 2 tablespoons Cheddar. 4. Fold over the rectangle to cover the egg and meat mixture. Pinch, roll, or use a wet fork to close the edges completely. 5. Cut a piece of parchment to fit your air fryer basket and place the calzones onto the parchment. Place parchment into the air fryer basket. 6. Adjust the temperature to 380ºF (193ºC) and air fry for 15 minutes. 7. Flip the calzones halfway through the cooking time. When done, calzones should be golden in color. Serve immediately.

New York Strip Steaks with Eggs

Prep time: 8 minutes | Cook time: 14 minutes per batch | Serves 4

- Cooking oil spray
- 4 (4-ounce / 113-g) New York strip steaks
- 1 teaspoon granulated garlic, divided
- 1 teaspoon salt, divided
- 1 teaspoon freshly ground black pepper, divided
- 4 eggs
- ½ teaspoon paprika

1. Insert the crisper plate into the basket and the basket into the unit. Preheat the unit by selecting AIR FRY, setting the temperature to 360ºF (182ºC), and setting the time to 3 minutes. Select START/STOP to begin. 2. Once the unit is preheated, spray the crisper plate with cooking oil. Place 2 steaks into the basket; do not oil or season them at this time. 3. Select AIR FRY, set the temperature to 360ºF (182ºC), and set the time to 9 minutes. Select START/STOP to begin. 4. After 5 minutes, open the unit and flip the steaks. Sprinkle each with ¼ teaspoon of granulated garlic, ¼ teaspoon of salt, and ¼ teaspoon of pepper. Resume cooking until the steaks register at least 145ºF (63ºC) on a food thermometer. 5. When the cooking is complete, transfer the steaks to a plate and tent with aluminum foil to keep warm. Repeat steps 2, 3, and 4 with the remaining steaks. 6. Spray 4 ramekins with olive oil. Crack 1 egg into each ramekin. Sprinkle the eggs with the paprika and remaining ½ teaspoon each of salt and pepper. Working in batches, place 2 ramekins into the basket. 7. Select BAKE, set the temperature to 330ºF (166ºC), and set the time to 5 minutes. Select START/STOP to begin. 8. When the cooking is complete and the eggs are cooked to 160ºF (71ºC), remove the ramekins and repeat step 7 with the remaining 2 ramekins. 9. Serve the eggs with the steaks.

Blueberry Cobbler

Prep time: 5 minutes | Cook time: 15 minutes | Serves 4

- ⅓ cup whole-wheat pastry flour
- ¾ teaspoon baking powder
- Dash sea salt
- ½ cup 2% milk
- 2 tablespoons pure maple syrup
- ½ teaspoon vanilla extract
- Cooking oil spray
- ½ cup fresh blueberries
- ¼ cup granola

1. In a medium bowl, whisk the flour, baking powder, and salt. Add the milk, maple syrup, and vanilla and gently whisk, just until thoroughly combined. 2. Preheat the unit by selecting BAKE, setting the temperature to 350ºF (177ºC), and setting the time to 3 minutes. Select START/STOP to begin. 3. Spray a 6-by-2-inch round baking pan with cooking oil and pour the batter into the pan. Top evenly with the blueberries and granola. 4. Once the unit is preheated, place the pan into the basket. 5. Select BAKE, set the temperature to 350ºF (177ºC), and set the time to 15 minutes. Select START/STOP to begin. 6. When the cooking is complete, the cobbler should be nicely browned and a knife inserted into the middle should come out clean. Enjoy plain or topped with a little vanilla yogurt.

Coconut Brown Rice Porridge with Dates

Prep time: 10 minutes | Cook time: 23 minutes | Serves 1 to 2

- 1 cup canned coconut milk
- ½ cup cooked brown rice
- ¼ cup unsweetened shredded coconut
- ¼ cup packed dark brown sugar
- ½ teaspoon kosher salt
- ¼ teaspoon ground cardamom
- 4 large Medjool dates, pitted and roughly chopped
- Heavy cream, for serving (optional)

1. In a cake pan, stir together the coconut milk, rice, shredded coconut, brown sugar, salt, cardamom, and dates and place in the air fryer. Bake at 375ºF (191ºC) until reduced and thickened and browned on top, about 23 minutes, stirring halfway through. 2. Remove the pan from the air fryer and divide the porridge among bowls. Drizzle the porridge with cream, if you like, and serve hot.

Hearty Cheddar Biscuits

Prep time: 10 minutes | Cook time: 22 minutes | Makes 8 biscuits

- 2⅓ cups self-rising flour
- 2 tablespoons sugar
- ½ cup butter (1 stick), frozen for 15 minutes
- ½ cup grated Cheddar cheese, plus more to melt
- on top
- 1⅓ cups buttermilk
- 1 cup all-purpose flour, for shaping
- 1 tablespoon butter, melted

1. Line a buttered 7-inch metal cake pan with parchment paper or a silicone liner. 2. Combine the flour and sugar in a large mixing bowl. Grate the butter into the flour. Add the grated cheese and stir to coat the cheese and butter with flour. Then add the buttermilk and stir just until you can no longer see streaks of flour. The dough should be quite wet. 3. Spread the all-purpose (not self-rising) flour out on a small cookie sheet. With a spoon, scoop 8 evenly sized balls of dough into the flour, making sure they don't touch each other. With floured hands, coat each dough ball with flour and toss them gently from hand to hand to shake off any excess flour. Put each floured dough ball into the prepared pan, right up next to the other. This will help the biscuits rise, rather than spreading out. 4. Preheat the air fryer to 380°F (193°C). 5. Transfer the cake pan to the basket of the air fryer. Let the ends of the aluminum foil sling hang across the cake pan before returning the basket to the air fryer. 6. Air fry for 20 minutes. Check the biscuits twice to make sure they are not getting too brown on top. If they are, re-arrange the aluminum foil strips to cover any brown parts. After 20 minutes, check the biscuits by inserting a toothpick into the center of the biscuits. It should come out clean. If it needs a little more time, continue to air fry for two extra minutes. Brush the tops of the biscuits with some melted butter and sprinkle a little more grated cheese on top if desired. Pop the basket back into the air fryer for another 2 minutes. 7. Remove the cake pan from the air fryer. Let the biscuits cool for just a minute or two and then turn them out onto a plate and pull apart. Serve immediately.

Buffalo Chicken Breakfast Muffins

Prep time: 7 minutes | Cook time: 13 to 16 minutes | Serves 10

- 6 ounces (170 g) shredded cooked chicken
- 3 ounces (85 g) blue cheese, crumbled
- 2 tablespoons unsalted butter, melted
- ⅓ cup Buffalo hot sauce,
- such as Frank's RedHot
- 1 teaspoon minced garlic
- 6 large eggs
- Sea salt and freshly ground black pepper, to taste
- Avocado oil spray

1. In a large bowl, stir together the chicken, blue cheese, melted butter, hot sauce, and garlic. 2. In a medium bowl or large liquid measuring cup, beat the eggs. Season with salt and pepper. 3. Spray 10 silicone muffin cups with oil. Divide the chicken mixture among the cups, and pour the egg mixture over top. 4. Place the cups in the air fryer and set to 300°F (149°C). Bake for 13 to 16 minutes, until the muffins are set and cooked through. (Depending on the size of your air fryer, you may need to cook the muffins in batches.)

Italian Egg Cups

Prep time: 5 minutes | Cook time: 10 minutes | Serves 4

- Olive oil
- 1 cup marinara sauce
- 4 eggs
- 4 tablespoons shredded Mozzarella cheese
- 4 teaspoons grated
- Parmesan cheese
- Salt and freshly ground black pepper, to taste
- Chopped fresh basil, for garnish

1. Lightly spray 4 individual ramekins with olive oil. 2. Pour ¼ cup of marinara sauce into each ramekin. 3. Crack one egg into each ramekin on top of the marinara sauce. 4. Sprinkle 1 tablespoon of Mozzarella and 1 tablespoon of Parmesan on top of each egg. Season with salt and pepper. 5. Cover each ramekin with aluminum foil. Place two of the ramekins in the air fryer basket. 6. Air fry at 350°F (177°C) for 5 minutes and remove the aluminum foil. Air fry until the top is lightly browned and the egg white is cooked, another 2 to 4 minutes. If you prefer the yolk to be firmer, cook for 3 to 5 more minutes. 7. Repeat with the remaining two ramekins. Garnish with basil and serve.

Gluten-Free Granola Cereal

Prep time: 7 minutes | Cook time: 30 minutes | Makes 3½ cups

- Oil, for spraying
- 1½ cups gluten-free rolled oats
- ½ cup chopped walnuts
- ½ cup chopped almonds
- ½ cup pumpkin seeds
- ¼ cup maple syrup or
- honey
- 1 tablespoon toasted sesame oil or vegetable oil
- 1 teaspoon ground cinnamon
- ½ teaspoon salt
- ½ cup dried cranberries

1. Preheat the air fryer to 250°F (121°C). Line the air fryer basket with parchment and spray lightly with oil. (Do not skip the step of lining the basket; the parchment will keep the granola from falling through the holes.) 2. In a large bowl, mix together the oats, walnuts, almonds, pumpkin seeds, maple syrup, sesame oil, cinnamon, and salt. 3. Spread the mixture in an even layer in the prepared basket. 4. Cook for 30 minutes, stirring every 10 minutes. 5. Transfer the granola to a bowl, add the dried cranberries, and toss to combine. 6. Let cool to room temperature before storing in an airtight container.

Pork Sausage Eggs with Mustard Sauce

Prep time: 20 minutes | Cook time: 12 minutes | Serves 8

- 1 pound (454 g) pork sausage
- 8 soft-boiled or hard-boiled eggs, peeled
- 1 large egg
- 2 tablespoons milk
- 1 cup crushed pork rinds
- Smoky Mustard Sauce:
- ¼ cup mayonnaise
- 2 tablespoons sour cream
- 1 tablespoon Dijon mustard
- 1 teaspoon chipotle hot sauce

1. Preheat the air fryer to 390°F (199°C). 2. Divide the sausage into 8 portions. Take each portion of sausage, pat it down into a patty, and place 1 egg in the middle, gently wrapping the sausage around the egg until the egg is completely covered. (Wet your hands slightly if you find the sausage to be too sticky.) Repeat with the remaining eggs and sausage. 3. In a small shallow bowl, whisk the egg and milk until frothy. In another shallow bowl, place the crushed pork rinds. Working one at a time, dip a sausage-wrapped egg into the beaten egg and then into the pork rinds, gently rolling to coat evenly. Repeat with the remaining sausage-wrapped eggs. 4. Arrange the eggs in a single layer in the air fryer basket, and lightly spray with olive oil. Air fry for 10 to 12 minutes, pausing halfway through the baking time to turn the eggs, until the eggs are hot and the sausage is cooked through. 5. To make the sauce: In a small bowl, combine the mayonnaise, sour cream, Dijon, and hot sauce. Whisk until thoroughly combined. Serve with the Scotch eggs.

Turkey Breakfast Sausage Patties

Prep time: 5 minutes | Cook time: 10 minutes | Serves 4

- 1 tablespoon chopped fresh thyme
- 1 tablespoon chopped fresh sage
- 1¼ teaspoons kosher salt
- 1 teaspoon chopped fennel seeds
- ¾ teaspoon smoked paprika
- ½ teaspoon onion powder
- ½ teaspoon garlic powder
- ⅛ teaspoon crushed red pepper flakes
- ⅛ teaspoon freshly ground black pepper
- 1 pound (454 g) 93% lean ground turkey
- ½ cup finely minced sweet apple (peeled)

1. Thoroughly combine the thyme, sage, salt, fennel seeds, paprika, onion powder, garlic powder, red pepper flakes, and black pepper in a medium bowl. 2. Add the ground turkey and apple and stir until well incorporated. Divide the mixture into 8 equal portions and shape into patties with your hands, each about ¼ inch thick and 3 inches in diameter. 3. Preheat the

air fryer to 400°F (204°C). 4. Place the patties in the air fryer basket in a single layer. You may need to work in batches to avoid overcrowding. 5. Air fry for 5 minutes. Flip the patties and air fry for 5 minutes, or until the patties are nicely browned and cooked through. 6. Remove from the basket to a plate and repeat with the remaining patties. 7. Serve warm.

Asparagus and Bell Pepper Strata

Prep time: 10 minutes | Cook time: 14 to 20 minutes | Serves 4

- 8 large asparagus spears, trimmed and cut into 2-inch pieces
- ⅓ cup shredded carrot
- ½ cup chopped red bell pepper
- 2 slices low-sodium whole-
- wheat bread, cut into ½-inch cubes
- 3 egg whites
- 1 egg
- 3 tablespoons 1% milk
- ½ teaspoon dried thyme

1. In a baking pan, combine the asparagus, carrot, red bell pepper, and 1 tablespoon of water. Bake in the air fryer at 330°F (166°C) for 3 to 5 minutes, or until crisp-tender. Drain well. 2. Add the bread cubes to the vegetables and gently toss. 3. In a medium bowl, whisk the egg whites, egg, milk, and thyme until frothy. 4. Pour the egg mixture into the pan. Bake for 11 to 15 minutes, or until the strata is slightly puffy and set and the top starts to brown. Serve.

Quesadillas

Prep time: 10 minutes | Cook time: 15 minutes | Serves 4

- 4 eggs
- 2 tablespoons skim milk
- Salt and pepper, to taste
- Oil for misting or cooking spray
- 4 flour tortillas
- 4 tablespoons salsa
- 2 ounces (57 g) Cheddar cheese, grated
- ½ small avocado, peeled and thinly sliced

1. Preheat the air fryer to 270°F (132°C). 2. Beat together eggs, milk, salt, and pepper. 3. Spray a baking pan lightly with cooking spray and add egg mixture. 4. Bake for 8 to 9 minutes, stirring every 1 to 2 minutes, until eggs are scrambled to your liking. Remove and set aside. 5. Spray one side of each tortilla with oil or cooking spray. Flip over. 6. Divide eggs, salsa, cheese, and avocado among the tortillas, covering only half of each tortilla. 7. Fold each tortilla in half and press down lightly. 8. Place 2 tortillas in air fryer basket and air fry at 390°F (199°C) for 3 minutes or until cheese melts and outside feels slightly crispy. Repeat with remaining two tortillas. 9. Cut each cooked tortilla into halves or thirds.

Breakfast Hash

Prep time: 10 minutes | Cook time: 30 minutes | Serves 6

- Oil, for spraying
- 3 medium russet potatoes, diced
- ½ yellow onion, diced
- 1 green bell pepper, seeded and diced
- 2 tablespoons olive oil
- 2 teaspoons granulated garlic
- 1 teaspoon salt
- ½ teaspoon freshly ground black pepper

1. Line the air fryer basket with parchment and spray lightly with oil. 2. In a large bowl, mix together the potatoes, onion, bell pepper, and olive oil. 3. Add the garlic, salt, and black pepper and stir until evenly coated. 4. Transfer the mixture to the prepared basket. 5. Air fry at 400°F (204°C) for 20 to 30 minutes, shaking or stirring every 10 minutes, until browned and crispy. If you spray the potatoes with a little oil each time you stir, they will get even crispier.

Ham and Cheese Crescents

Prep time: 5 minutes | Cook time: 7 minutes | Makes 8 rolls

- Oil, for spraying
- 1 (8 ounces / 227 g) can refrigerated crescent rolls
- 4 slices deli ham
- 8 slices American cheese
- 2 tablespoons unsalted butter, melted

1. Line the air fryer basket with parchment and spray lightly with oil. 2. Separate the dough into 8 pieces. 3. Tear the ham slices in half and place 1 piece on each piece of dough. Top each with 1 slice of cheese. 4. Roll up each piece of dough, starting on the wider side. 5. Place the rolls in the prepared basket. Brush with the melted butter. 6. Air fry at 320°F (160°C) for 6 to 7 minutes, or until puffed and golden brown and the cheese is melted.

Fried Cheese Grits

Prep time: 10 minutes | Cook time: 10 to 12 minutes | Serves 4

- ⅔ cup instant grits
- 1 teaspoon salt
- 1 teaspoon freshly ground black pepper
- ¾ cup whole or 2% milk
- 3 ounces (85 g) cream cheese, at room temperature
- 1 large egg, beaten
- 1 tablespoon butter, melted
- 1 cup shredded mild Cheddar cheese
- Cooking spray

1. Mix the grits, salt, and black pepper in a large bowl. Add the milk, cream cheese, beaten egg, and melted butter and whisk to combine. Fold in the Cheddar cheese and stir well. 2. Preheat the air fryer to 400°F (204°C). Spray a baking pan with cooking spray. 3. Spread the grits mixture into the baking pan and place in the air fryer basket. 4. Air fry for 1o to 12 minutes, or until the grits are cooked and a knife inserted in the center comes out clean. Stir the mixture once halfway through the cooking time. 5. Rest for 5 minutes and serve warm.

Chapter 2
Family Favorites

Churro Bites

Prep time: 5 minutes | Cook time: 6 minutes | Makes 36 bites

- Oil, for spraying
- 1 (17¼ ounces / 489 g) package frozen puffed pastry, thawed
- 1 cup granulated sugar
- 1 tablespoon ground cinnamon
- ½ cup confectioners' sugar
- 1 tablespoon milk

1. Preheat the air fryer to 400°F (204°C). Line the air fryer basket with parchment and spray lightly with oil. 2. Unfold the puff pastry onto a clean work surface. Using a sharp knife, cut the dough into 36 bite-size pieces. 3. Place the dough pieces in one layer in the prepared basket, taking care not to let the pieces touch or overlap. 4. Cook for 3 minutes, flip, and cook for another 3 minutes, or until puffed and golden. 5. In a small bowl, mix together the granulated sugar and cinnamon. 6. In another small bowl, whisk together the confectioners' sugar and milk. 7. Dredge the bites in the cinnamon-sugar mixture until evenly coated. 8. Serve with the icing on the side for dipping.

Beignets

Prep time: 30 minutes | Cook time: 6 minutes | Makes 9 beignets

- Oil, for greasing and spraying
- 3 cups all-purpose flour, plus more for dusting
- 1½ teaspoons salt
- 1 (2¼ teaspoons) envelope active dry yeast
- 1 cup milk
- 2 tablespoons packed light brown sugar
- 1 tablespoon unsalted butter
- 1 large egg
- 1 cup confectioners' sugar

1. Oil a large bowl. 2. In a small bowl, mix together the flour, salt, and yeast. Set aside. 3. Pour the milk into a glass measuring cup and microwave in 1-minute intervals until it boils. 4. In a large bowl, mix together the brown sugar and butter. Pour in the hot milk and whisk until the sugar has dissolved. Let cool to room temperature. 5. Whisk the egg into the cooled milk mixture and fold in the flour mixture until a dough forms. 6. On a lightly floured work surface, knead the dough for 3 to 5 minutes. 7. Place the dough in the oiled bowl and cover with a clean kitchen towel. Let rise in a warm place for about 1 hour, or until doubled in size. 8. Roll the dough out on a lightly floured work surface until it's about ¼ inch thick. Cut the dough into 3-inch squares and place them on a lightly floured baking sheet. Cover loosely with a kitchen towel and let rise again until doubled in size, about 30 minutes. 9. Line the air fryer basket with parchment and spray lightly with oil. 10. Place the dough squares in the prepared basket and spray lightly with oil. You may need to work in batches, depending on the size of your air fryer. 11. Air fry at 390°F (199°C) for 3 minutes, flip, spray with oil, and cook for another 3 minutes, until crispy. 12. Dust with the confectioners' sugar before serving.

Phyllo Vegetable Triangles

Prep time: 15 minutes | Cook time: 6 to 11 minutes | Serves 6

- 3 tablespoons minced onion
- 2 garlic cloves, minced
- 2 tablespoons grated carrot
- 1 teaspoon olive oil
- 3 tablespoons frozen baby peas, thawed
- 2 tablespoons nonfat
- cream cheese, at room temperature
- 6 sheets frozen phyllo dough, thawed
- Olive oil spray, for coating the dough

1. In a baking pan, combine the onion, garlic, carrot, and olive oil. Air fry at 390°F (199°C) for 2 to 4 minutes, or until the vegetables are crisp-tender. Transfer to a bowl. 2. Stir in the peas and cream cheese to the vegetable mixture. Let cool while you prepare the dough. 3. Lay one sheet of phyllo on a work surface and lightly spray with olive oil spray. Top with another sheet of phyllo. Repeat with the remaining 4 phyllo sheets; you'll have 3 stacks with 2 layers each. Cut each stack lengthwise into 4 strips (12 strips total). 4. Place a scant 2 teaspoons of the filling near the bottom of each strip. Bring one corner up over the filling to make a triangle; continue folding the triangles over, as you would fold a flag. Seal the edge with a bit of water. Repeat with the remaining strips and filling. 5. Air fry the triangles, in 2 batches, for 4 to 7 minutes, or until golden brown. Serve.

Puffed Egg Tarts

Prep time: 10 minutes | Cook time: 42 minutes | Makes 4 tarts

- Oil, for spraying
- All-purpose flour, for dusting
- 1 (12 ounces / 340 g) sheet frozen puff pastry, thawed
- ¾ cup shredded Cheddar
- cheese, divided
- 4 large eggs
- 2 teaspoons chopped fresh parsley
- Salt and freshly ground black pepper, to taste

1. Preheat the air fryer to 390°F (199°C). Line the air fryer basket with parchment and spray lightly with oil. 2. Lightly dust your work surface with flour. Unfold the puff pastry and cut it into 4 equal squares. Place 2 squares in the prepared basket. 3. Cook for 10 minutes. 4. Remove the basket. Press the center of each tart shell with a spoon to make an indentation. 5. Sprinkle 3 tablespoons of cheese into each indentation and crack 1 egg into the center of each tart shell. 6. Cook for another 7 to 11 minutes, or until the eggs are cooked to your desired doneness. 7. Repeat with the remaining puff pastry squares, cheese, and eggs. 8. Sprinkle evenly with the parsley, and season with salt and black pepper. Serve immediately.

Meringue Cookies

Prep time: 15 minutes | Cook time: 1 hour 30 minutes | Makes 20 cookies

- Oil, for spraying
- 4 large egg whites
- 1 cup sugar
- Pinch cream of tartar

1. Preheat the air fryer to 140ºF (60ºC). Line the air fryer basket with parchment and spray lightly with oil. 2. In a small heatproof bowl, whisk together the egg whites and sugar. Fill a small saucepan halfway with water, place it over medium heat, and bring to a light simmer. Place the bowl with the egg whites on the saucepan, making sure the bottom of the bowl does not touch the water. Whisk the mixture until the sugar is dissolved. 3. Transfer the mixture to a large bowl and add the cream of tartar. Using an electric mixer, beat the mixture on high until it is glossy and stiff peaks form. Transfer the mixture to a piping bag or a zip-top plastic bag with a corner cut off. 4. Pipe rounds into the prepared basket. You may need to work in batches, depending on the size of your air fryer. 5. Cook for 1 hour 30 minutes. 6. Turn off the air fryer and let the meringues cool completely inside. The residual heat will continue to dry them out.

Old Bay Tilapia

Prep time: 15 minutes | Cook time: 6 minutes | Serves 4

- Oil, for spraying
- 1 cup panko bread crumbs
- 2 tablespoons Old Bay seasoning
- 2 teaspoons granulated garlic
- 1 teaspoon onion powder
- ½ teaspoon salt
- ¼ teaspoon freshly ground black pepper
- 1 large egg
- 4 tilapia fillets

1. Preheat the air fryer to 400ºF (204ºC). Line the air fryer basket with parchment and spray lightly with oil. 2. In a shallow bowl, mix together the bread crumbs, Old Bay, garlic, onion powder, salt, and black pepper. 3. In a small bowl, whisk the egg. 4. Coat the tilapia in the egg, then dredge in the bread crumb mixture until completely coated. 5. Place the tilapia in the prepared basket. You may need to work in batches, depending on the size of your air fryer. Spray lightly with oil. 6. Cook for 4 to 6 minutes, depending on the thickness of the fillets, until the internal temperature reaches 145ºF (63ºC). Serve immediately.

Fried Green Tomatoes

Prep time: 15 minutes | Cook time: 6 to 8 minutes | Serves 4

- 4 medium green tomatoes
- ⅓ cup all-purpose flour
- 2 egg whites
- ¼ cup almond milk
- 1 cup ground almonds
- ½ cup panko bread crumbs
- 2 teaspoons olive oil
- 1 teaspoon paprika
- 1 clove garlic, minced

1. Rinse the tomatoes and pat dry. Cut the tomatoes into ½-inch slices, discarding the thinner ends. 2. Put the flour on a plate. In a shallow bowl, beat the egg whites with the almond milk until frothy. And on another plate, combine the almonds, bread crumbs, olive oil, paprika, and garlic and mix well. 3. Dip the tomato slices into the flour, then into the egg white mixture, then into the almond mixture to coat. 4. Place four of the coated tomato slices in the air fryer basket. Air fry at 400ºF (204ºC) for 6 to 8 minutes or until the tomato coating is crisp and golden brown. Repeat with remaining tomato slices and serve immediately.

Coconut Chicken Tenders

Prep time: 10 minutes | Cook time: 12 minutes | Serves 4

- Oil, for spraying
- 2 large eggs
- ¼ cup milk
- 1 tablespoon hot sauce
- 1½ cups sweetened flaked coconut
- ¾ cup panko bread crumbs
- 1 teaspoon salt
- ½ teaspoon freshly ground black pepper
- 1 pound (454 g) chicken tenders

1. Line the air fryer basket with parchment and spray lightly with oil. 2. In a small bowl, whisk together the eggs, milk, and hot sauce. 3. In a shallow dish, mix together the coconut, bread crumbs, salt, and black pepper. 4. Coat the chicken in the egg mix, then dredge in the coconut mixture until evenly coated. 5. Place the chicken in the prepared basket and spray liberally with oil. 6. Air fry at 400ºF (204ºC) for 6 minutes, flip, spray with more oil, and cook for another 6 minutes, or until the internal temperature reaches 165ºF (74ºC).

Beef Jerky

Prep time: 30 minutes | Cook time: 2 hours | Serves 8

- Oil, for spraying
- 1 pound (454 g) round steak, cut into thin, short slices
- ¼ cup soy sauce
- 3 tablespoons packed light brown sugar
- 1 tablespoon minced garlic
- 1 teaspoon ground ginger
- 1 tablespoon water

1. Line the air fryer basket with parchment and spray lightly with oil. 2. Place the steak, soy sauce, brown sugar, garlic, ginger, and water in a zip-top plastic bag, seal, and shake well until evenly coated. Refrigerate for 30 minutes. 3. Place the steak in the prepared basket in a single layer. You may need to work in batches, depending on the size of your air fryer. 4. Air fry at 180ºF (82ºC) for at least 2 hours. Add more time if you like your jerky a bit tougher.

Steak Tips and Potatoes

Prep time: 10 minutes | Cook time: 20 minutes | Serves 4

- Oil, for spraying
- 8 ounces (227 g) baby gold potatoes, cut in half
- ½ teaspoon salt
- 1 pound (454 g) steak, cut into ½-inch pieces
- 1 teaspoon Worcestershire
- sauce
- 1 teaspoon granulated garlic
- ½ teaspoon salt
- ½ teaspoon freshly ground black pepper

1. Line the air fryer basket with parchment and spray lightly with oil. 2. In a microwave-safe bowl, combine the potatoes and salt, then pour in about ½ inch of water. Microwave for 7 minutes, or until the potatoes are nearly tender. Drain. 3. In a large bowl, gently mix together the steak, potatoes, Worcestershire sauce, garlic, salt, and black pepper. Spread the mixture in an even layer in the prepared basket. 4. Air fry at 400ºF (204ºC) for 12 to 17 minutes, stirring after 5 to 6 minutes. The cooking time will depend on the thickness of the meat and preferred doneness.

Avocado and Egg Burrito

Prep time: 10 minutes | Cook time: 3 to 5 minutes | Serves 4

- 2 hard-boiled egg whites, chopped
- 1 hard-boiled egg, chopped
- 1 avocado, peeled, pitted, and chopped
- 1 red bell pepper, chopped
- 3 tablespoons low-sodium salsa, plus additional for
- serving (optional)
- 1 (1.2 ounces / 34 g) slice low-sodium, low-fat American cheese, torn into pieces
- 4 low-sodium whole-wheat flour tortillas

1. In a medium bowl, thoroughly mix the egg whites, egg, avocado, red bell pepper, salsa, and cheese. 2. Place the tortillas on a work surface and evenly divide the filling among them. Fold in the edges and roll up. Secure the burritos with toothpicks if necessary. 3. Put the burritos in the air fryer basket. Air fry at 390ºF (199ºC) for 3 to 5 minutes, or until the burritos are light golden brown and crisp. Serve with more salsa (if using).

Bacon-Wrapped Hot Dogs

Prep time: 5 minutes | Cook time: 10 minutes | Serves 4

- Oil, for spraying
- 4 bacon slices
- 4 all-beef hot dogs
- 4 hot dog buns
- Toppings of choice

1. Line the air fryer basket with parchment and spray lightly with oil. 2. Wrap a strip of bacon tightly around each hot dog, taking care to cover the tips so they don't get too crispy. Secure with a toothpick at each end to keep the bacon from shrinking. 3. Place the hot dogs in the prepared basket. 4. Air fry at 380ºF (193ºC) for 8 to 9 minutes, depending on how crispy you like the bacon. For extra-crispy, cook the hot dogs at 400ºF (204ºC) for 6 to 8 minutes. 5. Place the hot dogs in the buns, return them to the air fryer, and cook for another 1 to 2 minutes, or until the buns are warm. Add your desired toppings and serve.

Cajun Shrimp

Prep time: 15 minutes | Cook time: 9 minutes | Serves 4

- Oil, for spraying
- 1 pound (454 g) jumbo raw shrimp, peeled and deveined
- 1 tablespoon Cajun seasoning
- 6 ounces (170 g) cooked kielbasa, cut into thick slices
- ½ medium zucchini, cut into ¼-inch-thick slices
- ½ medium yellow squash, cut into ¼-inch-thick slices
- 1 green bell pepper, seeded and cut into 1-inch pieces
- 2 tablespoons olive oil
- ½ teaspoon salt

1. Preheat the air fryer to 400ºF (204ºC). Line the air fryer basket with parchment and spray lightly with oil. 2. In a large bowl, toss together the shrimp and Cajun seasoning. Add the kielbasa, zucchini, squash, bell pepper, olive oil, and salt and mix well. 3. Transfer the mixture to the prepared basket, taking care not to overcrowd. You may need to work in batches, depending on the size of your air fryer. 4. Cook for 9 minutes, shaking and stirring every 3 minutes. Serve immediately.

Fish and Vegetable Tacos

Prep time: 15 minutes | Cook time: 9 to 12 minutes | Serves 4

- 1 pound (454 g) white fish fillets, such as sole or cod
- 2 teaspoons olive oil
- 3 tablespoons freshly squeezed lemon juice, divided
- 1½ cups chopped red
- cabbage
- 1 large carrot, grated
- ½ cup low-sodium salsa
- ⅓ cup low-fat Greek yogurt
- 4 soft low-sodium whole-wheat tortillas

1. Brush the fish with the olive oil and sprinkle with 1 tablespoon of lemon juice. Air fry in the air fryer basket at 390ºF (199ºC) for 9 to 12 minutes, or until the fish just flakes when tested with a fork. 2. Meanwhile, in a medium bowl, stir together the remaining 2 tablespoons of lemon juice, the red cabbage, carrot, salsa, and yogurt. 3. When the fish is cooked, remove it from the air fryer basket and break it up into large pieces. 4. Offer the fish, tortillas, and the cabbage mixture, and let each person assemble a taco.

Chinese-Inspired Spareribs

Prep time: 30 minutes | Cook time: 8 minutes | Serves 4

- Oil, for spraying
- 12 ounces (340 g) boneless pork spareribs, cut into 3-inch-long pieces
- 1 cup soy sauce
- ¾ cup sugar
- ½ cup beef or chicken stock
- ¼ cup honey
- 2 tablespoons minced garlic
- 1 teaspoon ground ginger
- 2 drops red food coloring (optional)

1. Line the air fryer basket with parchment and spray lightly with oil. 2. Combine the ribs, soy sauce, sugar, beef stock, honey, garlic, ginger, and food coloring (if using) in a large zip-top plastic bag, seal, and shake well until completely coated. Refrigerate for at least 30 minutes. 3. Place the ribs in the prepared basket. 4. Air fry at 375°F (191°C) for 8 minutes, or until the internal temperature reaches 165°F (74°C).

Buffalo Cauliflower

Prep time: 15 minutes | Cook time: 5 minutes | Serves 6

- 1 large head cauliflower, separated into small florets
- 1 tablespoon olive oil
- ½ teaspoon garlic powder
- ⅓ cup low-sodium hot wing sauce
- ⅔ cup nonfat Greek yogurt
- ½ teaspoons Tabasco sauce
- 1 celery stalk, chopped
- 1 tablespoon crumbled blue cheese

1. In a large bowl, toss the cauliflower florets with the olive oil. Sprinkle with the garlic powder and toss again to coat. Put half of the cauliflower in the air fryer basket. Air fry at 380°F (193°C) for 5 to 7 minutes, until the cauliflower is browned, shaking the basket once during cooking. 2. Transfer to a serving bowl and toss with half of the wing sauce. Repeat with the remaining cauliflower and wing sauce. 3. In a small bowl, stir together the yogurt, Tabasco sauce, celery, and blue cheese. Serve with the cauliflower for dipping.

Scallops with Green Vegetables

Prep time: 15 minutes | Cook time: 8 to 11 minutes | Serves 4

- 1 cup green beans
- 1 cup frozen peas
- 1 cup frozen chopped broccoli
- 2 teaspoons olive oil
- ½ teaspoon dried basil
- ½ teaspoon dried oregano
- 12 ounces (340 g) sea scallops

1. In a large bowl, toss the green beans, peas, and broccoli with the olive oil. Place in the air fryer basket. Air fry at 400°F (204°C) for 4 to 6 minutes, or until the vegetables are crisp-tender. 2. Remove the vegetables from the air fryer basket and sprinkle with the herbs. Set aside. 3. In the air fryer basket, put the scallops and air fry for 4 to 5 minutes, or until the scallops are firm and reach an internal temperature of just 145°F (63°C) on a meat thermometer. 4. Toss scallops with the vegetables and serve immediately.

Elephant Ears

Prep time: 5 minutes | Cook time: 5 minutes | Serves 8

- Oil, for spraying
- 1 (8 ounces / 227 g) can buttermilk biscuits
- 3 tablespoons sugar
- 1 tablespoon ground
- cinnamon
- 3 tablespoons unsalted butter, melted
- 8 scoops vanilla ice cream (optional)

1. Line the air fryer basket with parchment and spray lightly with oil. 2. Separate the dough. Using a rolling pin, roll out the biscuits into 6- to 8-inch circles. 3. Place the dough circles in the prepared basket and spray liberally with oil. You may need to work in batches, depending on the size of your air fryer. 4. Air fry at 350°F (177°C) for 5 minutes, or until lightly browned. 5. In a small bowl, mix together the sugar and cinnamon. 6. Brush the elephant ears with the melted butter and sprinkle with the cinnamon-sugar mixture. 7. Top each serving with a scoop of ice cream (if using).

Cheesy Roasted Sweet Potatoes

Prep time: 7 minutes | Cook time: 18 to 23 minutes | Serves 4

- 2 large sweet potatoes, peeled and sliced
- 1 teaspoon olive oil
- 1 tablespoon white
- balsamic vinegar
- 1 teaspoon dried thyme
- ¼ cup grated Parmesan cheese

1. In a large bowl, drizzle the sweet potato slices with the olive oil and toss. 2. Sprinkle with the balsamic vinegar and thyme and toss again. 3. Sprinkle the potatoes with the Parmesan cheese and toss to coat. 4. Roast the slices, in batches, in the air fryer basket at 400°F (204°C) for 18 to 23 minutes, tossing the sweet potato slices in the basket once during cooking, until tender. 5. Repeat with the remaining sweet potato slices. Serve immediately.

Steak and Vegetable Kebabs

Prep time: 15 minutes | Cook time: 5 to 7 minutes | Serves 4

- 2 tablespoons balsamic vinegar
- 2 teaspoons olive oil
- ½ teaspoon dried marjoram
- ⅛ teaspoon freshly ground black pepper
- ¾ pound (340 g) round steak, cut into 1-inch pieces
- 1 red bell pepper, sliced
- 16 button mushrooms
- 1 cup cherry tomatoes

1. In a medium bowl, stir together the balsamic vinegar, olive oil, marjoram, and black pepper. 2. Add the steak and stir to coat. Let stand for 10 minutes at room temperature. 3. Alternating items, thread the beef, red bell pepper, mushrooms, and tomatoes onto 8 bamboo or metal skewers that fit in the air fryer. 4. Air fry at 390°F (199°C) for 5 to 7 minutes, or until the beef is browned and reaches at least 145°F (63°C) on a meat thermometer. Serve immediately.

Chapter 3

Fast and Easy Everyday Favorites

Easy Roasted Asparagus

Prep time: 5 minutes | Cook time: 6 minutes | Serves 4

- 1 pound (454 g) asparagus, trimmed and halved crosswise
- 1 teaspoon extra-virgin
- olive oil
- Salt and pepper, to taste
- Lemon wedges, for serving

1. Preheat the air fryer to 400°F (204°C). 2. Toss the asparagus with the oil, ⅛ teaspoon salt, and ⅛ teaspoon pepper in bowl. Transfer to air fryer basket. 3. Place the basket in air fryer and roast for 6 to 8 minutes, or until tender and bright green, tossing halfway through cooking. 4. Season with salt and pepper and serve with lemon wedges.

Cheesy Jalapeño Cornbread

Prep time: 10 minutes | Cook time: 20 minutes | Serves 8

- ⅔ cup cornmeal
- ⅓ cup all-purpose flour
- ¾ teaspoon baking powder
- 2 tablespoons buttery spread, melted
- ½ teaspoon kosher salt
- 1 tablespoon granulated sugar
- ¾ cup whole milk
- 1 large egg, beaten
- 1 jalapeño pepper, thinly sliced
- ⅓ cup shredded sharp Cheddar cheese
- Cooking spray

1. Preheat the air fryer to 300°F (149°C). Spritz the air fryer basket with cooking spray. 2. Combine all the ingredients in a large bowl. Stir to mix well. Pour the mixture in a baking pan. 3. Arrange the pan in the preheated air fryer. Bake for 20 minutes or until a toothpick inserted in the center of the bread comes out clean. 4. When the cooking is complete, remove the baking pan from the air fryer and allow the bread to cool for a few minutes before slicing to serve.

Buttery Sweet Potatoes

Prep time: 5 minutes | Cook time: 10 minutes | Serves 4

- 2 tablespoons butter, melted
- 1 tablespoon light brown sugar
- 2 sweet potatoes, peeled and cut into ½-inch cubes
- Cooking spray

1. Preheat the air fryer to 400°F (204°C). Line the air fryer basket with parchment paper. 2. In a medium bowl, stir together the melted butter and brown sugar until blended. Toss the sweet potatoes in the butter mixture until coated. 3. Place the sweet potatoes on the parchment and spritz with oil. 4. Air fry for 5 minutes. Shake the basket, spritz the sweet potatoes with oil, and air fry for 5 minutes more until they're soft enough to cut

with a fork. 5. Serve immediately.

Cheesy Baked Grits

Prep time: 10 minutes | Cook time: 12 minutes | Serves 6

- ¾ cup hot water
- 2 (1-ounce / 28-g) packages instant grits
- 1 large egg, beaten
- 1 tablespoon butter, melted
- 2 cloves garlic, minced
- ½ to 1 teaspoon red pepper flakes
- 1 cup shredded Cheddar cheese or jalapeño Jack cheese

1. Preheat the air fryer to 400°F (204°C). 2. In a baking pan, combine the water, grits, egg, butter, garlic, and red pepper flakes. Stir until well combined. Stir in the shredded cheese. 3. Place the pan in the air fryer basket and air fry for 12 minutes, or until the grits have cooked through and a knife inserted near the center comes out clean. 4. Let stand for 5 minutes before serving.

Herb-Roasted Veggies

Prep time: 10 minutes | Cook time: 14 to 18 minutes | Serves 4

- 1 red bell pepper, sliced
- 1 (8 ounces / 227 g) package sliced mushrooms
- 1 cup green beans, cut into 2-inch pieces
- ⅓ cup diced red onion
- 3 garlic cloves, sliced
- 1 teaspoon olive oil
- ½ teaspoon dried basil
- ½ teaspoon dried tarragon

1. Preheat the air fryer to 350°F (177°C). 2. In a medium bowl, mix the red bell pepper, mushrooms, green beans, red onion, and garlic. Drizzle with the olive oil. Toss to coat. 3. Add the herbs and toss again. 4. Place the vegetables in the air fryer basket. Roast for 14 to 18 minutes, or until tender. Serve immediately.

Cheesy Chile Toast

Prep time: 5 minutes | Cook time: 5 minutes | Serves 1

- 2 tablespoons grated Parmesan cheese
- 2 tablespoons grated Mozzarella cheese
- 2 teaspoons salted butter, at
- room temperature
- 10 to 15 thin slices serrano chile or jalapeño
- 2 slices sourdough bread
- ½ teaspoon black pepper

1. Preheat the air fryer to 325°F (163°C). 2. In a small bowl, stir together the Parmesan, Mozzarella, butter, and chiles. 3. Spread half the mixture onto one side of each slice of bread. Sprinkle with the pepper. Place the slices, cheese-side up, in the air fryer basket. Bake for 5 minutes, or until the cheese has melted and started to brown slightly. 4. Serve immediately.

Southwest Corn and Bell Pepper Roast

Prep time: 10 minutes | Cook time: 10 minutes | Serves 4

- For the Corn:
- 1½ cups thawed frozen corn kernels
- 1 cup mixed diced bell peppers
- 1 jalapeño, diced
- 1 cup diced yellow onion
- ½ teaspoon ancho chile powder
- 1 tablespoon fresh lemon
- juice
- 1 teaspoon ground cumin
- ½ teaspoon kosher salt
- Cooking spray
- For Serving:
- ¼ cup feta cheese
- ¼ cup chopped fresh cilantro
- 1 tablespoon fresh lemon juice

1. Preheat the air fryer to 375ºF (191ºC). Spritz the air fryer with cooking spray. 2. Combine the ingredients for the corn in a large bowl. Stir to mix well. 3. Pout the mixture into the air fryer. Air fry for 10 minutes or until the corn and bell peppers are soft. Shake the basket halfway through the cooking time. 4. Transfer them onto a large plate, then spread with feta cheese and cilantro. Drizzle with lemon juice and serve.

Lemony and Garlicky Asparagus

Prep time: 5 minutes | Cook time: 10 minutes | Makes 10 spears

- 10 spears asparagus (about ½ pound / 227 g in total), snap the ends off
- 1 tablespoon lemon juice
- 2 teaspoons minced garlic
- ½ teaspoon salt
- ¼ teaspoon ground black pepper
- Cooking spray

1. Preheat the air fryer to 400ºF (204ºC). Line a parchment paper in the air fryer basket. 2. Put the asparagus spears in a large bowl. Drizzle with lemon juice and sprinkle with minced garlic, salt, and ground black pepper. Toss to coat well. 3. Transfer the asparagus in the preheated air fryer and spritz with cooking spray. Air fryer for 10 minutes or until wilted and soft. Flip the asparagus halfway through. 4. Serve immediately.

Indian-Style Sweet Potato Fries

Prep time: 5 minutes | Cook time: 8 minutes | Makes 20 fries

- Seasoning Mixture:
- ¾ teaspoon ground coriander
- ½ teaspoon garam masala
- ½ teaspoon garlic powder
- ½ teaspoon ground cumin
- ¼ teaspoon ground cayenne pepper
- Fries:
- 2 large sweet potatoes, peeled
- 2 teaspoons olive oil

1. Preheat the air fryer to 400ºF (204ºC). 2. In a small bowl, combine the coriander, garam masala, garlic powder, cumin, and cayenne pepper. 3. Slice the sweet potatoes into ¼-inch-thick fries. 4. In a large bowl, toss the sliced sweet potatoes with the olive oil and the seasoning mixture. 5. Transfer the seasoned sweet potatoes to the air fryer basket and fry for 8 minutes, until crispy. 6. Serve warm.

Crunchy Fried Okra

Prep time: 5 minutes | Cook time: 8 to 10 minutes | Serves 4

- 1 cup self-rising yellow cornmeal
- 1 teaspoon Italian-style seasoning
- 1 teaspoon paprika
- 1 teaspoon salt
- ½ teaspoon freshly ground black pepper
- 2 large eggs, beaten
- 2 cups okra slices
- Cooking spray

1. Preheat the air fryer to 400ºF (204ºC). Line the air fryer basket with parchment paper. 2. In a shallow bowl, whisk the cornmeal, Italian-style seasoning, paprika, salt, and pepper until blended. Place the beaten eggs in a second shallow bowl. 3. Add the okra to the beaten egg and stir to coat. Add the egg and okra mixture to the cornmeal mixture and stir until coated. 4. Place the okra on the parchment and spritz it with oil. 5. Air fry for 4 minutes. Shake the basket, spritz the okra with oil, and air fry for 4 to 6 minutes more until lightly browned and crispy. 6. Serve immediately.

Parsnip Fries with Garlic-Yogurt Dip

Prep time: 10 minutes | Cook time: 10 minutes | Serves 4

- 3 medium parsnips, peeled, cut into sticks
- ¼ teaspoon kosher salt
- 1 teaspoon olive oil
- 1 garlic clove, unpeeled
- Cooking spray
- Dip:
- ¼ cup plain Greek yogurt
- ⅛ teaspoon garlic powder
- 1 tablespoon sour cream
- ¼ teaspoon kosher salt
- Freshly ground black pepper, to taste

1. Preheat the air fryer to 360ºF (182ºC). Spritz the air fryer basket with cooking spray. 2. Put the parsnip sticks in a large bowl, then sprinkle with salt and drizzle with olive oil. 3. Transfer the parsnip into the preheated air fryer and add the garlic. 4. Air fry for 5 minutes, then remove the garlic from the air fryer and shake the basket. Air fry for 5 more minutes or until the parsnip sticks are crisp. 5. Meanwhile, peel the garlic and crush it. Combine the crushed garlic with the ingredients for the dip. Stir to mix well. 6. When the frying is complete, remove the parsnip fries from the air fryer and serve with the dipping sauce.

Classic Latkes

Prep time: 15 minutes | Cook time: 10 minutes | Makes 4 latkes

- 1 egg
- 2 tablespoons all-purpose flour
- 2 medium potatoes, peeled and shredded, rinsed and
- drained
- ¼ teaspoon granulated garlic
- ½ teaspoon salt
- Cooking spray

1. Preheat the air fryer to 380ºF (193ºC). Spritz the air fryer basket with cooking spray. 2. Whisk together the egg, flour, potatoes, garlic, and salt in a large bowl. Stir to mix well. 3. Divide the mixture into four parts, then flatten them into four circles. Arrange the circles into the preheated air fryer. 4. Spritz the circles with cooking spray, then air fry for 10 minutes or until golden brown and crispy. Flip the latkes halfway through. 5. Serve immediately.

Air Fried Shishito Peppers

Prep time: 5 minutes | Cook time: 5 minutes | Serves 4

- ½ pound (227 g) shishito peppers (about 24)
- 1 tablespoon olive oil
- Coarse sea salt, to taste
- Lemon wedges, for serving
- Cooking spray

1. Preheat the air fryer to 400ºF (204ºC). Spritz the air fryer basket with cooking spray. 2. Toss the peppers with olive oil in a large bowl to coat well. 3. Arrange the peppers in the preheated air fryer. 4. Air fryer for 5 minutes or until blistered and lightly charred. Shake the basket and sprinkle the peppers with salt halfway through the cooking time. 5. Transfer the peppers onto a plate and squeeze the lemon wedges on top before serving.

Sweet Corn and Carrot Fritters

Prep time: 10 minutes | Cook time: 8 to 11 minutes | Serves 4

- 1 medium-sized carrot, grated
- 1 yellow onion, finely chopped
- 4 ounces (113 g) canned sweet corn kernels, drained
- 1 teaspoon sea salt flakes
- 1 tablespoon chopped fresh cilantro
- 1 medium-sized egg, whisked
- 2 tablespoons plain milk
- 1 cup grated Parmesan cheese
- ¼ cup flour
- ⅓ teaspoon baking powder
- ⅓ teaspoon sugar
- Cooking spray

1. Preheat the air fryer to 350ºF (177ºC). 2. Place the grated carrot in a colander and press down to squeeze out any excess moisture. Dry it with a paper towel. 3. Combine the carrots with the remaining ingredients. 4. Mold 1 tablespoon of the mixture into a ball and press it down with your hand or a spoon to flatten it. Repeat until the rest of the mixture is used up. 5. Spritz the balls with cooking spray. 6. Arrange in the air fryer basket, taking care not to overlap any balls. Bake for 8 to 11 minutes, or until they're firm. 7. Serve warm.

Spicy Air Fried Old Bay Shrimp

Prep time: 7 minutes | Cook time: 10 minutes | Makes 2 cups

- ½ teaspoon Old Bay Seasoning
- 1 teaspoon ground cayenne pepper
- ½ teaspoon paprika
- 1 tablespoon olive oil
- ⅛ teaspoon salt
- ½ pound (227 g) shrimps, peeled and deveined
- Juice of half a lemon

1. Preheat the air fryer to 390ºF (199ºC). 2. Combine the Old Bay Seasoning, cayenne pepper, paprika, olive oil, and salt in a large bowl, then add the shrimps and toss to coat well. 3. Put the shrimps in the preheated air fryer. Air fry for 10 minutes or until opaque. Flip the shrimps halfway through. 4. Serve the shrimps with lemon juice on top.

Beef Bratwursts

Prep time: 5 minutes | Cook time: 15 minutes | Serves 4

- 4 (3-ounce / 85-g) beef bratwursts

1. Preheat the air fryer to 375ºF (191ºC). 2. Place the beef bratwursts in the air fryer basket and air fry for 15 minutes, turning once halfway through. 3. Serve hot.

Beet Salad with Lemon Vinaigrette

Prep time: 10 minutes | Cook time: 12 to 15 minutes | Serves 4

- 6 medium red and golden beets, peeled and sliced
- 1 teaspoon olive oil
- ¼ teaspoon kosher salt
- ½ cup crumbled feta cheese
- 8 cups mixed greens
- Cooking spray
- Vinaigrette:
- 2 teaspoons olive oil
- 2 tablespoons chopped fresh chives
- Juice of 1 lemon

1. Preheat the air fryer to 360ºF (182ºC). 2. In a large bowl, toss the beets, olive oil, and kosher salt. 3. Spray the air fryer basket with cooking spray, then place the beets in the basket and air fry for 12 to 15 minutes or until tender. 4. While the beets cook, make the vinaigrette in a large bowl by whisking together the olive oil, lemon juice, and chives. 5. Remove the beets from the air fryer, toss in the vinaigrette, and allow to cool for 5 minutes. Add the feta and serve on top of the mixed greens.

Bacon Pinwheels

Prep time: 10 minutes | Cook time: 10 minutes | Makes 8 pinwheels

- 1 sheet puff pastry
- 2 tablespoons maple syrup
- ¼ cup brown sugar
- 8 slices bacon
- Ground black pepper, to taste
- Cooking spray

1. Preheat the air fryer to 360ºF (182ºC). Spritz the air fryer basket with cooking spray. 2. Roll the puff pastry into a 10-inch square with a rolling pin on a clean work surface, then cut the pastry into 8 strips. 3. Brush the strips with maple syrup and sprinkle with sugar, leaving a 1-inch far end uncovered. 4. Arrange each slice of bacon on each strip, leaving a ⅛-inch length of bacon hang over the end close to you. Sprinkle with black pepper. 5. From the end close to you, roll the strips into pinwheels, then dab the uncovered end with water and seal the rolls. 6. Arrange the pinwheels in the preheated air fryer and spritz with cooking spray. 7. Air fry for 10 minutes or until golden brown. Flip the pinwheels halfway through. 8. Serve immediately.

Baked Halloumi with Greek Salsa

Prep time: 15 minutes | Cook time: 6 minutes | Serves 4

- Salsa:
- 1 small shallot, finely diced
- 3 garlic cloves, minced
- 2 tablespoons fresh lemon juice
- 2 tablespoons extra-virgin olive oil
- 1 teaspoon freshly cracked black pepper
- Pinch of kosher salt
- ½ cup finely diced English cucumber
- 1 plum tomato, deseeded and finely diced
- 2 teaspoons chopped fresh parsley
- 1 teaspoon snipped fresh dill
- 1 teaspoon snipped fresh oregano
- Cheese:
- 8 ounces (227 g) Halloumi cheese, sliced into ½-inch-thick pieces
- 1 tablespoon extra-virgin olive oil

1. Preheat the air fryer to 375ºF (191ºC). 2. For the salsa: Combine the shallot, garlic, lemon juice, olive oil, pepper, and salt in a medium bowl. Add the cucumber, tomato, parsley, dill, and oregano. Toss gently to combine; set aside. 3. For the cheese: Place the cheese slices in a medium bowl. Drizzle with the olive oil. Toss gently to coat. Arrange the cheese in a single layer in the air fryer basket. Bake for 6 minutes. 4. Divide the cheese among four serving plates. Top with the salsa and serve immediately.

Purple Potato Chips with Rosemary

Prep time: 10 minutes | Cook time: 9 to 14 minutes | Serves 6

- 1 cup Greek yogurt
- 2 chipotle chiles, minced
- 2 tablespoons adobo sauce
- 1 teaspoon paprika
- 1 tablespoon lemon juice
- 10 purple fingerling potatoes
- 1 teaspoon olive oil
- 2 teaspoons minced fresh rosemary leaves
- ⅛ teaspoon cayenne pepper
- ¼ teaspoon coarse sea salt

1. Preheat the air fryer to 400ºF (204ºC). 2. In a medium bowl, combine the yogurt, minced chiles, adobo sauce, paprika, and lemon juice. Mix well and refrigerate. 3. Wash the potatoes and dry them with paper towels. Slice the potatoes lengthwise, as thinly as possible. You can use a mandoline, a vegetable peeler, or a very sharp knife. 4. Combine the potato slices in a medium bowl and drizzle with the olive oil; toss to coat. 5. Air fry the chips, in batches, in the air fryer basket, for 9 to 14 minutes. Use tongs to gently rearrange the chips halfway during cooking time. 6. Sprinkle the chips with the rosemary, cayenne pepper, and sea salt. Serve with the chipotle sauce for dipping.

Chapter ④

Poultry

Thai Tacos with Peanut Sauce

Prep time: 10 minutes | Cook time: 6 minutes | Serves 4

- 1 pound (454 g) ground chicken
- ¼ cup diced onions (about

Sauce:

- ¼ cup creamy peanut butter, room temperature
- 2 tablespoons chicken broth, plus more if needed
- 2 tablespoons lime juice
- 2 tablespoons grated fresh

For Serving:

- 2 small heads butter lettuce, leaves separated

For Garnish (Optional):

- Cilantro leaves
- Shredded purple cabbage

- 1 small onion)
- 2 cloves garlic, minced
- ¼ teaspoon fine sea salt

- ginger
- 2 tablespoons wheat-free tamari or coconut aminos
- 1½ teaspoons hot sauce
- 5 drops liquid stevia (optional)

- Lime slices (optional)

- Sliced green onions

1. Preheat the air fryer to 350°F (177°C). 2. Place the ground chicken, onions, garlic, and salt in a pie pan or a dish that will fit in your air fryer. Break up the chicken with a spatula. Place in the air fryer and bake for 5 minutes, or until the chicken is browned and cooked through. Break up the chicken again into small crumbles. 3. Make the sauce: In a medium-sized bowl, stir together the peanut butter, broth, lime juice, ginger, tamari, hot sauce, and stevia (if using) until well combined. If the sauce is too thick, add another tablespoon or two of broth. Taste and add more hot sauce if desired. 4. Add half of the sauce to the pan with the chicken. Cook for another minute, until heated through, and stir well to combine. 5. Assemble the tacos: Place several lettuce leaves on a serving plate. Place a few tablespoons of the chicken mixture in each lettuce leaf and garnish with cilantro leaves, purple cabbage, and sliced green onions, if desired. Serve the remaining sauce on the side. Serve with lime slices, if desired. 6. Store leftover meat mixture in an airtight container in the refrigerator for up to 4 days; store leftover sauce, lettuce leaves, and garnishes separately. Reheat the meat mixture in a lightly greased pie pan in a preheated 350°F (177°C) air fryer for 3 minutes, or until heated through.

Crunchy Chicken with Roasted Carrots

Prep time: 10 minutes | Cook time: 22 minutes | Serves 4

- 4 bone-in, skin-on chicken thighs
- 2 carrots, cut into 2-inch pieces
- 2 tablespoons extra-virgin olive oil

- 2 teaspoons poultry spice
- 1 teaspoon sea salt, divided
- 2 teaspoons chopped fresh rosemary leaves
- Cooking oil spray
- 2 cups cooked white rice

1. Brush the chicken thighs and carrots with olive oil. Sprinkle both with the poultry spice, salt, and rosemary. 2. Insert the crisper plate into the basket and the basket into the unit. Preheat the unit by selecting AIR FRY, setting the temperature to 400°F (204°C), and setting the time to 3 minutes. Select START/STOP to begin. 3. Once the unit is preheated, spray the crisper plate with cooking oil. Place the carrots into the basket. Add the wire rack and arrange the chicken thighs on the rack. 4. Select AIR FRY, set the temperature to 400°F (204°C), and set the time to 20 minutes. Select START/STOP to begin. 5. When the cooking is complete, check the chicken temperature. If a food thermometer inserted into the chicken registers 165°F (74°C), remove the chicken from the air fryer, place it on a clean plate, and cover with aluminum foil to keep warm. Otherwise, resume cooking for 1 to 2 minutes longer. 6. The carrots can cook for 18 to 22 minutes and will be tender and caramelized; cooking time isn't as crucial for root vegetables. 7. Serve the chicken and carrots with the hot cooked rice.

French Garlic Chicken

Prep time: 30 minutes | Cook time: 27 minutes | Serves 4

- 2 tablespoon extra-virgin olive oil
- 1 tablespoon Dijon mustard
- 1 tablespoon apple cider vinegar
- 3 cloves garlic, minced
- 2 teaspoons herbes de Provence
- ½ teaspoon kosher salt

- 1 teaspoon black pepper
- 1 pound (454 g) boneless, skinless chicken thighs, halved crosswise
- 2 tablespoons butter
- 8 cloves garlic, chopped
- ¼ cup heavy whipping cream

1. In a small bowl, combine the olive oil, mustard, vinegar, minced garlic, herbes de Provence, salt, and pepper. Use a wire whisk to emulsify the mixture. 2. Pierce the chicken all over with a fork to allow the marinade to penetrate better. Place the chicken in a resealable plastic bag, pour the marinade over, and seal. Massage until the chicken is well coated. Marinate at room temperature for 30 minutes or in the refrigerator for up to 24 hours. 3. When you are ready to cook, place the butter and chopped garlic in a baking pan and place it in the air fryer basket. Set the air fryer to 400°F (204°C) for 5 minutes, or until the butter has melted and the garlic is sizzling. 4. Add the chicken and the marinade to the seasoned butter. Set the air fryer to 350°F (177°C) for 15 minutes. Use a meat thermometer to ensure the chicken has reached an internal temperature of 165°F (74°C). Transfer the chicken to a plate and cover lightly with foil to keep warm. 5. Add the cream to the pan, stirring to combine with the garlic, butter, and cooking juices. Place the pan in the air fryer basket. Set the air fryer to 350°F (177°C) for 7 minutes. 6. Pour the thickened sauce over the chicken and serve.

Garlic Soy Chicken Thighs

Prep time: 10 minutes | Cook time: 30 minutes | Serves 1 to 2

- 2 tablespoons chicken stock
- 2 tablespoons reduced-sodium soy sauce
- 1½ tablespoons sugar
- 4 garlic cloves, smashed and peeled
- 2 large scallions, cut into 2- to 3-inch batons, plus more, thinly sliced, for garnish
- 2 bone-in, skin-on chicken thighs (7 to 8 ounces / 198 to 227 g each)

1. Preheat the air fryer to 375°F (191°C). 2. In a metal cake pan, combine the chicken stock, soy sauce, and sugar and stir until the sugar dissolves. Add the garlic cloves, scallions, and chicken thighs, turning the thighs to coat them in the marinade, then resting them skin-side up. Place the pan in the air fryer and bake, flipping the thighs every 5 minutes after the first 10 minutes, until the chicken is cooked through and the marinade is reduced to a sticky glaze over the chicken, about 30 minutes. 3. Remove the pan from the air fryer and serve the chicken thighs warm, with any remaining glaze spooned over top and sprinkled with more sliced scallions.

Cobb Salad

Prep time: 15 minutes | Cook time: 8 minutes | Serves 4

- 8 slices reduced-sodium bacon
- 8 chicken breast tenders (about 1½ pounds / 680 g)
- 8 cups chopped romaine lettuce
- 1 cup cherry tomatoes, halved
- ¼ red onion, thinly sliced
- 2 hard-boiled eggs, peeled and sliced

Avocado-Lime Dressing:
- ½ cup plain Greek yogurt
- ¼ cup almond milk
- ½ avocado
- Juice of ½ lime
- 3 scallions, coarsely chopped
- 1 clove garlic
- 2 tablespoons fresh cilantro
- ⅛ teaspoon ground cumin
- Salt and freshly ground black pepper, to taste

1. Preheat the air fryer to 400°F (204°C). 2. Wrap a piece of bacon around each piece of chicken and secure with a toothpick. Working in batches if necessary, arrange the bacon-wrapped chicken in a single layer in the air fryer basket. Air fry for 8 minutes until the bacon is browned and a thermometer inserted into the thickest piece of chicken register 165°F (74°C). Let cool for a few minutes, then slice into bite-size pieces. 3. To make the dressing: In a blender or food processor, combine the yogurt, milk, avocado, lime juice, scallions, garlic, cilantro, and cumin. Purée until smooth. Season to taste with salt and freshly ground pepper. 4. To assemble the salad, in a large bowl, combine the lettuce, tomatoes, and onion. Drizzle the dressing over the vegetables and toss gently until thoroughly combined. Arrange the chicken and eggs on top just before serving.

Simply Terrific Turkey Meatballs

Prep time: 10 minutes | Cook time: 7 to 10 minutes | Serves 4

- 1 red bell pepper, seeded and coarsely chopped
- 2 cloves garlic, coarsely chopped
- ¼ cup chopped fresh parsley
- 1½ pounds (680 g) 85%
- lean ground turkey
- 1 egg, lightly beaten
- ½ cup grated Parmesan cheese
- 1 teaspoon salt
- ½ teaspoon freshly ground black pepper

1. Preheat the air fryer to 400°F (204°C). 2. In a food processor fitted with a metal blade, combine the bell pepper, garlic, and parsley. Pulse until finely chopped. Transfer the vegetables to a large mixing bowl. 3. Add the turkey, egg, Parmesan, salt, and black pepper. Mix gently until thoroughly combined. Shape the mixture into 1¼-inch meatballs. 4. Working in batches if necessary, arrange the meatballs in a single layer in the air fryer basket; coat lightly with olive oil spray. Pausing halfway through the cooking time to shake the basket, air fry for 7 to 10 minutes, until lightly browned and a thermometer inserted into the center of a meatball registers 165°F (74°C).

Herbed Turkey Breast with Simple Dijon Sauce

Prep time: 5 minutes | Cook time: 30 minutes | Serves 4

- 1 teaspoon chopped fresh sage
- 1 teaspoon chopped fresh tarragon
- 1 teaspoon chopped fresh thyme leaves
- 1 teaspoon chopped fresh rosemary leaves
- 1½ teaspoons sea salt
- 1 teaspoon ground black pepper
- 1 (2-pound / 907-g) turkey breast
- 3 tablespoons Dijon mustard
- 3 tablespoons butter, melted
- Cooking spray

1. Preheat the air fryer to 390°F (199°C). Spritz the air fryer basket with cooking spray. 2. Combine the herbs, salt, and black pepper in a small bowl. Stir to mix well. Set aside. 3. Combine the Dijon mustard and butter in a separate bowl. Stir to mix well. 4. Rub the turkey with the herb mixture on a clean work surface, then brush the turkey with Dijon mixture. 5. Arrange the turkey in the preheated air fryer basket. Air fry for 30 minutes or until an instant-read thermometer inserted in the thickest part of the turkey breast reaches at least 165°F (74°C). 6. Transfer the cooked turkey breast on a large plate and slice to serve.

Chicken Wellington

Prep time: 30 minutes | Cook time: 31 minutes | Serves 2

- 2 (5 ounces / 142 g) boneless, skinless chicken breasts
- ½ cup White Worcestershire sauce
- 3 tablespoons butter
- ½ cup finely diced onion (about ½ onion)
- 8 ounces (227 g) button mushrooms, finely chopped
- ¼ cup chicken stock
- 2 tablespoons White Worcestershire sauce (or white wine)
- Salt and freshly ground black pepper, to taste
- 1 tablespoon chopped fresh tarragon
- 2 sheets puff pastry, thawed
- 1 egg, beaten
- Vegetable oil

1. Place the chicken breasts in a shallow dish. Pour the White Worcestershire sauce over the chicken coating both sides and marinate for 30 minutes. 2. While the chicken is marinating, melt the butter in a large skillet over medium-high heat on the stovetop. Add the onion and sauté for a few minutes, until it starts to soften. Add the mushrooms and sauté for 3 to 5 minutes until the vegetables are brown and soft. Deglaze the skillet with the chicken stock, scraping up any bits from the bottom of the pan. Add the White Worcestershire sauce and simmer for 2 to 3 minutes until the mixture reduces and starts to thicken. Season with salt and freshly ground black pepper. Remove the mushroom mixture from the heat and stir in the fresh tarragon. Let the mushroom mixture cool. 3. Preheat the air fryer to 360ºF (182ºC). 4. Remove the chicken from the marinade and transfer it to the air fryer basket. Tuck the small end of the chicken breast under the thicker part to shape it into a circle rather than an oval. Pour the marinade over the chicken and air fry for 10 minutes. 5. Roll out the puff pastry and cut out two 6-inch squares. Brush the perimeter of each square with the egg wash. Place half of the mushroom mixture in the center of each puff pastry square. Place the chicken breasts, top side down on the mushroom mixture. Starting with one corner of puff pastry and working in one direction, pull the pastry up over the chicken to enclose it and press the ends of the pastry together in the middle. Brush the pastry with the egg wash to seal the edges. Turn the Wellingtons over and set aside. 6. Make a decorative design with the remaining puff pastry, cut out four 10-inch strips. For each Wellington, twist two of the strips together, place them over the chicken breast wrapped in puff pastry, and tuck the ends underneath to seal it. Brush the entire top and sides of the Wellingtons with the egg wash. 7. Preheat the air fryer to 350ºF (177ºC). 8. Spray or brush the air fryer basket with vegetable oil. Air fry the chicken Wellingtons for 13 minutes. Carefully turn the Wellingtons over. Air fry for another 8 minutes. Transfer to serving plates, light a candle and enjoy!

Italian Chicken Thighs

Prep time: 5 minutes | Cook time: 20 minutes | Serves 2

- 4 bone-in, skin-on chicken thighs
- 2 tablespoons unsalted butter, melted
- 1 teaspoon dried parsley
- 1 teaspoon dried basil
- ½ teaspoon garlic powder
- ¼ teaspoon onion powder
- ¼ teaspoon dried oregano

1. Brush chicken thighs with butter and sprinkle remaining ingredients over thighs. Place thighs into the air fryer basket. 2. Adjust the temperature to 380ºF (193ºC) and roast for 20 minutes. 3. Halfway through the cooking time, flip the thighs. 4. When fully cooked, internal temperature will be at least 165ºF (74ºC) and skin will be crispy. Serve warm.

Jalapeño Chicken Balls

Prep time: 10 minutes | Cook time: 25 minutes | Serves 4

- 1 medium red onion, minced
- 2 garlic cloves, minced
- 1 jalapeño pepper, minced
- 2 teaspoons extra-virgin olive oil
- 3 tablespoons ground
- almonds
- 1 egg
- 1 teaspoon dried thyme
- 1 pound (454 g) ground chicken breast
- Cooking oil spray

1. Insert the crisper plate into the basket and the basket into the unit. Preheat the unit by selecting BAKE, setting the temperature to 400ºF (204ºC), and setting the time to 3 minutes. Select START/STOP to begin. 2. In a 6-by-2-inch round pan, combine the red onion, garlic, jalapeño, and olive oil. 3. Once the unit is preheated, place the pan into the basket. 4. Select BAKE, set the temperature to 400ºF (204ºC), and set the time to 4 minutes. Select START/STOP to begin. 5. When the cooking is complete, the vegetables should be crisp-tender. Transfer to a medium bowl. 6. Mix the almonds, egg, and thyme into the vegetable mixture. Add the chicken and mix until just combined. Form the chicken mixture into about 24 (1-inch) balls. 7. Insert the crisper plate into the basket and the basket into the unit. Preheat the unit by selecting BAKE, setting the temperature to 400ºF (204ºC), and setting the time to 3 minutes. Select START/STOP to begin. 8. Once the unit is preheated, spray the crisper plate with cooking oil. Working in batches, place half the meatballs in a single layer, not touching, into the basket. 9. Select BAKE, set the temperature to 400ºF (204ºC), and set the time to 10 minutes. Select START/STOP to begin. 10. When the cooking is complete, a food thermometer inserted into the meatballs should register at least 165ºF (74ºC). 11. Repeat steps 8 and 9 with the remaining meatballs. Serve warm.

Buttermilk Breaded Chicken

Prep time: 7 minutes | Cook time: 20 to 25 minutes | Serves 4

- 1 cup all-purpose flour
- 2 teaspoons paprika
- Pinch salt
- Freshly ground black pepper, to taste
- ⅓ cup buttermilk
- 2 eggs
- 2 tablespoons extra-virgin olive oil
- 1½ cups bread crumbs
- 6 chicken pieces, drumsticks, breasts, and thighs, patted dry
- Cooking oil spray

1. In a shallow bowl, stir together the flour, paprika, salt, and pepper. 2. In another bowl, beat the buttermilk and eggs until smooth. 3. In a third bowl, stir together the olive oil and bread crumbs until mixed. 4. Dredge the chicken in the flour, dip in the eggs to coat, and finally press into the bread crumbs, patting the crumbs firmly onto the chicken skin. 5. Insert the crisper plate into the basket and the basket into the unit. Preheat the unit by selecting AIR FRY, setting the temperature to 375°F (191°C), and setting the time to 3 minutes. Select START/STOP to begin. 6. Once the unit is preheated, spray the crisper plate with cooking oil. Place the chicken into the basket. 7. Select AIR FRY, set the temperature to 375°F (191°C), and set the time to 25 minutes. Select START/STOP to begin. 8. After 10 minutes, flip the chicken. Resume cooking. After 10 minutes more, check the chicken. If a food thermometer inserted into the chicken registers 165°F (74°C) and the chicken is brown and crisp, it is done. Otherwise, resume cooking for up to 5 minutes longer. 9. When the cooking is complete, let cool for 5 minutes, then serve.

Hawaiian Huli Huli Chicken

Prep time: 30 minutes | Cook time: 15 minutes | Serves 4

- 4 boneless, skinless chicken thighs (about 1½ pounds / 680 g)
- 1 (8 ounces / 227 g) can pineapple chunks in juice, drained, ¼ cup juice reserved
- ¼ cup soy sauce
- ¼ cup sugar
- 2 tablespoons ketchup
- 1 tablespoon minced fresh ginger
- 1 tablespoon minced garlic
- ¼ cup chopped scallions

1. Use a fork to pierce the chicken all over to allow the marinade to penetrate better. Place the chicken in a large bowl or large resealable plastic bag. 2. Set the drained pineapple chunks aside. In a small microwave-safe bowl, combine the pineapple juice, soy sauce, sugar, ketchup, ginger, and garlic. Pour half the sauce over the chicken; toss to coat. Reserve the remaining sauce. Marinate the chicken at room temperature for 30 minutes, or cover and refrigerate for up to 24 hours. 3. Place the chicken in the air fryer basket. (Discard marinade.) Set the air fryer to 350°F (177°C) for 15 minutes, turning halfway through the cooking time. 4. Meanwhile, microwave the reserved sauce on high for 45 to 60 seconds, stirring every 15 seconds, until the sauce has the consistency of a thick glaze. 5. At the end of the cooking time, use a meat thermometer to ensure the chicken has reached an internal temperature of 165°F (74°C). 6. Transfer the chicken to a serving platter. Pour the sauce over the chicken. Garnish with the pineapple chunks and scallions.

Chicken Cordon Bleu

Prep time: 20 minutes | Cook time: 15 to 20 minutes | Serves 4

- 4 small boneless, skinless chicken breasts
- Salt and pepper, to taste
- 4 slices deli ham
- 4 slices deli Swiss cheese
- (about 3 to 4 inches square)
- 2 tablespoons olive oil
- 2 teaspoons marjoram
- ¼ teaspoon paprika

1. Split each chicken breast horizontally almost in two, leaving one edge intact. 2. Lay breasts open flat and sprinkle with salt and pepper to taste. 3. Place a ham slice on top of each chicken breast. 4. Cut cheese slices in half and place one half atop each breast. Set aside remaining halves of cheese slices. 5. Roll up chicken breasts to enclose cheese and ham and secure with toothpicks. 6. Mix together the olive oil, marjoram, and paprika. Rub all over outsides of chicken breasts. 7. Place chicken in air fryer basket and air fry at 360°F (182°C) for 15 to 20 minutes, until well done and juices run clear. 8. Remove all toothpicks. To avoid burns, place chicken breasts on a plate to remove toothpicks, then immediately return them to the air fryer basket. 9. Place a half cheese slice on top of each chicken breast and cook for a minute or so just to melt cheese.

Classic Whole Chicken

Prep time: 5 minutes | Cook time: 50 minutes | Serves 4

- Oil, for spraying
- 1 (4-pound / 1.8-kg) whole chicken, giblets removed
- 1 tablespoon olive oil
- 1 teaspoon paprika
- ½ teaspoon granulated
- garlic
- ½ teaspoon salt
- ½ teaspoon freshly ground black pepper
- ¼ teaspoon finely chopped fresh parsley, for garnish

1. Line the air fryer basket with parchment and spray lightly with oil. 2. Pat the chicken dry with paper towels. Rub it with the olive oil until evenly coated. 3. In a small bowl, mix together the paprika, garlic, salt, and black pepper and sprinkle it evenly over the chicken. 4. Place the chicken in the prepared basket, breast-side down. 5. Air fry at 360°F (182°C) for 30 minutes, flip, and cook for another 20 minutes, or until the internal temperature reaches 165°F (74°C) and the juices run clear. 6. Sprinkle with the parsley before serving.

Hawaiian Chicken Bites

Prep time: 1 hour 15 minutes | Cook time: 15 minutes | Serves 4

- ½ cup pineapple juice
- 2 tablespoons apple cider vinegar
- ½ tablespoon minced ginger
- ½ cup ketchup
- 2 garlic cloves, minced
- ½ cup brown sugar
- 2 tablespoons sherry
- ½ cup soy sauce
- 4 chicken breasts, cubed
- Cooking spray

1. Combine the pineapple juice, cider vinegar, ginger, ketchup, garlic, and sugar in a saucepan. Stir to mix well. Heat over low heat for 5 minutes or until thickened. Fold in the sherry and soy sauce. 2. Dunk the chicken cubes in the mixture. Press to submerge. Wrap the bowl in plastic and refrigerate to marinate for at least an hour. 3. Preheat the air fryer to 360ºF (182ºC). Spritz the air fryer basket with cooking spray. 4. Remove the chicken cubes from the marinade. Shake the excess off and put in the preheated air fryer. Spritz with cooking spray. 5. Air fry for 15 minutes or until the chicken cubes are glazed and well browned. Shake the basket at least three times during the frying. 6. Serve immediately.

Crispy Duck with Cherry Sauce

Prep time: 10 minutes | Cook time: 33 minutes | Serves 2 to 4

- 1 whole duck (up to 5 pounds / 2.3 kg), split in half, back and rib bones removed
- **Cherry Sauce:**
- 1 tablespoon butter
- 1 shallot, minced
- ½ cup sherry
- ¾ cup cherry preserves
- 1 cup chicken stock
- 1 teaspoon white wine

- 1 teaspoon olive oil
- Salt and freshly ground black pepper, to taste

  vinegar
- 1 teaspoon fresh thyme leaves
- Salt and freshly ground black pepper, to taste

1. Preheat the air fryer to 400ºF (204ºC). 2. Trim some of the fat from the duck. Rub olive oil on the duck and season with salt and pepper. Place the duck halves in the air fryer basket, breast side up and facing the center of the basket. 3. Air fry the duck for 20 minutes. Turn the duck over and air fry for another 6 minutes. 4. While duck is air frying, make the cherry sauce. Melt the butter in a large sauté pan. Add the shallot and sauté until it is just starting to brown, about 2 to 3 minutes. Add the sherry and deglaze the pan by scraping up any brown bits from the bottom of the pan. Simmer the liquid for a few minutes, until it has reduced by half. Add the cherry preserves, chicken stock and white wine vinegar. Whisk well to combine all the ingredients. Simmer the sauce until it thickens and coats the back of a spoon, about 5 to 7 minutes. Season with salt and pepper and stir in the fresh thyme leaves. 5. When the air fryer timer goes off, spoon some cherry sauce over the duck and continue to air fry at 400ºF (204ºC) for 4 more minutes. Then, turn the duck halves back over so that the breast side is facing up. Spoon more cherry sauce over the top of the duck, covering the skin completely. Air fry for 3 more minutes and then remove the duck to a plate to rest for a few minutes. 6. Serve the duck in halves, or cut each piece in half again for a smaller serving. Spoon any additional sauce over the duck or serve it on the side.

Chicken Manchurian

Prep time: 10 minutes | Cook time: 20 minutes | Serves 2

- 1 pound (454 g) boneless, skinless chicken breasts, cut into 1-inch pieces
- ¼ cup ketchup
- 1 tablespoon tomato-based chili sauce, such as Heinz
- 1 tablespoon soy sauce
- 1 tablespoon rice vinegar

- 2 teaspoons vegetable oil
- 1 teaspoon hot sauce, such as Tabasco
- ½ teaspoon garlic powder
- ¼ teaspoon cayenne pepper
- 2 scallions, thinly sliced
- Cooked white rice, for serving

1. Preheat the air fryer to 350ºF (177ºC). 2. In a bowl, combine the chicken, ketchup, chili sauce, soy sauce, vinegar, oil, hot sauce, garlic powder, cayenne, and three-quarters of the scallions and toss until evenly coated. 3. Scrape the chicken and sauce into a metal cake pan and place the pan in the air fryer. Bake until the chicken is cooked through and the sauce is reduced to a thick glaze, about 20 minutes, flipping the chicken pieces halfway through. 4. Remove the pan from the air fryer. Spoon the chicken and sauce over rice and top with the remaining scallions. Serve immediately.

Almond-Crusted Chicken

Prep time: 15 minutes | Cook time: 25 minutes | Serves 4

- ¼ cup slivered almonds
- 2 (6-ounce / 170-g) boneless, skinless chicken breasts

- 2 tablespoons full-fat mayonnaise
- 1 tablespoon Dijon mustard

1. Pulse the almonds in a food processor or chop until finely chopped. Place almonds evenly on a plate and set aside. 2. Completely slice each chicken breast in half lengthwise. 3. Mix the mayonnaise and mustard in a small bowl and then coat chicken with the mixture. 4. Lay each piece of chicken in the chopped almonds to fully coat. Carefully move the pieces into the air fryer basket. 5. Adjust the temperature to 350ºF (177ºC) and air fry for 25 minutes. 6. Chicken will be done when it has reached an internal temperature of 165ºF (74ºC) or more. Serve warm.

Chicken and Gruyère Cordon Bleu

Prep time: 15 minutes | Cook time: 15 minutes | Serves 4

- 4 chicken breast filets
- ¼ cup chopped ham
- ⅓ cup grated Swiss cheese, or Gruyère cheese
- ¼ cup all-purpose flour
- Pinch salt
- Freshly ground black pepper, to taste
- ½ teaspoon dried marjoram
- 1 egg
- 1 cup panko bread crumbs
- Olive oil spray

1. Put the chicken breast filets on a work surface and gently press them with the palm of your hand to make them a bit thinner. Don't tear the meat. 2. In a small bowl, combine the ham and cheese. Divide this mixture among the chicken filets. Wrap the chicken around the filling to enclose it, using toothpicks to hold the chicken together. 3. In a shallow bowl, stir together the flour, salt, pepper, and marjoram. 4. In another bowl, beat the egg. 5. Spread the panko on a plate. 6. Dip the chicken in the flour mixture, in the egg, and in the panko to coat thoroughly. Press the crumbs into the chicken so they stick well. 7. Insert the crisper plate into the basket and the basket into the unit. Preheat the unit by selecting BAKE, setting the temperature to 375°F (191°C), and setting the time to 3 minutes. Select START/STOP to begin. 8. Once the unit is preheated, spray the crisper plate with olive oil. Place the chicken into the basket and spray it with olive oil. 9. Select BAKE, set the temperature to 375°F (191°C), and set the time to 15 minutes. Select START/STOP to begin. 10. When the cooking is complete, the chicken should be cooked through and a food thermometer inserted into the chicken should register 165°F (74°C). Carefully remove the toothpicks and serve.

Tex-Mex Turkey Burgers

Prep time: 10 minutes | Cook time: 14 to 16 minutes | Serves 4

- ⅓ cup finely crushed corn tortilla chips
- 1 egg, beaten
- ¼ cup salsa
- ⅓ cup shredded pepper Jack cheese
- Pinch salt
- Freshly ground black pepper, to taste
- 1 pound (454 g) ground turkey
- 1 tablespoon olive oil
- 1 teaspoon paprika

1. Preheat the air fryer to 330°F (166°C). 2. In a medium bowl, combine the tortilla chips, egg, salsa, cheese, salt, and pepper, and mix well. 3. Add the turkey and mix gently but thoroughly with clean hands. 4. Form the meat mixture into patties about ½ inch thick. Make an indentation in the center of each patty with your thumb so the burgers don't puff up while cooking. 5. Brush the patties on both sides with the olive oil and sprinkle with paprika. 6. Put in the air fryer basket and air fry for 14 to

16 minutes or until the meat registers at least 165°F (74°C). 7. Let sit for 5 minutes before serving.

Thai-Style Cornish Game Hens

Prep time: 30 minutes | Cook time: 20 minutes | Serves 4

- 1 cup chopped fresh cilantro leaves and stems
- ¼ cup fish sauce
- 1 tablespoon soy sauce
- 1 serrano chile, seeded and chopped
- 8 garlic cloves, smashed
- 2 tablespoons sugar
- 2 tablespoons lemongrass
- paste
- 2 teaspoons black pepper
- 2 teaspoons ground coriander
- 1 teaspoon kosher salt
- 1 teaspoon ground turmeric
- 2 Cornish game hens, giblets removed, split in half lengthwise

1. In a blender, combine the cilantro, fish sauce, soy sauce, serrano, garlic, sugar, lemongrass, black pepper, coriander, salt, and turmeric. Blend until smooth. 2. Place the game hen halves in a large bowl. Pour the cilantro mixture over the hen halves and toss to coat. Marinate at room temperature for 30 minutes, or cover and refrigerate for up to 24 hours. 3. Arrange the hen halves in a single layer in the air fryer basket. Set the air fryer to 400°F (204°C) for 20 minutes. Use a meat thermometer to ensure the game hens have reached an internal temperature of 165°F (74°C).

Barbecue Chicken and Coleslaw Tostadas

Prep time: 15 minutes | Cook time: 40 minutes | Makes 4 tostadas

Coleslaw:

- ¼ cup sour cream
- ¼ small green cabbage, finely chopped
- ½ tablespoon white vinegar
- ½ teaspoon garlic powder
- ½ teaspoon salt
- ¼ teaspoon ground black pepper

Tostadas:

- 2 cups pulled rotisserie chicken
- ½ cup barbecue sauce
- 4 corn tortillas
- ½ cup shredded Mozzarella cheese
- Cooking spray

Make the Coleslaw: 1. Combine the ingredients for the coleslaw in a large bowl. Toss to mix well. 2. Refrigerate until ready to serve. Make the Tostadas: 1. Preheat the air fryer to 370°F (188°C). Spritz the air fryer basket with cooking spray. 2. Toss the chicken with barbecue sauce in a separate large bowl to combine well. Set aside. 3. Place one tortilla in the preheated air fryer and spritz with cooking spray. Work in batches to avoid overcrowding. 4. Air fry the tortilla for 5 minutes or until lightly browned, then spread a quarter of the barbecue chicken and cheese over. 5. Air fry for another 5 minutes or until the cheese melts. Repeat with remaining tortillas, chicken, and cheese. 6. Serve the tostadas with coleslaw on top.

Pomegranate-Glazed Chicken with Couscous Salad

Prep time: 25 minutes | Cook time: 20 minutes | Serves 4

- 3 tablespoons plus 2 teaspoons pomegranate molasses
- ½ teaspoon ground cinnamon
- 1 teaspoon minced fresh thyme
- Salt and ground black pepper, to taste
- 2 (12-ounce / 340-g) bone-in split chicken breasts, trimmed
- ¼ cup chicken broth
- ¼ cup water
- ½ cup couscous
- 1 tablespoon minced fresh parsley
- 2 ounces (57 g) cherry tomatoes, quartered
- 1 scallion, white part minced, green part sliced thin on bias
- 1 tablespoon extra-virgin olive oil
- 1 ounce (28 g) feta cheese, crumbled
- Cooking spray

1. Preheat the air fryer to 350ºF (177ºC). Spritz the air fryer basket with cooking spray. 2. Combine 3 tablespoons of pomegranate molasses, cinnamon, thyme, and ⅛ teaspoon of salt in a small bowl. Stir to mix well. Set aside. 3. Place the chicken breasts in the preheated air fryer, skin side down, and spritz with cooking spray. Sprinkle with salt and ground black pepper. 4. Air fry the chicken for 10 minutes, then brush the chicken with half of pomegranate molasses mixture and flip. Air fry for 5 more minutes. 5. Brush the chicken with remaining pomegranate molasses mixture and flip. Air fry for another 5 minutes or until the internal temperature of the chicken breasts reaches at least 165ºF (74ºC). 6. Meanwhile, pour the broth and water in a pot and bring to a boil over medium-high heat. Add the couscous and sprinkle with salt. Cover and simmer for 7 minutes or until the liquid is almost absorbed. 7. Combine the remaining ingredients, except for the cheese, with cooked couscous in a large bowl. Toss to mix well. Scatter with the feta cheese. 8. When the air frying is complete, remove the chicken from the air fryer and allow to cool for 10 minutes. Serve with vegetable and couscous salad.

Blackened Chicken

Prep time: 10 minutes | Cook time: 20 minutes | Serves 4

- 1 large egg, beaten
- ¾ cup Blackened seasoning
- 2 whole boneless, skinless
- chicken breasts (about 1 pound / 454 g each), halved
- 1 to 2 tablespoons oil

1. Place the beaten egg in one shallow bowl and the Blackened seasoning in another shallow bowl. 2. One at a time, dip chicken pieces in the beaten egg and the Blackened seasoning, coating thoroughly. 3. Preheat the air fryer to 360ºF (182ºC). Line the air fryer basket with parchment paper. 4. Place the chicken pieces on the parchment and spritz with oil. 5. Cook for 10 minutes. Flip the chicken, spritz it with oil, and cook for 10 minutes more until the internal temperature reaches 165ºF (74ºC) and the chicken is no longer pink inside. Let sit for 5 minutes before serving.

Bacon Lovers' Stuffed Chicken

Prep time: 10 minutes | Cook time: 20 minutes | Serves 4

- 4 (5-ounce / 142-g) boneless, skinless chicken breasts, pounded to ¼ inch thick
- 2 (5.2-ounce / 147-g) packages Boursin cheese (or Kite Hill brand chive
- cream cheese style spread, softened, for dairy-free)
- 8 slices thin-cut bacon or beef bacon
- Sprig of fresh cilantro, for garnish (optional)

1. Spray the air fryer basket with avocado oil. Preheat the air fryer to 400ºF (204ºC). 2. Place one of the chicken breasts on a cutting board. With a sharp knife held parallel to the cutting board, make a 1-inch-wide incision at the top of the breast. Carefully cut into the breast to form a large pocket, leaving a ½-inch border along the sides and bottom. Repeat with the other 3 chicken breasts. 3. Snip the corner of a large resealable plastic bag to form a ¾-inch hole. Place the Boursin cheese in the bag and pipe the cheese into the pockets in the chicken breasts, dividing the cheese evenly among them. 4. Wrap 2 slices of bacon around each chicken breast and secure the ends with toothpicks. Place the bacon-wrapped chicken in the air fryer basket and air fry until the bacon is crisp and the chicken's internal temperature reaches 165ºF (74ºC), about 18 to 20 minutes, flipping after 10 minutes. Garnish with a sprig of cilantro before serving, if desired. 5. Store leftovers in an airtight container in the refrigerator for up to 4 days. Reheat in a preheated 400ºF (204ºC) air fryer for 5 minutes, or until warmed through.

Garlic Dill Wings

Prep time: 5 minutes | Cook time: 25 minutes | Serves 4

- 2 pounds (907 g) bone-in chicken wings, separated at joints
- ½ teaspoon salt
- ½ teaspoon ground black
- pepper
- ½ teaspoon onion powder
- ½ teaspoon garlic powder
- 1 teaspoon dried dill

1. In a large bowl, toss wings with salt, pepper, onion powder, garlic powder, and dill until evenly coated. Place wings into ungreased air fryer basket in a single layer, working in batches if needed. 2. Adjust the temperature to 400ºF (204ºC) and air fry for 25 minutes, shaking the basket every 7 minutes during cooking. Wings should have an internal temperature of at least 165ºF (74ºC) and be golden brown when done. Serve warm.

Quick Chicken Fajitas

Prep time: 10 minutes | Cook time: 15 minutes | Serves 2

- 10 ounces (283 g) boneless, skinless chicken breast, sliced into ¼-inch strips
- 2 tablespoons coconut oil, melted
- 1 tablespoon chili powder
- ½ teaspoon cumin
- ½ teaspoon paprika
- ½ teaspoon garlic powder
- ¼ medium onion, peeled and sliced
- ½ medium green bell pepper, seeded and sliced
- ½ medium red bell pepper, seeded and sliced

1. Place chicken and coconut oil into a large bowl and sprinkle with chili powder, cumin, paprika, and garlic powder. Toss chicken until well coated with seasoning. Place chicken into the air fryer basket. 2. Adjust the temperature to 350°F (177°C) and air fry for 15 minutes. 3. Add onion and peppers into the basket when the cooking time has 7 minutes remaining. 4. Toss the chicken two or three times during cooking. Vegetables should be tender and chicken fully cooked to at least 165°F (74°C) internal temperature when finished. Serve warm.

Chicken Breasts with Asparagus, Beans, and Arugula

Prep time: 20 minutes | Cook time: 25 minutes | Serves 2

- 1 cup canned cannellini beans, rinsed
- 1½ tablespoons red wine vinegar
- 1 garlic clove, minced
- 2 tablespoons extra-virgin olive oil, divided
- Salt and ground black pepper, to taste
- ½ red onion, sliced thinly
- 8 ounces (227 g) asparagus,
- trimmed and cut into 1-inch lengths
- 2 (8-ounce / 227-g) boneless, skinless chicken breasts, trimmed
- ¼ teaspoon paprika
- ½ teaspoon ground coriander
- 2 ounces (57 g) baby arugula, rinsed and drained

1. Preheat the air fryer to 400°F (204°C). 2. Warm the beans in microwave for 1 minutes and combine with red wine vinegar, garlic, 1 tablespoon of olive oil, ¼ teaspoon of salt, and ¼ teaspoon of ground black pepper in a bowl. Stir to mix well. 3. Combine the onion with ⅛ teaspoon of salt, ⅛ teaspoon of ground black pepper, and 2 teaspoons of olive oil in a separate bowl. Toss to coat well. 4. Place the onion in the air fryer and air fry for 2 minutes, then add the asparagus and air fry for 8 more minutes or until the asparagus is tender. Shake the basket halfway through. Transfer the onion and asparagus to the bowl with beans. Set aside. 5. Toss the chicken breasts with remaining ingredients, except for the baby arugula, in a large bowl. 6. Put the chicken breasts in the air fryer and air fry for 14 minutes or until the internal temperature of the chicken reaches at least

165°F (74°C). Flip the breasts halfway through. 7. Remove the chicken from the air fryer and serve on an aluminum foil with asparagus, beans, onion, and arugula. Sprinkle with salt and ground black pepper. Toss to serve.

Lemon-Dijon Boneless Chicken

Prep time: 30 minutes | Cook time: 13 to 16 minutes | Serves 6

- ½ cup sugar-free mayonnaise
- 1 tablespoon Dijon mustard
- 1 tablespoon freshly squeezed lemon juice (optional)
- 1 tablespoon coconut aminos
- 1 teaspoon Italian
- seasoning
- 1 teaspoon sea salt
- ½ teaspoon freshly ground black pepper
- ¼ teaspoon cayenne pepper
- 1½ pounds (680 g) boneless, skinless chicken breasts or thighs

1. In a small bowl, combine the mayonnaise, mustard, lemon juice (if using), coconut aminos, Italian seasoning, salt, black pepper, and cayenne pepper. 2. Place the chicken in a shallow dish or large zip-top plastic bag. Add the marinade, making sure all the pieces are coated. Cover and refrigerate for at least 30 minutes or up to 4 hours. 3. Set the air fryer to 400°F (204°C). Arrange the chicken in a single layer in the air fryer basket, working in batches if necessary. Air fry for 7 minutes. Flip the chicken and continue cooking for 6 to 9 minutes more, until an instant-read thermometer reads 160°F (71°C).

Bell Pepper Stuffed Chicken Roll-Ups

Prep time: 10 minutes | Cook time: 12 minutes | Serves 4

- 2 (4-ounce / 113-g) boneless, skinless chicken breasts, slice in half horizontally
- 1 tablespoon olive oil
- Juice of ½ lime
- 2 tablespoons taco
- seasoning
- ½ green bell pepper, cut into strips
- ½ red bell pepper, cut into strips
- ¼ onion, sliced

1. Preheat the air fryer to 400°F (204°C). 2. Unfold the chicken breast slices on a clean work surface. Rub with olive oil, then drizzle with lime juice and sprinkle with taco seasoning. 3. Top the chicken slices with equal amount of bell peppers and onion. Roll them up and secure with toothpicks. 4. Arrange the chicken roll-ups in the preheated air fryer. Air fry for 12 minutes or until the internal temperature of the chicken reaches at least 165°F (74°C). Flip the chicken roll-ups halfway through. 5. Remove the chicken from the air fryer. Discard the toothpicks and serve immediately.

Honey-Glazed Chicken Thighs

Prep time: 5 minutes | Cook time: 14 minutes | Serves 4

- Oil, for spraying
- 4 boneless, skinless chicken thighs, fat trimmed
- 3 tablespoons soy sauce
- 1 tablespoon balsamic
- vinegar
- 2 teaspoons honey
- 2 teaspoons minced garlic
- 1 teaspoon ground ginger

1. Preheat the air fryer to 400°F (204°C). Line the air fryer basket with parchment and spray lightly with oil. 2. Place the chicken in the prepared basket. 3. Cook for 7 minutes, flip, and cook for another 7 minutes, or until the internal temperature reaches 165°F (74°C) and the juices run clear. 4. In a small saucepan, combine the soy sauce, balsamic vinegar, honey, garlic, and ginger and cook over low heat for 1 to 2 minutes, until warmed through. 5. Transfer the chicken to a serving plate and drizzle with the sauce just before serving.

Buffalo Crispy Chicken Strips

Prep time: 15 minutes | Cook time: 13 to 17 minutes per batch | Serves 4

- ¾ cup all-purpose flour
- 2 eggs
- 2 tablespoons water
- 1 cup seasoned panko bread crumbs
- 2 teaspoons granulated garlic
- 1 teaspoon salt
- 1 teaspoon freshly ground
- black pepper
- 16 chicken breast strips, or 3 large boneless, skinless chicken breasts, cut into 1-inch strips
- Olive oil spray
- ¼ cup Buffalo sauce, plus more as needed

1. Put the flour in a small bowl. 2. In another small bowl, whisk the eggs and the water. 3. In a third bowl, stir together the panko, granulated garlic, salt, and pepper. 4. Dip each chicken strip in the flour, in the egg, and in the panko mixture to coat. Press the crumbs onto the chicken with your fingers. 5. Insert the crisper plate into the basket and the basket into the unit. Preheat the unit by selecting AIR FRY, setting the temperature to 375°F (191°C), and setting the time to 3 minutes. Select START/STOP to begin. 6. Once the unit is preheated, place a parchment paper liner into the basket. Working in batches if needed, place the chicken strips into the basket. Do not stack unless using a wire rack for the second layer. Spray the top of the chicken with olive oil. 7. Select AIR FRY, set the temperature to 375°F (191°C), and set the time to 17 minutes. Select START/STOP to begin. 8. After 10 or 12 minutes, remove the basket, flip the chicken, and spray again with olive oil. Reinsert the basket to resume cooking. 9. When the cooking is complete, the chicken should be golden brown and crispy and a food thermometer inserted into the chicken should register 165°F (74°C). 10. Repeat steps 6, 7, and 8 with any remaining chicken. 11. Transfer the chicken to a large bowl.

Drizzle the Buffalo sauce over the top of the cooked chicken, toss to coat, and serve.

Chicken and Broccoli Casserole

Prep time: 5 minutes | Cook time: 20 to 25 minutes | Serves 4

- ½ pound (227 g) broccoli, chopped into florets
- 2 cups shredded cooked chicken
- 4 ounces (113 g) cream cheese
- ⅓ cup heavy cream
- 1½ teaspoons Dijon
- mustard
- ½ teaspoon garlic powder
- Salt and freshly ground black pepper, to taste
- 2 tablespoons chopped fresh basil
- 1 cup shredded Cheddar cheese

1. Preheat the air fryer to 390°F (199°C). Lightly coat a casserole dish that will fit in air fryer, with olive oil and set aside. 2. Place the broccoli in a large glass bowl with 1 tablespoon of water and cover with a microwavable plate. Microwave on high for 2 to 3 minutes until the broccoli is bright green but not mushy. Drain if necessary and add to another large bowl along with the shredded chicken. 3. In the same glass bowl used to microwave the broccoli, combine the cream cheese and cream. Microwave for 30 seconds to 1 minute on high and stir until smooth. Add the mustard and garlic powder and season to taste with salt and freshly ground black pepper. Whisk until the sauce is smooth. 4. Pour the warm sauce over the broccoli and chicken mixture and then add the basil. Using a silicone spatula, gently fold the mixture until thoroughly combined. 5. Transfer the chicken mixture to the prepared casserole dish and top with the cheese. Air fry for 20 to 25 minutes until warmed through and the cheese has browned.

Jerk Chicken Kebabs

Prep time: 10 minutes | Cook time: 14 minutes | Serves 4

- 8 ounces (227 g) boneless, skinless chicken thighs, cut into 1-inch cubes
- 2 tablespoons jerk seasoning
- 2 tablespoons coconut oil
- ½ medium red bell pepper,
- seeded and cut into 1-inch pieces
- ¼ medium red onion, peeled and cut into 1-inch pieces
- ½ teaspoon salt

1. Place chicken in a medium bowl and sprinkle with jerk seasoning and coconut oil. Toss to coat on all sides. 2. Using eight (6-inch) skewers, build skewers by alternating chicken, pepper, and onion pieces, about three repetitions per skewer. 3. Sprinkle salt over skewers and place into ungreased air fryer basket. Adjust the temperature to 370°F (188°C) and air fry for 14 minutes, turning skewers halfway through cooking. Chicken will be golden and have an internal temperature of at least 165°F (74°C) when done. Serve warm.

Pickle Brined Fried Chicken

Prep time: 30 minutes | Cook time: 47 minutes | Serves 4

- 4 bone-in, skin-on chicken legs, cut into drumsticks and thighs (about 3½ pounds / 1.6 kg)
- Pickle juice from 1 (24 ounces / 680 g) jar kosher dill pickles
- ½ cup flour
- Salt and freshly ground black pepper, to taste
- 2 eggs
- 1 cup fine bread crumbs
- 1 teaspoon salt
- 1 teaspoon freshly ground black pepper
- ½ teaspoon ground paprika
- ⅛ teaspoon ground cayenne pepper
- Vegetable or canola oil

1. Place the chicken in a shallow dish and pour the pickle juice over the top. Cover and transfer the chicken to the refrigerator to brine in the pickle juice for 3 to 8 hours. 2. When you are ready to cook, remove the chicken from the refrigerator to let it come to room temperature while you set up a dredging station. Place the flour in a shallow dish and season well with salt and freshly ground black pepper. Whisk the eggs in a second shallow dish. In a third shallow dish, combine the bread crumbs, salt, pepper, paprika and cayenne pepper. 3. Preheat the air fryer to 370°F (188°C). 4. Remove the chicken from the pickle brine and gently dry it with a clean kitchen towel. Dredge each piece of chicken in the flour, then dip it into the egg mixture, and finally press it into the bread crumb mixture to coat all sides of the chicken. Place the breaded chicken on a plate or baking sheet and spray each piece all over with vegetable oil. 5. Air fry the chicken in two batches. Place two chicken thighs and two drumsticks into the air fryer basket. Air fry for 10 minutes. Then, gently turn the chicken pieces over and air fry for another 10 minutes. Remove the chicken pieces and let them rest on plate, do not cover. Repeat with the second batch of chicken, air frying for 20 minutes, turning the chicken over halfway through. 6. Lower the temperature of the air fryer to 340°F (171°C). Place the first batch of chicken on top of the second batch already in the basket and air fry for an additional 7 minutes. Serve warm and enjoy.

Chicken Pesto Pizzas

Prep time: 10 minutes | Cook time: 12 minutes | Serves 4

- 1 pound (454 g) ground chicken thighs
- ¼ teaspoon salt
- ⅛ teaspoon ground black pepper
- ¼ cup basil pesto
- 1 cup shredded Mozzarella cheese
- 4 grape tomatoes, sliced

1. Cut four squares of parchment paper to fit into your air fryer basket. 2. Place ground chicken in a large bowl and mix with salt and pepper. Divide mixture into four equal sections. 3. Wet your hands with water to prevent sticking, then press each section into a 6-inch circle onto a piece of ungreased parchment. Place each chicken crust into air fryer basket, working in batches if needed. 4. Adjust the temperature to 350°F (177°C) and air fry for 10 minutes, turning crusts halfway through cooking. 5. Spread 1 tablespoon pesto across the top of each crust, then sprinkle with ¼ cup Mozzarella and top with 1 sliced tomato. Continue cooking at 350°F (177°C) for 2 minutes. Cheese will be melted and brown when done. Serve warm.

Crunchy Chicken Tenders

Prep time: 5 minutes | Cook time: 12 minutes | Serves 4

- 1 egg
- ¼ cup unsweetened almond milk
- ¼ cup whole wheat flour
- ¼ cup whole wheat bread crumbs
- ½ teaspoon salt
- ½ teaspoon black pepper
- ½ teaspoon dried thyme
- ½ teaspoon dried sage
- ½ teaspoon garlic powder
- 1 pound (454 g) chicken tenderloins
- 1 lemon, quartered

1. Preheat the air fryer to 360°F(182°C). 2. In a shallow bowl, beat together the egg and almond milk until frothy. 3. In a separate shallow bowl, whisk together the flour, bread crumbs, salt, pepper, thyme, sage, and garlic powder. 4. Dip each chicken tenderloin into the egg mixture, then into the bread crumb mixture, coating the outside with the crumbs. Place the breaded chicken tenderloins into the bottom of the air fryer basket in an even layer, making sure that they don't touch each other. 5. Cook for 6 minutes, then turn and cook for an additional 5 to 6 minutes. Serve with lemon slices.

Chicken Burgers with Ham and Cheese

Prep time: 12 minutes | Cook time: 13 to 16 minutes | Serves 4

- ⅓ cup soft bread crumbs
- 3 tablespoons milk
- 1 egg, beaten
- ½ teaspoon dried thyme
- Pinch salt
- Freshly ground black
- pepper, to taste
- 1¼ pounds (567 g) ground chicken
- ¼ cup finely chopped ham
- ⅓ cup grated Havarti cheese
- Olive oil for misting

1. Preheat the air fryer to 350°F (177°C). 2. In a medium bowl, combine the bread crumbs, milk, egg, thyme, salt, and pepper. Add the chicken and mix gently but thoroughly with clean hands. 3. Form the chicken into eight thin patties and place on waxed paper. 4. Top four of the patties with the ham and cheese. Top with remaining four patties and gently press the edges together to seal, so the ham and cheese mixture is in the middle of the burger. 5. Place the burgers in the basket and mist with olive oil. Bake for 13 to 16 minutes or until the chicken is thoroughly cooked to 165°F (74°C) as measured with a meat thermometer. Serve immediately.

Ranch Chicken Wings

Prep time: 10 minutes | Cook time: 40 minutes | Serves 4

- 2 tablespoons water
- 2 tablespoons hot pepper sauce
- 2 tablespoons unsalted butter, melted
- 2 tablespoons apple cider vinegar
- 1 (1-ounce / 28-g) envelope ranch salad dressing mix
- 1 teaspoon paprika
- 4 pounds (1.8 kg) chicken wings, tips removed
- Cooking oil spray

1. In a large bowl, whisk the water, hot pepper sauce, melted butter, vinegar, salad dressing mix, and paprika until combined. 2. Add the wings and toss to coat. At this point, you can cover the bowl and marinate the wings in the refrigerator for 4 to 24 hours for best results. However, you can just let the wings stand for 30 minutes in the refrigerator. 3. Insert the crisper plate into the basket and the basket into the unit. Preheat the unit by selecting AIR FRY, setting the temperature to 400°F (204°C), and setting the time to 3 minutes. Select START/STOP to begin. 4. Once the unit is preheated, spray the crisper plate with cooking oil. Working in batches, put half the wings into the basket; it is okay to stack them. Refrigerate the remaining wings. 5. Select AIR FRY, set the temperature to 400°F (204°C), and set the time to 20 minutes. Select START/STOP to begin. 6. After 5 minutes, remove the basket and shake it. Reinsert the basket to resume cooking. Remove and shake the basket every 5 minutes, three more times, until the chicken is browned and glazed and a food thermometer inserted into the wings registers 165°F (74°C). 7. Repeat steps 4, 5, and 6 with the remaining wings. 8. When the cooking is complete, serve warm.

Chicken with Lettuce

Prep time: 15 minutes | Cook time: 14 minutes | Serves 4

- 1 pound (454 g) chicken breast tenders, chopped into bite-size pieces
- ½ onion, thinly sliced
- ½ red bell pepper, seeded and thinly sliced
- ½ green bell pepper, seeded and thinly sliced
- 1 tablespoon olive oil
- 1 tablespoon fajita seasoning
- 1 teaspoon kosher salt
- Juice of ½ lime
- 8 large lettuce leaves
- 1 cup prepared guacamole

1. Preheat the air fryer to 400°F (204°C). 2. In a large bowl, combine the chicken, onion, and peppers. Drizzle with the olive oil and toss until thoroughly coated. Add the fajita seasoning and salt and toss again. 3. Working in batches if necessary, arrange the chicken and vegetables in a single layer in the air fryer basket. Pausing halfway through the cooking time to shake the basket, air fry for 14 minutes, or until the vegetables are tender and a thermometer inserted into the thickest piece of chicken registers 165°F (74°C). 4. Transfer the mixture to a serving platter and drizzle with the fresh lime juice. Serve with the lettuce leaves and top with the guacamole.

Chapter 5

Beef, Pork, and Lamb

Almond and Caraway Crust Steak

Prep time: 16 minutes | Cook time: 10 minutes | Serves 4

- ⅓ cup almond flour
- 2 eggs
- 2 teaspoons caraway seeds
- 4 beef steaks
- 2 teaspoons garlic powder
- 1 tablespoon melted butter
- Fine sea salt and cayenne pepper, to taste

1. Generously coat steaks with garlic powder, caraway seeds, salt, and cayenne pepper. 2. In a mixing dish, thoroughly combine melted butter with seasoned crumbs. In another bowl, beat the eggs until they're well whisked. 3. First, coat steaks with the beaten egg; then, coat beef steaks with the buttered crumb mixture. Place the steaks in the air fryer basket; cook for 10 minutes at 355ºF (179ºC). Bon appétit!

Swedish Meatloaf

Prep time: 10 minutes | Cook time: 35 minutes | Serves 8

- 1½ pounds (680 g) ground beef (85% lean)
- ¼ pound (113 g) ground pork
- 1 large egg (omit for egg-free)
- ½ cup minced onions

Sauce:

- ½ cup (1 stick) unsalted butter
- ½ cup shredded Swiss or mild Cheddar cheese (about 2 ounces / 57 g)
- 2 ounces (57 g) cream

- ¼ cup tomato sauce
- 2 tablespoons dry mustard
- 2 cloves garlic, minced
- 2 teaspoons fine sea salt
- 1 teaspoon ground black pepper, plus more for garnish

cheese (¼ cup), softened
- ⅓ cup beef broth
- ⅛ teaspoon ground nutmeg
- Halved cherry tomatoes, for serving (optional)

1. Preheat the air fryer to 390ºF (199ºC). 2. In a large bowl, combine the ground beef, ground pork, egg, onions, tomato sauce, dry mustard, garlic, salt, and pepper. Using your hands, mix until well combined. 3. Place the meatloaf mixture in a loaf pan and place it in the air fryer. Bake for 35 minutes, or until cooked through and the internal temperature reaches 145ºF (63ºC). Check the meatloaf after 25 minutes; if it's getting too brown on the top, cover it loosely with foil to prevent burning. 4. While the meatloaf cooks, make the sauce: Heat the butter in a saucepan over medium-high heat until it sizzles and brown flecks appear, stirring constantly to keep the butter from burning. Turn the heat down to low and whisk in the Swiss cheese, cream cheese, broth, and nutmeg. Simmer for at least 10 minutes. The longer it simmers, the more the flavors open up. 5. When the meatloaf is done, transfer it to a serving tray and pour the sauce over it. Garnish with ground black pepper and serve with cherry tomatoes, if desired. Allow the meatloaf

to rest for 10 minutes before slicing so it doesn't crumble apart. 6. Store leftovers in an airtight container in the fridge for 3 days or in the freezer for up to a month. Reheat in a preheated 350ºF (177ºC) air fryer for 4 minutes, or until heated through.

Rack of Lamb with Pistachio Crust

Prep time: 10 minutes | Cook time: 19 minutes | Serves 2

- ½ cup finely chopped pistachios
- 3 tablespoons panko bread crumbs
- 1 teaspoon chopped fresh rosemary
- 2 teaspoons chopped fresh

oregano
- Salt and freshly ground black pepper, to taste
- 1 tablespoon olive oil
- 1 rack of lamb, bones trimmed of fat and frenched
- 1 tablespoon Dijon mustard

1. Preheat the air fryer to 380ºF (193ºC). 2. Combine the pistachios, bread crumbs, rosemary, oregano, salt and pepper in a small bowl. (This is a good job for your food processor if you have one.) Drizzle in the olive oil and stir to combine. 3. Season the rack of lamb with salt and pepper on all sides and transfer it to the air fryer basket with the fat side facing up. Air fry the lamb for 12 minutes. Remove the lamb from the air fryer and brush the fat side of the lamb rack with the Dijon mustard. Coat the rack with the pistachio mixture, pressing the bread crumbs onto the lamb with your hands and rolling the bottom of the rack in any of the crumbs that fall off. 4. Return the rack of lamb to the air fryer and air fry for another 3 to 7 minutes or until an instant read thermometer reads 140ºF (60ºC) for medium. Add or subtract a couple of minutes for lamb that is more or less well cooked. (Your time will vary depending on how big the rack of lamb is.) 5. Let the lamb rest for at least 5 minutes. Then, slice into chops and serve.

Beef and Spinach Rolls

Prep time: 10 minutes | Cook time: 14 minutes | Serves 2

- 3 teaspoons pesto
- 2 pounds (907 g) beef flank steak
- 6 slices provolone cheese
- 3 ounces (85 g) roasted red

bell peppers
- ¾ cup baby spinach
- 1 teaspoon sea salt
- 1 teaspoon black pepper

1. Preheat the air fryer to 400ºF (204ºC). 2. Spoon equal amounts of the pesto onto each flank steak and spread it across evenly. 3. Put the cheese, roasted red peppers and spinach on top of the meat, about three-quarters of the way down. 4. Roll the steak up, holding it in place with toothpicks. Sprinkle with the sea salt and pepper. 5. Put inside the air fryer and air fry for 14 minutes, turning halfway through the cooking time. 6. Allow the beef to rest for 10 minutes before slicing up and serving.

Sesame Beef Lettuce Tacos

Prep time: 30 minutes | Cook time: 8 to 10 minutes | Serves 4

- ¼ cup coconut aminos
- ¼ cup avocado oil
- 2 tablespoons cooking sherry
- 1 tablespoon Swerve
- 1 tablespoon ground cumin
- 1 teaspoon minced garlic
- Sea salt and freshly ground black pepper, to taste
- 1 pound (454 g) flank steak
- 8 butter lettuce leaves
- 2 scallions, sliced
- 1 tablespoon toasted sesame seeds
- Hot sauce, for serving
- Lime wedges, for serving
- Flaky sea salt (optional)

1. In a small bowl, whisk together the coconut aminos, avocado oil, cooking sherry, Swerve, cumin, garlic, and salt and pepper to taste. 2. Place the steak in a shallow dish. Pour the marinade over the beef. Cover the dish with plastic wrap and let it marinate in the refrigerator for at least 2 hours or overnight. 3. Remove the flank steak from the dish and discard the marinade. 4. Set the air fryer to 400ºF (204ºC). Place the steak in the air fryer basket and air fry for 4 to 6 minutes. Flip the steak and cook for 4 minutes more, until an instant-read thermometer reads 120ºF (49ºC) at the thickest part (or cook it to your desired doneness). Allow the steak to rest for 10 minutes, then slice it thinly against the grain. 5. Stack 2 lettuce leaves on top of each other and add some sliced meat. Top with scallions and sesame seeds. Drizzle with hot sauce and lime juice, and finish with a little flaky salt (if using). Repeat with the remaining lettuce leaves and fillings.

Italian Sausages with Peppers and Onions

Prep time: 5 minutes | Cook time: 28 minutes | Serves 3

- 1 medium onion, thinly sliced
- 1 yellow or orange bell pepper, thinly sliced
- 1 red bell pepper, thinly sliced
- ¼ cup avocado oil or melted coconut oil
- 1 teaspoon fine sea salt
- 6 Italian sausages
- Dijon mustard, for serving (optional)

1. Preheat the air fryer to 400ºF (204ºC). 2. Place the onion and peppers in a large bowl. Drizzle with the oil and toss well to coat the veggies. Season with the salt. 3. Place the onion and peppers in a pie pan and cook in the air fryer for 8 minutes, stirring halfway through. Remove from the air fryer and set aside. 4. Spray the air fryer basket with avocado oil. Place the sausages in the air fryer basket and air fry for 20 minutes, or until crispy and golden brown. During the last minute or two of cooking, add the onion and peppers to the basket with the sausages to warm them through. 5. Place the onion and peppers on a serving platter and arrange the sausages on top.

Serve Dijon mustard on the side, if desired. 6. Store leftovers in an airtight container in the fridge for up to 7 days or in the freezer for up to a month. Reheat in a preheated 390ºF (199ºC) air fryer for 3 minutes, or until heated through.

Short Ribs with Chimichurri

Prep time: 30 minutes | Cook time: 13 minutes | Serves 4

- 1 pound (454 g) boneless short ribs
- 1½ teaspoons sea salt, divided
- ½ teaspoon freshly ground black pepper, divided
- ½ cup fresh parsley leaves
- ½ cup fresh cilantro leaves
- 1 teaspoon minced garlic
- 1 tablespoon freshly squeezed lemon juice
- ½ teaspoon ground cumin
- ¼ teaspoon red pepper flakes
- 2 tablespoons extra-virgin olive oil
- Avocado oil spray

1. Pat the short ribs dry with paper towels. Sprinkle the ribs all over with 1 teaspoon salt and ¼ teaspoon black pepper. Let sit at room temperature for 45 minutes. 2. Meanwhile, place the parsley, cilantro, garlic, lemon juice, cumin, red pepper flakes, the remaining ½ teaspoon salt, and the remaining ¼ teaspoon black pepper in a blender or food processor. With the blender running, slowly drizzle in the olive oil. Blend for about 1 minute, until the mixture is smooth and well combined. 3. Set the air fryer to 400ºF (204ºC). Spray both sides of the ribs with oil. Place in the basket and air fry for 8 minutes. Flip and cook for another 5 minutes, until an instant-read thermometer reads 125ºF (52ºC) for medium-rare (or to your desired doneness). 4. Allow the meat to rest for 5 to 10 minutes, then slice. Serve warm with the chimichurri sauce.

Carne Asada

Prep time: 5 minutes | Cook time: 15 minutes | Serves 4

- 3 chipotle peppers in adobo, chopped
- ⅓ cup chopped fresh oregano
- ⅓ cup chopped fresh parsley
- 4 cloves garlic, minced
- Juice of 2 limes
- 1 teaspoon ground cumin seeds
- ⅓ cup olive oil
- 1 to 1½ pounds (454 g to 680 g) flank steak
- Salt, to taste

1. Combine the chipotle, oregano, parsley, garlic, lime juice, cumin, and olive oil in a large bowl. Stir to mix well. 2. Dunk the flank steak in the mixture and press to coat well. Wrap the bowl in plastic and marinate under room temperature for at least 30 minutes. 3. Preheat the air fryer to 390ºF (199ºC). 4. Discard the marinade and place the steak in the preheated air fryer. Sprinkle with salt. 5. Air fry for 15 minutes or until the steak is medium-rare or it reaches your desired doneness. Flip the steak halfway through the cooking time. 6. Remove the steak from the air fryer and slice to serve.

Spicy Sirloin Tip Steak

Prep time: 25 minutes | Cook time: 12 to 18 minutes | Serves 4

- 2 tablespoons salsa
- 1 tablespoon minced chipotle pepper
- 1 tablespoon apple cider vinegar
- 1 teaspoon ground cumin
- ⅛ teaspoon freshly ground black pepper
- ⅛ teaspoon red pepper flakes
- 12 ounces (340 g) sirloin tip steak, cut into 4 pieces and gently pounded to about ⅓ inch thick
- Cooking oil spray

1. In a small bowl, thoroughly mix the salsa, chipotle pepper, vinegar, cumin, black pepper, and red pepper flakes. Rub this mixture into both sides of each steak piece. Let stand for 15 minutes at room temperature. 2. Insert the crisper plate into the basket and place the basket into the unit. Preheat the unit by selecting AIR FRY, setting the temperature to 390ºF (199ºC), and setting the time to 3 minutes. Select START/STOP to begin. 3. Once the unit is preheated, spray the crisper plate with cooking oil. Working in batches, place 2 steaks into the basket. 4. Select AIR FRY, set the temperature to 390ºF (199ºC), and set the time to 9 minutes. Select START/STOP to begin. 5. After about 6 minutes, check the steaks. If a food thermometer inserted into the meat registers at least 145ºF (63ºC), they are done. If not, resume cooking. 6. When the cooking is done, transfer the steaks to a clean plate and cover with aluminum foil to keep warm. Repeat steps 3, 4, and 5 with the remaining steaks. 7. Thinly slice the steaks against the grain and serve.

Smothered Chops

Prep time: 20 minutes | Cook time: 30 minutes | Serves 4

- 4 bone-in pork chops (8 ounces / 227 g each)
- 2 teaspoons salt, divided
- 1½ teaspoons freshly ground black pepper, divided
- 1 teaspoon garlic powder
- 1 cup tomato purée
- 1½ teaspoons Italian seasoning
- 1 tablespoon sugar
- 1 tablespoon cornstarch
- ½ cup chopped onion
- ½ cup chopped green bell pepper
- 1 to 2 tablespoons oil

1. Evenly season the pork chops with 1 teaspoon salt, 1 teaspoon pepper, and the garlic powder. 2. In a medium bowl, stir together the tomato purée, Italian seasoning, sugar, remaining 1 teaspoon of salt, and remaining ½ teaspoon of pepper. 3. In a small bowl, whisk ¾ cup water and the cornstarch until blended. Stir this slurry into the tomato purée, with the onion and green bell pepper. Transfer to a baking pan. 4. Preheat the air fryer to 350ºF (177ºC). 5. Place the sauce in the fryer and cook for 10 minutes. Stir and cook for 10 minutes more. Remove the pan and keep warm. 6. Increase the air fryer temperature to 400ºF (204ºC). Line the air fryer basket with parchment paper. 7. Place the pork chops on the parchment and spritz with oil. 8. Cook for 5 minutes. Flip and spritz the chops with oil and cook for 5 minutes more, until the internal temperature reaches 145ºF (63ºC). Serve with the tomato mixture spooned on top.

Panko Crusted Calf's Liver Strips

Prep time: 15 minutes | Cook time: 23 to 25 minutes | Serves 4

- 1 pound (454 g) sliced calf's liver, cut into ½-inch wide strips
- 2 eggs
- 2 tablespoons milk
- ½ cup whole wheat flour
- 2 cups panko breadcrumbs
- Salt and ground black pepper, to taste
- Cooking spray

1. Preheat the air fryer to 390ºF (199ºC) and spritz with cooking spray. 2. Rub the calf's liver strips with salt and ground black pepper on a clean work surface. 3. Whisk the eggs with milk in a large bowl. Pour the flour in a shallow dish. Pour the panko on a separate shallow dish. 4. Dunk the liver strips in the flour, then in the egg mixture. Shake the excess off and roll the strips over the panko to coat well. 5. Arrange half of the liver strips in a single layer in the preheated air fryer and spritz with cooking spray. 6. Air fry for 5 minutes or until browned. Flip the strips halfway through. Repeat with the remaining strips. 7. Serve immediately.

Sweet and Spicy Country-Style Ribs

Prep time: 10 minutes | Cook time: 25 minutes | Serves 4

- 2 tablespoons brown sugar
- 2 tablespoons smoked paprika
- 1 teaspoon garlic powder
- 1 teaspoon onion powder
- 1 teaspoon dry mustard
- 1 teaspoon ground cumin
- 1 teaspoon kosher salt
- 1 teaspoon black pepper
- ¼ to ½ teaspoon cayenne pepper
- 1½ pounds (680 g) boneless country-style pork ribs
- 1 cup barbecue sauce

1. In a small bowl, stir together the brown sugar, paprika, garlic powder, onion powder, dry mustard, cumin, salt, black pepper, and cayenne. Mix until well combined. 2. Pat the ribs dry with a paper towel. Generously sprinkle the rub evenly over both sides of the ribs and rub in with your fingers. 3. Place the ribs in the air fryer basket. Set the air fryer to 350ºF (177ºC) for 15 minutes. Turn the ribs and brush with ½ cup of the barbecue sauce. Cook for an additional 10 minutes. Use a meat thermometer to ensure the pork has reached an internal temperature of 145ºF (63ºC). 4. Serve with remaining barbecue sauce.

Spicy Flank Steak with Zhoug

Prep time: 30 minutes | Cook time: 8 minutes | Serves 4

Marinade and Steak:

- ½ cup dark beer or orange juice
- ¼ cup fresh lemon juice
- 3 cloves garlic, minced
- 2 tablespoons extra-virgin olive oil
- 2 tablespoons Sriracha
- 2 tablespoons brown sugar
- 2 teaspoons ground cumin
- 2 teaspoons smoked paprika
- 1 tablespoon kosher salt
- 1 teaspoon black pepper
- 1½ pounds (680 g) flank steak, trimmed and cut into 3 pieces

Zhoug:

- 1 cup packed fresh cilantro leaves
- 2 cloves garlic, peeled
- 2 jalapeño or serrano chiles, stemmed and coarsely chopped
- ½ teaspoon ground cumin
- ¼ teaspoon ground coriander
- ¼ teaspoon kosher salt
- 2 to 4 tablespoons extra-virgin olive oil

1. For the marinade and steak: In a small bowl, whisk together the beer, lemon juice, garlic, olive oil, Sriracha, brown sugar, cumin, paprika, salt, and pepper. Place the steak in a large resealable plastic bag. Pour the marinade over the steak, seal the bag, and massage the steak to coat. Marinate in the refrigerator for 1 hour or up to 24 hours, turning the bag occasionally. 2. Meanwhile, for the zhoug: In a food processor, combine the cilantro, garlic, jalapeños, cumin, coriander, and salt. Process until finely chopped. Add 2 tablespoons olive oil and pulse to form a loose paste, adding up to 2 tablespoons more olive oil if needed. Transfer the zhoug to a glass container. Cover and store in the refrigerator until 30 minutes before serving if marinating more than 1 hour. 3. Remove the steak from the marinade and discard the marinade. Place the steak in the air fryer basket and set the air fryer to 400ºF (204ºC) for 8 minutes. Use a meat thermometer to ensure the steak has reached an internal temperature of 150ºF / 66ºC (for medium). 4. Transfer the steak to a cutting board and let rest for 5 minutes. Slice the steak across the grain and serve with the zhoug.

Smoky Pork Tenderloin

Prep time: 5 minutes | Cook time: 19 to 22 minutes | Serves 6

- 1½ pounds (680 g) pork tenderloin
- 1 tablespoon avocado oil
- 1 teaspoon chili powder
- 1 teaspoon smoked paprika
- 1 teaspoon garlic powder
- 1 teaspoon sea salt
- 1 teaspoon freshly ground black pepper

1. Pierce the tenderloin all over with a fork and rub the oil all over the meat. 2. In a small dish, stir together the chili powder, smoked paprika, garlic powder, salt, and pepper. 3. Rub the spice mixture all over the tenderloin. 4. Set the air fryer to 400ºF (204ºC). Place the pork in the air fryer basket and air fry for 10 minutes. Flip the tenderloin and cook for 9 to 12 minutes more, until an instant-read thermometer reads at least 145ºF (63ºC). 5. Allow the tenderloin to rest for 5 minutes, then slice and serve.

Sausage-Stuffed Peppers

Prep time: 15 minutes | Cook time: 28 to 30 minutes | Serves 6

- Avocado oil spray
- 8 ounces (227 g) Italian sausage, casings removed
- ½ cup chopped mushrooms
- ¼ cup diced onion
- 1 teaspoon Italian seasoning
- Sea salt and freshly ground
- black pepper, to taste
- 1 cup keto-friendly marinara sauce
- 3 bell peppers, halved and seeded
- 3 ounces (85 g) provolone cheese, shredded

1. Spray a large skillet with oil and place it over medium-high heat. Add the sausage and cook for 5 minutes, breaking up the meat with a wooden spoon. Add the mushrooms, onion, and Italian seasoning, and season with salt and pepper. Cook for 5 minutes more. Stir in the marinara sauce and cook until heated through. 2. Scoop the sausage filling into the bell pepper halves. 3. Set the air fryer to 350ºF (177ºC). Arrange the peppers in a single layer in the air fryer basket, working in batches if necessary. Air fry for 15 minutes. 4. Top the stuffed peppers with the cheese and air fry for 3 to 5 minutes more, until the cheese is melted and the peppers are tender.

Ham with Sweet Potatoes

Prep time: 20 minutes | Cook time: 15 to 17 minutes | Serves 4

- 1 cup freshly squeezed orange juice
- ½ cup packed light brown sugar
- 1 tablespoon Dijon mustard
- ½ teaspoon salt
- ½ teaspoon freshly ground
- black pepper
- 3 sweet potatoes, cut into small wedges
- 2 ham steaks (8 ounces / 227 g each), halved
- 1 to 2 tablespoons oil

1. In a large bowl, whisk the orange juice, brown sugar, Dijon, salt, and pepper until blended. Toss the sweet potato wedges with the brown sugar mixture. 2. Preheat the air fryer to 400ºF (204ºC). Line the air fryer basket with parchment paper and spritz with oil. 3. Place the sweet potato wedges on the parchment. 4. Cook for 10 minutes. 5. Place ham steaks on top of the sweet potatoes and brush everything with more of the orange juice mixture. 6. Cook for 3 minutes. Flip the ham and cook or 2 to 4 minutes more until the sweet potatoes are soft and the glaze has thickened. Cut the ham steaks in half to serve.

Spicy Lamb Sirloin Chops

Prep time: 30 minutes | Cook time: 15 minutes | Serves 4

- ½ yellow onion, coarsely chopped
- 4 coin-size slices peeled fresh ginger
- 5 garlic cloves
- 1 teaspoon garam masala
- 1 teaspoon ground fennel
- 1 teaspoon ground cinnamon
- 1 teaspoon ground turmeric
- ½ to 1 teaspoon cayenne pepper
- ½ teaspoon ground cardamom
- 1 teaspoon kosher salt
- 1 pound (454 g) lamb sirloin chops

1. In a blender, combine the onion, ginger, garlic, garam masala, fennel, cinnamon, turmeric, cayenne, cardamom, and salt. Pulse until the onion is finely minced and the mixture forms a thick paste, 3 to 4 minutes. 2. Place the lamb chops in a large bowl. Slash the meat and fat with a sharp knife several times to allow the marinade to penetrate better. Add the spice paste to the bowl and toss the lamb to coat. Marinate at room temperature for 30 minutes or cover and refrigerate for up to 24 hours. 3. Place the lamb chops in a single layer in the air fryer basket. Set the air fryer to 325°F (163°C) for 15 minutes, turning the chops halfway through the cooking time. Use a meat thermometer to ensure the lamb has reached an internal temperature of 145°F (63°C) (medium-rare).

Kheema Burgers

Prep time: 15 minutes | Cook time: 12 minutes | Serves 4

Burgers:
- 1 pound (454 g) 85% lean ground beef or ground lamb
- 2 large eggs, lightly beaten
- 1 medium yellow onion, diced
- ¼ cup chopped fresh cilantro
- 1 tablespoon minced fresh ginger
- 3 cloves garlic, minced
- 2 teaspoons garam masala
- 1 teaspoon ground turmeric
- ½ teaspoon ground cinnamon
- ⅛ teaspoon ground cardamom
- 1 teaspoon kosher salt
- 1 teaspoon cayenne pepper

Raita Sauce:
- 1 cup grated cucumber
- ½ cup sour cream
- ¼ teaspoon kosher salt
- ¼ teaspoon black pepper

For Serving:
- 4 lettuce leaves, hamburger buns, or naan breads

1. For the burgers: In a large bowl, combine the ground beef, eggs, onion, cilantro, ginger, garlic, garam masala, turmeric, cinnamon, cardamom, salt, and cayenne. Gently mix until ingredients are thoroughly combined. 2. Divide the meat into four portions and form into round patties. Make a slight depression in the middle of each patty with your thumb to prevent them from puffing up into a dome shape while cooking. 3. Place the patties in the air fryer basket. Set the air

fryer to 350°F (177°C) for 12 minutes. Use a meat thermometer to ensure the burgers have reached an internal temperature of 160°F / 71°C (for medium). 4. Meanwhile, for the sauce: In a small bowl, combine the cucumber, sour cream, salt, and pepper. 5. To serve: Place the burgers on the lettuce, buns, or naan and top with the sauce.

Herb-Roasted Beef Tips with Onions

Prep time: 5 minutes | Cook time: 10 minutes | Serves 4

- 1 pound (454 g) rib eye steak, cubed
- 2 garlic cloves, minced
- 2 tablespoons olive oil
- 1 tablespoon fresh oregano
- 1 teaspoon salt
- ½ teaspoon black pepper
- 1 yellow onion, thinly sliced

1. Preheat the air fryer to 380°F(193°C). 2. In a medium bowl, combine the steak, garlic, olive oil, oregano, salt, pepper, and onion. Mix until all of the beef and onion are well coated. 3. Put the seasoned steak mixture into the air fryer basket. Roast for 5 minutes. Stir and roast for 5 minutes more. 4. Let rest for 5 minutes before serving with some favorite sides.

Mustard and Rosemary Pork Tenderloin

Prep time: 10 minutes | Cook time: 26 minutes | Serves 2 to 3

- 1 pork tenderloin (about 1 pound / 454 g)
- 2 tablespoons coarse brown mustard
- Salt and freshly ground black pepper, to taste
- 1½ teaspoons finely
- chopped fresh rosemary, plus sprigs for garnish
- 2 apples, cored and cut into 8 wedges
- 1 tablespoon butter, melted
- 1 teaspoon brown sugar

1. Preheat the air fryer to 370°F (188°C). 2. Cut the pork tenderloin in half so that you have two pieces that fit into the air fryer basket. Brush the mustard onto both halves of the pork tenderloin and then season with salt, pepper and the fresh rosemary. Place the pork tenderloin halves into the air fryer basket and air fry for 10 minutes. Turn the pork over and air fry for an additional 5 to 8 minutes or until the internal temperature of the pork registers 155°F (68°C) on an instant read thermometer. If your pork tenderloin is especially thick, you may need to add a minute or two, but it's better to check the pork and add time, than to overcook it. 3. Let the pork rest for 5 minutes. In the meantime, toss the apple wedges with the butter and brown sugar and air fry at 400°F (204°C) for 8 minutes, shaking the basket once or twice during the cooking process so the apples cook and brown evenly. 4. Slice the pork on the bias. Serve with the fried apples scattered over the top and a few sprigs of rosemary as garnish.

Teriyaki Rump Steak with Broccoli and Capsicum

Prep time: 5 minutes | Cook time: 13 minutes | Serves 4

- ½ pound (227 g) rump steak
- ⅓ cup teriyaki marinade
- 1½ teaspoons sesame oil
- ½ head broccoli, cut into florets
- 2 red capsicums, sliced
- Fine sea salt and ground black pepper, to taste
- Cooking spray

1. Toss the rump steak in a large bowl with teriyaki marinade. Wrap the bowl in plastic and refrigerate to marinate for at least an hour. 2. Preheat the air fryer to 400°F (204°C) and spritz with cooking spray. 3. Discard the marinade and transfer the steak in the preheated air fryer. Spritz with cooking spray. 4. Air fry for 13 minutes or until well browned. Flip the steak halfway through. 5. Meanwhile, heat the sesame oil in a nonstick skillet over medium heat. Add the broccoli and capsicum. Sprinkle with salt and ground black pepper. Sauté for 5 minutes or until the broccoli is tender. 6. Transfer the air fried rump steak on a plate and top with the sautéed broccoli and capsicum. Serve hot.

Savory Sausage Cobbler

Prep time: 15 minutes | Cook time: 34 minutes | Serves 4

Filling:
- 1 pound (454 g) ground Italian sausage
- 1 cup sliced mushrooms

- 1 teaspoon fine sea salt
- 2 cups marinara sauce

Biscuits:
- 3 large egg whites
- ¾ cup blanched almond flour
- 1 teaspoon baking powder
- ¼ teaspoon fine sea salt

- 2½ tablespoons very cold unsalted butter, cut into ¼-inch pieces
- Fresh basil leaves, for garnish

1. Preheat the air fryer to 400°F (204°C). 2. Place the sausage in a pie pan (or a pan that fits into your air fryer). Use your hands to break up the sausage and spread it evenly on the bottom of the pan. Place the pan in the air fryer and air fry for 5 minutes. 3. Remove the pan from the air fryer and use a fork or metal spatula to crumble the sausage more. Season the mushrooms with the salt and add them to the pie pan. Stir to combine the mushrooms and sausage, then return the pan to the air fryer and air fry for 4 minutes, or until the mushrooms are soft and the sausage is cooked through. 4. Remove the pan from the air fryer. Add the marinara sauce and stir well. Set aside. 5. Make the biscuits: Place the egg whites in a large mixing bowl or the bowl of a stand mixer. Using a hand mixer or stand mixer, whip the egg whites until stiff peaks form. 6. In a medium-sized bowl, whisk together the almond flour, baking powder, and salt, then cut in the butter. Gently fold the flour mixture into the egg whites with a rubber spatula. 7. Using a large spoon or ice cream scoop, spoon one-quarter of the dough on top of the sausage mixture, making sure the butter stays in separate clumps. Repeat with the remaining dough, spacing the biscuits about 1 inch apart. 8. Place the pan in the air fryer and cook for 5 minutes, then lower the heat to 325°F (163°C) and bake for another 15 to 20 minutes, until the biscuits are golden brown. Serve garnished with fresh basil leaves. 9. Store leftovers in an airtight container in the refrigerator for up to 3 days. Reheat in a preheated 350°F (177°C) air fryer for 5 minutes, or until warmed through.

Parmesan Herb Filet Mignon

Prep time: 20 minutes | Cook time: 13 minutes | Serves 4

- 1 pound (454 g) filet mignon
- Sea salt and ground black pepper, to taste
- ½ teaspoon cayenne pepper
- 1 teaspoon dried basil
- 1 teaspoon dried rosemary

- 1 teaspoon dried thyme
- 1 tablespoon sesame oil
- 1 small-sized egg, well-whisked
- ½ cup Parmesan cheese, grated

1. Season the filet mignon with salt, black pepper, cayenne pepper, basil, rosemary, and thyme. Brush with sesame oil. 2. Put the egg in a shallow plate. Now, place the Parmesan cheese in another plate. 3. Coat the filet mignon with the egg; then lay it into the Parmesan cheese. Set the air fryer to 360°F (182°C). 4. Cook for 10 to 13 minutes or until golden. Serve with mixed salad leaves and enjoy!

Spinach and Provolone Steak Rolls

Prep time: 10 minutes | Cook time: 12 minutes | Makes 8 rolls

- 1 (1 pound / 454 g) flank steak, butterflied
- 8 (1 ounce / 28 g, ¼-inch-thick) deli slices provolone cheese
- 1 cup fresh spinach leaves
- ½ teaspoon salt
- ¼ teaspoon ground black pepper

1. Place steak on a large plate. Place provolone slices to cover steak, leaving 1-inch at the edges. Lay spinach leaves over cheese. Gently roll steak and tie with kitchen twine or secure with toothpicks. Carefully slice into eight pieces. Sprinkle each with salt and pepper. 2. Place rolls into ungreased air fryer basket, cut side up. Adjust the temperature to 400°F (204°C) and air fry for 12 minutes. Steak rolls will be browned and cheese will be melted when done and have an internal temperature of at least 150°F (66°C) for medium steak and 180°F (82°C) for well-done steak. Serve warm.

Kale and Beef Omelet

Prep time: 15 minutes | Cook time: 16 minutes | Serves 4

- ½ pound (227 g) leftover beef, coarsely chopped
- 2 garlic cloves, pressed
- 1 cup kale, torn into pieces and wilted
- 1 tomato, chopped
- ¼ teaspoon sugar
- 4 eggs, beaten
- 4 tablespoons heavy cream
- ½ teaspoon turmeric powder
- Salt and ground black pepper, to taste
- ⅛ teaspoon ground allspice
- Cooking spray

1. Preheat the air fryer to 360ºF (182ºC). Spritz four ramekins with cooking spray. 2. Put equal amounts of each of the ingredients into each ramekin and mix well. 3. Air fry for 16 minutes. Serve immediately.

Bacon, Cheese and Pear Stuffed Pork

Prep time: 10 minutes | Cook time: 24 minutes | Serves 3

- 4 slices bacon, chopped
- 1 tablespoon butter
- ½ cup finely diced onion
- ⅓ cup chicken stock
- 1½ cups seasoned stuffing cubes
- 1 egg, beaten
- ½ teaspoon dried thyme
- ½ teaspoon salt
- ⅛ teaspoon black pepper
- 1 pear, finely diced
- ⅓ cup crumbled blue cheese
- 3 boneless center-cut pork chops (2-inch thick)
- Olive oil
- Salt and freshly ground black pepper, to taste

1. Preheat the air fryer to 400ºF (204ºC). 2. Place the bacon into the air fryer basket and air fry for 6 minutes, stirring halfway through the cooking time. Remove the bacon and set it aside on a paper towel. Pour out the grease from the bottom of the air fryer. 3. Make the stuffing: Melt the butter in a medium saucepan over medium heat on the stovetop. Add the onion and sauté for a few minutes, until it starts to soften. Add the chicken stock and simmer for 1 minute. Remove the pan from the heat and add the stuffing cubes. Stir until the stock has been absorbed. Add the egg, dried thyme, salt and freshly ground black pepper, and stir until combined. Fold in the diced pear and crumbled blue cheese. 4. Place the pork chops on a cutting board. Using the palm of your hand to hold the chop flat and steady, slice into the side of the pork chop to make a pocket in the center of the chop. Leave about an inch of chop uncut and make sure you don't cut all the way through the pork chop. Brush both sides of the pork chops with olive oil and season with salt and freshly ground black pepper. Stuff each pork chop with a third of the stuffing, packing the stuffing tightly inside the pocket. 5. Preheat the air fryer to 360ºF (182ºC). 6. Spray or brush the sides of the air fryer basket with oil. Place the pork chops in the air fryer basket with the open stuffed edge of the pork chop facing the outside edges of the basket. 7. Air fry the pork chops for 18 minutes, turning the pork chops over halfway through the cooking time. When the chops are done, let them rest for 5 minutes and then transfer to a serving platter.

Herbed Beef

Prep time: 5 minutes | Cook time: 22 minutes | Serves 6

- 1 teaspoon dried dill
- 1 teaspoon dried thyme
- 1 teaspoon garlic powder
- 2 pounds (907 g) beef steak
- 3 tablespoons butter

1. Preheat the air fryer to 360ºF (182ºC). 2. Combine the dill, thyme, and garlic powder in a small bowl, and massage into the steak. 3. Air fry the steak in the air fryer for 20 minutes, then remove, shred, and return to the air fryer. 4. Add the butter and air fry the shredded steak for a further 2 minutes at 365ºF (185ºC). Make sure the beef is coated in the butter before serving.

Currywurst

Prep time: 15 minutes | Cook time: 12 minutes | Serves 4

- 1 cup tomato sauce
- 2 tablespoons cider vinegar
- 2 teaspoons curry powder
- 2 teaspoons sweet paprika
- 1 teaspoon sugar
- ¼ teaspoon cayenne pepper
- 1 small onion, diced
- 1 pound (454 g) bratwurst, sliced diagonally into 1-inch pieces

1. In a large bowl, combine the tomato sauce, vinegar, curry powder, paprika, sugar, and cayenne. Whisk until well combined. Stir in the onion and bratwurst. 2. Transfer the mixture to a baking pan. Place the pan in the air fryer basket. Set the air fryer to 400ºF (204ºC) for 12 minutes, or until the sausage is heated through and the sauce is bubbling.

Beef and Pork Sausage Meatloaf

Prep time: 20 minutes | Cook time: 25 minutes | Serves 4

- ¾ pound (340 g) ground chuck
- 4 ounces (113 g) ground pork sausage
- 1 cup shallots, finely chopped
- 2 eggs, well beaten
- 3 tablespoons plain milk
- 1 tablespoon oyster sauce
- 1 teaspoon porcini mushrooms
- ½ teaspoon cumin powder
- 1 teaspoon garlic paste
- 1 tablespoon fresh parsley
- Salt and crushed red pepper flakes, to taste
- 1 cup crushed saltines
- Cooking spray

1. Preheat the air fryer to 360ºF (182ºC). Spritz a baking dish with cooking spray. 2. Mix all the ingredients in a large bowl, combining everything well. 3. Transfer to the baking dish and bake in the air fryer for 25 minutes. 4. Serve hot.

Fruited Ham

Prep time: 15 minutes | Cook time: 8 to 10 minutes | Serves 4

- 1 cup orange marmalade
- ¼ cup packed light brown sugar
- ¼ teaspoon ground cloves
- ½ teaspoon dry mustard
- 1 to 2 tablespoons oil
- 1 pound (454 g) cooked ham, cut into 1-inch cubes
- ½ cup canned mandarin oranges, drained and chopped

1. In a small bowl, stir together the orange marmalade, brown sugar, cloves, and dry mustard until blended. Set aside. 2. Preheat the air fryer to 320ºF (160ºC). Spritz a baking pan with oil. 3. Place the ham cubes in the prepared pan. Pour the marmalade sauce over the ham to glaze it. 4. Cook for 4 minutes. Stir and cook for 2 minutes more. 5. Add the mandarin oranges and cook for 2 to 4 minutes more until the sauce begins to thicken and the ham is tender.

Sausage and Cauliflower Arancini

Prep time: 30 minutes | Cook time: 28 to 32 minutes | Serves 6

- Avocado oil spray
- 6 ounces (170 g) Italian sausage, casings removed
- ¼ cup diced onion
- 1 teaspoon minced garlic
- 1 teaspoon dried thyme
- Sea salt and freshly ground black pepper, to taste
- 2½ cups cauliflower rice
- 3 ounces (85 g) cream
- cheese
- 4 ounces (113 g) Cheddar cheese, shredded
- 1 large egg
- ½ cup finely ground blanched almond flour
- ¼ cup finely grated Parmesan cheese
- Keto-friendly marinara sauce, for serving

1. Spray a large skillet with oil and place it over medium-high heat. Once the skillet is hot, put the sausage in the skillet and cook for 7 minutes, breaking up the meat with the back of a spoon. 2. Reduce the heat to medium and add the onion. Cook for 5 minutes, then add the garlic, thyme, and salt and pepper to taste. Cook for 1 minute more. 3. Add the cauliflower rice and cream cheese to the skillet. Cook for 7 minutes, stirring frequently, until the cream cheese melts and the cauliflower is tender. 4. Remove the skillet from the heat and stir in the Cheddar cheese. Using a cookie scoop, form the mixture into 1½-inch balls. Place the balls on a parchment paper-lined baking sheet. Freeze for 30 minutes. 5. Place the egg in a shallow bowl and beat it with a fork. In a separate bowl, stir together the almond flour and Parmesan cheese. 6. Dip the cauliflower balls into the egg, then coat them with the almond flour mixture, gently pressing the mixture to the balls to adhere. 7. Set the air fryer to 400ºF (204ºC). Spray the cauliflower rice balls with oil, and arrange them in a single layer in the air fryer basket, working in batches if necessary. Air fry for 5 minutes. Flip the rice balls and spray them with more oil. Air fry for 3 to 7 minutes longer, until the balls are golden brown. 8. Serve warm with marinara sauce.

Pork Milanese

Prep time: 10 minutes | Cook time: 12 minutes | Serves 4

- 4 (1-inch) boneless pork chops
- Fine sea salt and ground black pepper, to taste
- 2 large eggs
- ¾ cup powdered Parmesan cheese
- Chopped fresh parsley, for garnish
- Lemon slices, for serving

1. Spray the air fryer basket with avocado oil. Preheat the air fryer to 400ºF (204ºC). 2. Place the pork chops between 2 sheets of plastic wrap and pound them with the flat side of a meat tenderizer until they're ¼ inch thick. Lightly season both sides of the chops with salt and pepper. 3. Lightly beat the eggs in a shallow bowl. Divide the Parmesan cheese evenly between 2 bowls and set the bowls in this order: Parmesan, eggs, Parmesan. Dredge a chop in the first bowl of Parmesan, then dip it in the eggs, and then dredge it again in the second bowl of Parmesan, making sure both sides and all edges are well coated. Repeat with the remaining chops. 4. Place the chops in the air fryer basket and air fry for 12 minutes, or until the internal temperature reaches 145ºF (63ºC), flipping halfway through. 5. Garnish with fresh parsley and serve immediately with lemon slices. Store leftovers in an airtight container in the refrigerator for up to 3 days. Reheat in a preheated 390ºF (199ºC) air fryer for 5 minutes, or until warmed through.

Mongolian-Style Beef

Prep time: 10 minutes | Cook time: 10 minutes | Serves 4

- Oil, for spraying
- ¼ cup cornstarch
- 1 pound (454 g) flank steak, thinly sliced
- ¾ cup packed light brown sugar
- ½ cup soy sauce
- 2 teaspoons toasted sesame oil
- 1 tablespoon minced garlic
- ½ teaspoon ground ginger
- ½ cup water
- Cooked white rice or ramen noodles, for serving

1. Line the air fryer basket with parchment and spray lightly with oil. 2. Place the cornstarch in a bowl and dredge the steak until evenly coated. Shake off any excess cornstarch. 3. Place the steak in the prepared basket and spray lightly with oil. 4. Roast at 390ºF (199ºC) for 5 minutes, flip, and cook for another 5 minutes. 5. In a small saucepan, combine the brown sugar, soy sauce, sesame oil, garlic, ginger, and water and bring to a boil over medium-high heat, stirring frequently. Remove from the heat. 6. Transfer the meat to the sauce and toss until evenly coated. Let sit for about 5 minutes so the steak absorbs the flavors. Serve with white rice or ramen noodles.

Simple Ground Beef with Zucchini

Prep time: 5 minutes | Cook time: 12 minutes | Serves 4

- 1½ pounds (680 g) ground beef
- 1 pound (454 g) chopped zucchini
- 2 tablespoons extra-virgin olive oil
- 1 teaspoon dried oregano
- 1 teaspoon dried basil
- 1 teaspoon dried rosemary
- 2 tablespoons fresh chives, chopped

1. Preheat the air fryer to 400°F (204°C). 2. In a large bowl, combine all the ingredients, except for the chives, until well blended. 3. Place the beef and zucchini mixture in the baking pan. Air fry for 12 minutes, or until the beef is browned and the zucchini is tender. 4. Divide the beef and zucchini mixture among four serving dishes. Top with fresh chives and serve hot.

Ham Hock Mac and Cheese

Prep time: 20 minutes | Cook time: 25 minutes | Serves 4

- 2 large eggs, beaten
- 2 cups cottage cheese, whole milk or 2%
- 2 cups grated sharp Cheddar cheese, divided
- 1 cup sour cream
- ½ teaspoon salt
- 1 teaspoon freshly ground
- black pepper
- 2 cups uncooked elbow macaroni
- 2 ham hocks (about 11 ounces / 312 g each), meat removed and diced
- 1 to 2 tablespoons oil

1. In a large bowl, stir together the eggs, cottage cheese, 1 cup of the Cheddar cheese, sour cream, salt, and pepper. 2. Stir in the macaroni and the diced meat. 3. Preheat the air fryer to 360°F (182°C). Spritz a baking pan with oil. 4. Pour the macaroni mixture into the prepared pan, making sure all noodles are covered with sauce. 5. Cook for 12 minutes. Stir in the remaining 1 cup of Cheddar cheese, making sure all the noodles are covered with sauce. Cook for 13 minutes more, until the noodles are tender. Let rest for 5 minutes before serving.

Rosemary Ribeye Steaks

Prep time: 10 minutes | Cook time: 15 minutes | Serves 2

- ¼ cup butter
- 1 clove garlic, minced
- Salt and ground black pepper, to taste
- 1½ tablespoons balsamic vinegar
- ¼ cup rosemary, chopped
- 2 ribeye steaks

1. Melt the butter in a skillet over medium heat. Add the garlic and fry until fragrant. 2. Remove the skillet from the heat and add the salt, pepper, and vinegar. Allow it to cool. 3. Add the rosemary, then pour the mixture into a Ziploc bag. 4. Put the ribeye steaks in the bag and shake well, coating the meat well. Refrigerate for an hour, then allow to sit for a further twenty minutes. 5. Preheat the air fryer to 400°F (204°C). 6. Air fry the ribeye steaks for 15 minutes. 7. Take care when removing the steaks from the air fryer and plate up. 8. Serve immediately.

Italian Pork Loin

Prep time: 30 minutes | Cook time: 16 minutes | Serves 3

- 1 teaspoon Celtic sea salt
- ½ teaspoon black pepper, freshly cracked
- ¼ cup red wine
- 2 tablespoons mustard
- 2 garlic cloves, minced
- 1 pound (454 g) pork top loin
- 1 tablespoon Italian herb seasoning blend

1. In a ceramic bowl, mix the salt, black pepper, red wine, mustard, and garlic. Add the pork top loin and let it marinate at least 30 minutes. 2. Spritz the sides and bottom of the air fryer basket with nonstick cooking spray. 3. Place the pork top loin in the basket; sprinkle with the Italian herb seasoning blend. 4. Cook the pork tenderloin at 370°F (188°C) for 10 minutes. Flip halfway through, spraying with cooking oil and cook for 5 to 6 minutes more. Serve immediately.

Greek Pork with Tzatziki Sauce

Prep time: 30 minutes | Cook time: 50 minutes | Serves 4

- Greek Pork:
- 2 pounds (907 g) pork sirloin roast
- Salt and black pepper, to taste
- 1 teaspoon smoked paprika
- ½ teaspoon mustard seeds
- ½ teaspoon celery seeds

Tzatziki:
- ½ cucumber, finely chopped and squeezed
- 1 cup full-fat Greek yogurt
- 1 garlic clove, minced
- 1 tablespoon extra-virgin
- 1 teaspoon fennel seeds
- 1 teaspoon Ancho chili powder
- 1 teaspoon turmeric powder
- ½ teaspoon ground ginger
- 2 tablespoons olive oil
- 2 cloves garlic, finely chopped

- olive oil
- 1 teaspoon balsamic vinegar
- 1 teaspoon minced fresh dill
- A pinch of salt

1. Toss all ingredients for Greek pork in a large mixing bowl. Toss until the meat is well coated. 2. Cook in the preheated air fryer at 360°F (182°C) for 30 minutes; turn over and cook another 20 minutes. 3. Meanwhile, prepare the tzatziki by mixing all the tzatziki ingredients. Place in your refrigerator until ready to use. 4. Serve the pork sirloin roast with the chilled tzatziki on the side. Enjoy!

Bone-in Pork Chops

Prep time: 5 minutes | Cook time: 10 to 12 minutes | Serves 2

- 1 pound (454 g) bone-in pork chops
- 1 tablespoon avocado oil
- 1 teaspoon smoked paprika
- ½ teaspoon onion powder
- ¼ teaspoon cayenne pepper
- Sea salt and freshly ground black pepper, to taste

1. Brush the pork chops with the avocado oil. In a small dish, mix together the smoked paprika, onion powder, cayenne pepper, and salt and black pepper to taste. Sprinkle the seasonings over both sides of the pork chops. 2. Set the air fryer to 400ºF (204ºC). Place the chops in the air fryer basket in a single layer, working in batches if necessary. Air fry for 10 to 12 minutes, until an instant-read thermometer reads 145ºF (63ºC) at the chops' thickest point. 3. Remove the chops from the air fryer and allow them to rest for 5 minutes before serving.

Italian Sausage Links

Prep time: 10 minutes | Cook time: 24 minutes | Serves 4

- 1 bell pepper (any color), sliced
- 1 medium onion, sliced
- 1 tablespoon avocado oil
- 1 teaspoon Italian seasoning
- Sea salt and freshly ground black pepper, to taste
- 1 pound (454 g) Italian sausage links

1. Place the bell pepper and onion in a medium bowl, and toss with the avocado oil, Italian seasoning, and salt and pepper to taste. 2. Set the air fryer to 400ºF (204ºC). Put the vegetables in the air fryer basket and cook for 12 minutes. 3. Push the vegetables to the side of the basket and arrange the sausage links in the bottom of the basket in a single layer. Spoon the vegetables over the sausages. Cook for 12 minutes, tossing halfway through, until an instant-read thermometer inserted into the sausage reads 160ºF (71ºC).

Chapter 6
Fish and Seafood

Shrimp Curry

Prep time: 30 minutes | Cook time: 10 minutes | Serves 4

- ¾ cup unsweetened full-fat coconut milk
- ¼ cup finely chopped yellow onion
- 2 teaspoons garam masala
- 1 tablespoon minced fresh ginger
- 1 tablespoon minced garlic
- 1 teaspoon ground turmeric
- 1 teaspoon salt
- ¼ to ½ teaspoon cayenne pepper
- 1 pound (454 g) raw shrimp (21 to 25 count), peeled and deveined
- 2 teaspoons chopped fresh cilantro

1. In a large bowl, stir together the coconut milk, onion, garam masala, ginger, garlic, turmeric, salt and cayenne, until well blended. 2. Add the shrimp and toss until coated with sauce on all sides. Marinate at room temperature for 30 minutes. 3. Transfer the shrimp and marinade to a baking pan. Place the pan in the air fryer basket. Set the air fryer to 375ºF (191ºC) for 10 minutes, stirring halfway through the cooking time. 4. Transfer the shrimp to a serving bowl or platter. Sprinkle with the cilantro and serve.

Panko-Crusted Fish Sticks

Prep time: 10 minutes | Cook time: 15 minutes | Serves 4

Tartar Sauce:
- 2 cups mayonnaise
- 2 tablespoons dill pickle relish
- 1 tablespoon dried minced onions

Fish Sticks:
- Oil, for spraying
- 1 pound (454 g) tilapia fillets
- ½ cup all-purpose flour
- 2 cups panko bread crumbs
- 2 tablespoons Creole seasoning
- 2 teaspoons granulated garlic
- 1 teaspoon onion powder
- ½ teaspoon salt
- ¼ teaspoon freshly ground black pepper
- 1 large egg

Make the Tartar Sauce 1. In a small bowl, whisk together the mayonnaise, pickle relish, and onions. Cover with plastic wrap and refrigerate until ready to serve. You can make this sauce ahead of time; the flavors will intensify as it chills. Make the Fish Sticks 2. Preheat the air fryer to 350ºF (177ºC). Line the air fryer basket with parchment and spray lightly with oil. 3. Cut the fillets into equal-size sticks and place them in a zip-top plastic bag. 4. Add the flour to the bag, seal, and shake well until evenly coated. 5. In a shallow bowl, mix together the bread crumbs, Creole seasoning, garlic, onion powder, salt, and black pepper. 6. In a small bowl, whisk the egg. 7. Dip the fish sticks in the egg, then dredge in the bread crumb mixture until completely coated. 8. Place the fish sticks in the prepared basket. You may need to work in batches, depending on the size of your air fryer. Do not overcrowd. Spray lightly with oil. 9. Cook for 12 to 15 minutes, or until browned and cooked through. Serve with the tartar sauce.

Confetti Salmon Burgers

Prep time: 10 minutes | Cook time: 12 minutes | Serves 4

- 14 ounces (397 g) cooked fresh or canned salmon, flaked with a fork
- ¼ cup minced scallion, white and light green parts only
- ¼ cup minced red bell pepper
- ¼ cup minced celery
- 2 small lemons
- 1 teaspoon crab boil seasoning such as Old Bay
- ½ teaspoon kosher salt
- ½ teaspoon black pepper
- 1 egg, beaten
- ½ cup fresh bread crumbs
- Vegetable oil, for spraying

1. In a large bowl, combine the salmon, vegetables, the zest and juice of 1 of the lemons, crab boil seasoning, salt, and pepper. Add the egg and bread crumbs and stir to combine. Form the mixture into 4 patties weighing approximately 5 ounces (142 g) each. Chill until firm, about 15 minutes. 2. Preheat the air fryer to 400ºF (204ºC). 3. Spray the salmon patties with oil on all sides and spray the air fryer basket to prevent sticking. Air fry for 12 minutes, flipping halfway through, until the burgers are browned and cooked through. Cut the remaining lemon into 4 wedges and serve with the burgers.

Browned Shrimp Patties

Prep time: 15 minutes | Cook time: 10 to 12 minutes | Serves 4

- ½ pound (227 g) raw shrimp, shelled, deveined, and chopped finely
- 2 cups cooked sushi rice
- ¼ cup chopped red bell pepper
- ¼ cup chopped celery
- ¼ cup chopped green onion
- 2 teaspoons Worcestershire sauce
- ½ teaspoon salt
- ½ teaspoon garlic powder
- ½ teaspoon Old Bay seasoning
- ½ cup plain bread crumbs
- Cooking spray

1. Preheat the air fryer to 390ºF (199ºC). 2. Put all the ingredients except the bread crumbs and oil in a large bowl and stir to incorporate. 3. Scoop out the shrimp mixture and shape into 8 equal-sized patties with your hands, no more than ½-inch thick. Roll the patties in the bread crumbs on a plate and spray both sides with cooking spray. 4. Place the patties in the air fryer basket. You may need to work in batches to avoid overcrowding. 5. Air fry for 10 to 12 minutes, flipping the patties halfway through, or until the outside is crispy brown. 6. Divide the patties among four plates and serve warm.

Garlic Shrimp

Prep time: 15 minutes | Cook time: 10 minutes | Serves 3

Shrimp:

- Oil, for spraying
- 1 pound (454 g) medium raw shrimp, peeled and deveined
- 6 tablespoons unsalted butter, melted
- 1 cup panko bread crumbs
- 2 tablespoons granulated garlic
- 1 teaspoon salt
- ½ teaspoon freshly ground black pepper

Garlic Butter Sauce:

- ½ cup unsalted butter
- 2 teaspoons granulated garlic
- ¾ teaspoon salt (omit if using salted butter)

Make the Shrimp 1. Preheat the air fryer to 400ºF (204ºC). Line the air fryer basket with parchment and spray lightly with oil. 2. Place the shrimp and melted butter in a zip-top plastic bag, seal, and shake well, until evenly coated. 3. In a medium bowl, mix together the bread crumbs, garlic, salt, and black pepper. 4. Add the shrimp to the panko mixture and toss until evenly coated. Shake off any excess coating. 5. Place the shrimp in the prepared basket and spray lightly with oil. 6. Cook for 8 to 10 minutes, flipping and spraying with oil after 4 to 5 minutes, until golden brown and crispy. Make the Garlic Butter Sauce 7. In a microwave-safe bowl, combine the butter, garlic, and salt and microwave on 50% power for 30 to 60 seconds, stirring every 15 seconds, until completely melted. 8. Serve the shrimp immediately with the garlic butter sauce on the side for dipping.

Scallops Gratiné with Parmesan

Prep time: 10 minutes | Cook time: 9 minutes | Serves 2

Scallops:

- ½ cup half-and-half
- ½ cup grated Parmesan cheese
- ¼ cup thinly sliced green onions
- ¼ cup chopped fresh
- parsley
- 3 cloves garlic, minced
- ½ teaspoon kosher salt
- ½ teaspoon black pepper
- 1 pound (454 g) sea scallops

Topping:

- ¼ cup crushed pork rinds or panko bread crumbs
- ¼ cup grated Parmesan
- cheese
- Vegetable oil spray

For Serving:

- Lemon wedges
- Crusty French bread
- (optional)

1. For the scallops: In a baking pan, combine the half-and-half, cheese, green onions, parsley, garlic, salt, and pepper. Stir in the scallops. 2. For the topping: In a small bowl, combine the pork rinds or bread crumbs and cheese. Sprinkle evenly over the scallops. Spray the topping with vegetable oil spray. 3. Place the pan in the air fryer basket. Set the air fryer to 325ºF (163ºC) for 6 minutes. Set the air fryer to 400ºF (204ºC) for 3 minutes until the topping has browned. 4. To serve: Squeeze the lemon wedges over the gratin and serve with crusty French bread, if desired.

Cod with Creamy Mustard Sauce

Prep time: 10 minutes | Cook time: 10 minutes | Serves 4

Fish:

- Oil, for spraying
- 1 pound (454 g) cod fillets
- 2 tablespoons olive oil
- 1 tablespoon lemon juice
- 1 teaspoon salt
- ½ teaspoon freshly ground black pepper

Mustard Sauce:

- ½ cup heavy cream
- 3 tablespoons Dijon mustard
- 1 tablespoon unsalted butter
- 1 teaspoon salt

Make the Fish: 1. Line the air fryer basket with parchment and spray lightly with oil. 2. Rub the cod with the olive oil and lemon juice. Season with the salt and black pepper. 3. Place the cod in the prepared basket. You may need to work in batches, depending on the size of your air fryer. 4. Roast at 350ºF (177ºC) for 5 minutes. Increase the temperature to 400ºF (204ºC) and cook for another 5 minutes, until flaky and the internal temperature reaches 145ºF (63ºC). Make the Mustard Sauce: 5. In a small saucepan, mix together the heavy cream, mustard, butter, and salt and bring to a simmer over low heat. Cook for 3 to 4 minutes, or until the sauce starts to thicken. 6. Transfer the cod to a serving plate and drizzle with the mustard sauce. Serve immediately.

Snapper with Fruit

Prep time: 15 minutes | Cook time: 9 to 13 minutes | Serves 4

- 4 (4-ounce / 113-g) red snapper fillets
- 2 teaspoons olive oil
- 3 nectarines, halved and pitted
- 3 plums, halved and pitted
- 1 cup red grapes
- 1 tablespoon freshly squeezed lemon juice
- 1 tablespoon honey
- ½ teaspoon dried thyme

1. Put the red snapper in the air fryer basket and drizzle with the olive oil. Air fry at 390ºF (199ºC) for 4 minutes. 2. Remove the basket and add the nectarines and plums. Scatter the grapes over all. 3. Drizzle with the lemon juice and honey and sprinkle with the thyme. 4. Return the basket to the air fryer and air fry for 5 to 9 minutes more, or until the fish flakes when tested with a fork and the fruit is tender. Serve immediately.

Country Shrimp

Prep time: 10 minutes | Cook time: 15 to 20 minutes | Serves 4

- 1 pound (454 g) large shrimp, deveined, with tails on
- 1 pound (454 g) smoked turkey sausage, cut into thick slices
- 2 corn cobs, quartered
- 1 zucchini, cut into bite-
- sized pieces
- 1 red bell pepper, cut into chunks
- 1 tablespoon Old Bay seasoning
- 2 tablespoons olive oil
- Cooking spray

1. Preheat the air fryer to 400°F (204°C). Spray the air fryer basket lightly with cooking spray. 2. In a large bowl, mix the shrimp, turkey sausage, corn, zucchini, bell pepper, and Old Bay seasoning, and toss to coat with the spices. Add the olive oil and toss again until evenly coated. 3. Spread the mixture in the air fryer basket in a single layer. You will need to cook in batches. 4. Air fry for 15 to 20 minutes, or until cooked through, shaking the basket every 5 minutes for even cooking. 5. Serve immediately.

Tilapia with Pecans

Prep time: 20 minutes | Cook time: 16 minutes | Serves 5

- 2 tablespoons ground flaxseeds
- 1 teaspoon paprika
- Sea salt and white pepper, to taste
- 1 teaspoon garlic paste
- 2 tablespoons extra-virgin olive oil
- ½ cup pecans, ground
- 5 tilapia fillets, sliced into halves

1. Combine the ground flaxseeds, paprika, salt, white pepper, garlic paste, olive oil, and ground pecans in a Ziploc bag. Add the fish fillets and shake to coat well. 2. Spritz the air fryer basket with cooking spray. Cook in the preheated air fryer at 400°F (204°C) for 10 minutes; turn them over and cook for 6 minutes more. Work in batches. 3. Serve with lemon wedges, if desired. Enjoy!

Chilean Sea Bass with Olive Relish

Prep time: 10 minutes | Cook time: 10 minutes | Serves 2

- Olive oil spray
- 2 (6-ounce / 170-g) Chilean sea bass fillets or other firm-fleshed white fish
- 3 tablespoons extra-virgin olive oil
- ½ teaspoon ground cumin
- ½ teaspoon kosher salt
- ½ teaspoon black pepper
- ⅓ cup pitted green olives, diced
- ¼ cup finely diced onion
- 1 teaspoon chopped capers

1. Spray the air fryer basket with the olive oil spray. Drizzle the fillets with the olive oil and sprinkle with the cumin, salt, and pepper. Place the fish in the air fryer basket. Set the air fryer to 325°F (163°C) for 10 minutes, or until the fish flakes easily with a fork. 2. Meanwhile, in a small bowl, stir together the olives, onion, and capers. 3. Serve the fish topped with the relish.

Marinated Swordfish Skewers

Prep time: 30 minutes | Cook time: 6 to 8 minutes | Serves 4

- 1 pound (454 g) filleted swordfish
- ¼ cup avocado oil
- 2 tablespoons freshly squeezed lemon juice
- 1 tablespoon minced fresh
- parsley
- 2 teaspoons Dijon mustard
- Sea salt and freshly ground black pepper, to taste
- 3 ounces (85 g) cherry tomatoes

1. Cut the fish into 1½-inch chunks, picking out any remaining bones. 2. In a large bowl, whisk together the oil, lemon juice, parsley, and Dijon mustard. Season to taste with salt and pepper. Add the fish and toss to coat the pieces. Cover and marinate the fish chunks in the refrigerator for 30 minutes. 3. Remove the fish from the marinade. Thread the fish and cherry tomatoes on 4 skewers, alternating as you go. 4. Set the air fryer to 400°F (204°C). Place the skewers in the air fryer basket and air fry for 3 minutes. Flip the skewers and cook for 3 to 5 minutes longer, until the fish is cooked through and an instant-read thermometer reads 140°F (60°C).

Golden Beer-Battered Cod

Prep time: 5 minutes | Cook time: 15 minutes | Serves 4

- 2 eggs
- 1 cup malty beer
- 1 cup all-purpose flour
- ½ cup cornstarch
- 1 teaspoon garlic powder
- Salt and pepper, to taste
- 4 (4-ounce / 113-g) cod fillets
- Cooking spray

1. Preheat the air fryer to 400°F (204°C). 2. In a shallow bowl, beat together the eggs with the beer. In another shallow bowl, thoroughly combine the flour and cornstarch. Sprinkle with the garlic powder, salt, and pepper. 3. Dredge each cod fillet in the flour mixture, then in the egg mixture. Dip each piece of fish in the flour mixture a second time. 4. Spritz the air fryer basket with cooking spray. Arrange the cod fillets in the basket in a single layer. 5. Air fry in batches for 15 minutes until the cod reaches an internal temperature of 145°F (63°C) on a meat thermometer and the outside is crispy. Flip the fillets halfway through the cooking time. 6. Let the fish cool for 5 minutes and serve.

Simple Buttery Cod

Prep time: 5 minutes | Cook time: 8 minutes | Serves 2

- 2 (4-ounce / 113-g) cod fillets
- 2 tablespoons salted butter, melted
- 1 teaspoon Old Bay seasoning
- ½ medium lemon, sliced

1. Place cod fillets into a round baking dish. Brush each fillet with butter and sprinkle with Old Bay seasoning. Lay two lemon slices on each fillet. Cover the dish with foil and place into the air fryer basket. 2. Adjust the temperature to 350ºF (177ºC) and bake for 8 minutes. 3. Flip halfway through the cooking time. When cooked, internal temperature should be at least 145ºF (63ºC). Serve warm.

Parmesan Mackerel with Coriander

Prep time: 10 minutes | Cook time: 7 minutes | Serves 2

- 12 ounces (340 g) mackerel fillet
- 2 ounces (57 g) Parmesan, grated
- 1 teaspoon ground coriander
- 1 tablespoon olive oil

1. Sprinkle the mackerel fillet with olive oil and put it in the air fryer basket. 2. Top the fish with ground coriander and Parmesan. 3. Cook the fish at 390ºF (199ºC) for 7 minutes.

Rainbow Salmon Kebabs

Prep time: 10 minutes | Cook time: 8 minutes | Serves 2

- 6 ounces (170 g) boneless, skinless salmon, cut into 1-inch cubes
- ¼ medium red onion, peeled and cut into 1-inch pieces
- ½ medium yellow bell pepper, seeded and cut into
- 1-inch pieces
- ½ medium zucchini, trimmed and cut into ½-inch slices
- 1 tablespoon olive oil
- ½ teaspoon salt
- ¼ teaspoon ground black pepper

1. Using one (6-inch) skewer, skewer 1 piece salmon, then 1 piece onion, 1 piece bell pepper, and finally 1 piece zucchini. Repeat this pattern with additional skewers to make four kebabs total. Drizzle with olive oil and sprinkle with salt and black pepper. 2. Place kebabs into ungreased air fryer basket. Adjust the temperature to 400ºF (204ºC) and air fry for 8 minutes, turning kebabs halfway through cooking. Salmon will easily flake and have an internal temperature of at least 145ºF (63ºC) when done; vegetables will be tender. Serve warm.

Almond Catfish

Prep time: 10 minutes | Cook time: 12 minutes | Serves 4

- 2 pounds (907 g) catfish fillet
- ½ cup almond flour
- 2 eggs, beaten
- 1 teaspoon salt
- 1 teaspoon avocado oil

1. Sprinkle the catfish fillet with salt and dip in the eggs. 2. Then coat the fish in the almond flour and put in the air fryer basket. Sprinkle the fish with avocado oil. 3. Cook the fish for 6 minutes per side at 380ºF (193ºC).

Tex-Mex Salmon Bowl

Prep time: 15 minutes | Cook time: 9 to 14 minutes | Serves 4

- 12 ounces (340 g) salmon fillets, cut into 1½-inch cubes
- 1 red onion, chopped
- 1 jalapeño pepper, minced
- 1 red bell pepper, chopped
- ¼ cup low-sodium salsa
- 2 teaspoons peanut oil or safflower oil
- 2 tablespoons low-sodium tomato juice
- 1 teaspoon chili powder

1. Preheat the air fryer to 370ºF (188ºC). 2. Mix together the salmon cubes, red onion, jalapeño, red bell pepper, salsa, peanut oil, tomato juice, chili powder in a medium metal bowl and stir until well incorporated. 3. Transfer the bowl to the air fryer basket and bake for 9 to 14 minutes, stirring once, or until the salmon is cooked through and the veggies are fork-tender. 4. Serve warm.

Roasted Halibut Steaks with Parsley

Prep time: 5 minutes | Cook time: 10 minutes | Serves 4

- 1 pound (454 g) halibut steaks
- ¼ cup vegetable oil
- 2½ tablespoons Worcester sauce
- 2 tablespoons honey
- 2 tablespoons vermouth
- 1 tablespoon freshly squeezed lemon juice
- 1 tablespoon fresh parsley leaves, coarsely chopped
- Salt and pepper, to taste
- 1 teaspoon dried basil

1. Preheat the air fryer to 390ºF (199ºC). 2. Put all the ingredients in a large mixing dish and gently stir until the fish is coated evenly. 3. Transfer the fish to the air fryer basket and roast for 10 minutes, flipping the fish halfway through, or until the fish reaches an internal temperature of at least 145ºF (63ºC) on a meat thermometer. 4. Let the fish cool for 5 minutes and serve.

Blackened Fish

Prep time: 15 minutes | Cook time: 8 minutes | Serves 4

- 1 large egg, beaten
- Blackened seasoning, as needed
- 2 tablespoons light brown sugar
- 4 (4-ounce / 113- g) tilapia fillets
- Cooking spray

1. In a shallow bowl, place the beaten egg. In a second shallow bowl, stir together the Blackened seasoning and the brown sugar. 2. One at a time, dip the fish fillets in the egg, then the brown sugar mixture, coating thoroughly. 3. Preheat the air fryer to 300°F (149°C). Line the air fryer basket with parchment paper. 4. Place the coated fish on the parchment and spritz with oil. 5. Bake for 4 minutes. Flip the fish, spritz it with oil, and bake for 4 to 6 minutes more until the fish is white inside and flakes easily with a fork. 6. Serve immediately.

Blackened Red Snapper

Prep time: 13 minutes | Cook time: 8 to 10 minutes | Serves 4

- 1½ teaspoons black pepper
- ¼ teaspoon thyme
- ¼ teaspoon garlic powder
- ⅛ teaspoon cayenne pepper
- 1 teaspoon olive oil
- 4 (4 ounces / 113 g) red snapper fillet portions, skin on
- 4 thin slices lemon
- Cooking spray

1. Mix the spices and oil together to make a paste. Rub into both sides of the fish. 2. Spray the air fryer basket with nonstick cooking spray and lay snapper steaks in basket, skin-side down. 3. Place a lemon slice on each piece of fish. 4. Roast at 390°F (199°C) for 8 to 10 minutes. The fish will not flake when done, but it should be white through the center.

Sole and Cauliflower Fritters

Prep time: 5 minutes | Cook time: 24 minutes | Serves 2

- ½ pound (227 g) sole fillets
- ½ pound (227 g) mashed cauliflower
- ½ cup red onion, chopped
- 1 bell pepper, finely chopped
- 1 egg, beaten
- 2 garlic cloves, minced
- 2 tablespoons fresh parsley, chopped
- 1 tablespoon olive oil
- 1 tablespoon coconut aminos
- ½ teaspoon scotch bonnet pepper, minced
- ½ teaspoon paprika
- Salt and white pepper, to taste
- Cooking spray

1. Preheat the air fryer to 395°F (202°C). Spray the air fryer basket with cooking spray. 2. Place the sole fillets in the basket and air fry for 10 minutes, flipping them halfway through. 3.

When the fillets are done, transfer them to a large bowl. Mash the fillets into flakes. Add the remaining ingredients and stir to combine. 4. Make the fritters: Scoop out 2 tablespoons of the fish mixture and shape into a patty about ½ inch thick with your hands. Repeat with the remaining fish mixture. 5. Arrange the patties in the air fryer basket and bake for 14 minutes, flipping the patties halfway through, or until they are golden brown and cooked through. 6. Cool for 5 minutes and serve on a plate.

Air Fried Spring Rolls

Prep time: 10 minutes | Cook time: 17 to 22 minutes | Serves 4

- 2 teaspoons minced garlic
- 2 cups finely sliced cabbage
- 1 cup matchstick cut carrots
- 2 (4-ounce / 113-g) cans tiny shrimp, drained
- 4 teaspoons soy sauce
- Salt and freshly ground black pepper, to taste
- 16 square spring roll wrappers
- Cooking spray

1. Preheat the air fryer to 370°F (188°C). 2. Spray the air fryer basket lightly with cooking spray. Spray a medium sauté pan with cooking spray. 3. Add the garlic to the sauté pan and cook over medium heat until fragrant, 30 to 45 seconds. Add the cabbage and carrots and sauté until the vegetables are slightly tender, about 5 minutes. 4. Add the shrimp and soy sauce and season with salt and pepper, then stir to combine. Sauté until the moisture has evaporated, 2 more minutes. Set aside to cool. 5. Place a spring roll wrapper on a work surface so it looks like a diamond. Place 1 tablespoon of the shrimp mixture on the lower end of the wrapper. 6. Roll the wrapper away from you halfway, then fold in the right and left sides, like an envelope. Continue to roll to the very end, using a little water to seal the edge. Repeat with the remaining wrappers and filling. 7. Place the spring rolls in the air fryer basket in a single layer, leaving room between each roll. Lightly spray with cooking spray. You may need to cook them in batches. 8. Air fry for 5 minutes. Turn the rolls over, lightly spray with cooking spray, and air fry until heated through and the rolls start to brown, 5 to 10 more minutes. Cool for 5 minutes before serving.

Salmon with Cauliflower

Prep time: 10 minutes | Cook time: 25 minutes | Serves 4

- 1 pound (454 g) salmon fillet, diced
- 1 cup cauliflower, shredded
- 1 tablespoon dried cilantro
- 1 tablespoon coconut oil, melted
- 1 teaspoon ground turmeric
- ¼ cup coconut cream

1. Mix salmon with cauliflower, dried cilantro, ground turmeric, coconut cream, and coconut oil. 2. Transfer the salmon mixture into the air fryer and cook the meal at 350°F (177°C) for 25 minutes. Stir the meal every 5 minutes to avoid the burning.

Almond Pesto Salmon

Prep time: 5 minutes | Cook time: 12 minutes | Serves 2

- ¼ cup pesto
- ¼ cup sliced almonds, roughly chopped
- 2 (1½-inch-thick) salmon
- fillets (about 4 ounces / 113 g each)
- 2 tablespoons unsalted butter, melted

1. In a small bowl, mix pesto and almonds. Set aside. 2. Place fillets into a round baking dish. 3. Brush each fillet with butter and place half of the pesto mixture on the top of each fillet. Place dish into the air fryer basket. 4. Adjust the temperature to 390ºF (199ºC) and set the timer for 12 minutes. 5. Salmon will easily flake when fully cooked and reach an internal temperature of at least 145ºF (63ºC). Serve warm.

Pesto Shrimp with Wild Rice Pilaf

Prep time: 5 minutes | Cook time: 5 minutes | Serves 4

- 1 pound (454 g) medium shrimp, peeled and deveined
- ¼ cup pesto sauce
- 1 lemon, sliced
- 2 cups cooked wild rice pilaf

1. Preheat the air fryer to 360ºF(182ºC). 2. In a medium bowl, toss the shrimp with the pesto sauce until well coated. 3. Place the shrimp in a single layer in the air fryer basket. Put the lemon slices over the shrimp and roast for 5 minutes. 4. Remove the lemons and discard. Serve a quarter of the shrimp over ½ cup wild rice with some favorite steamed vegetables.

Herbed Shrimp Pita

Prep time: 5 minutes | Cook time: 8 minutes | Serves 4

- 1 pound (454 g) medium shrimp, peeled and deveined
- 2 tablespoons olive oil
- 1 teaspoon dried oregano
- ½ teaspoon dried thyme
- ½ teaspoon garlic powder
- ¼ teaspoon onion powder
- ½ teaspoon salt
- ¼ teaspoon black pepper
- 4 whole wheat pitas
- 4 ounces (113 g) feta cheese, crumbled
- 1 cup shredded lettuce
- 1 tomato, diced
- ¼ cup black olives, sliced
- 1 lemon

1. Preheat the oven to 380ºF(193ºC). 2. In a medium bowl, combine the shrimp with the olive oil, oregano, thyme, garlic powder, onion powder, salt, and black pepper. 3. Pour shrimp in a single layer in the air fryer basket and roast for 6 to 8 minutes, or until cooked through. 4. Remove from the air fryer and divide into warmed pitas with feta, lettuce, tomato, olives,

and a squeeze of lemon.

Scallops and Spinach with Cream Sauce

Prep time: 5 minutes | Cook time: 10 minutes | Serves 2

- Vegetable oil spray
- 1 (10-ounce / 283-g) package frozen spinach, thawed and drained
- 8 jumbo sea scallops
- Kosher salt and black
- pepper, to taste
- ¾ cup heavy cream
- 1 tablespoon tomato paste
- 1 tablespoon chopped fresh basil
- 1 teaspoon minced garlic

1. Spray a baking pan with vegetable oil spray. Spread the thawed spinach in an even layer in the bottom of the pan. 2. Spray both sides of the scallops with vegetable oil spray. Season lightly with salt and pepper. Arrange the scallops on top of the spinach. 3. In a small bowl, whisk together the cream, tomato paste, basil, garlic, ½ teaspoon salt, and ½ teaspoon pepper. Pour the sauce over the scallops and spinach. 4. Place the pan in the air fryer basket. Set the air fryer to 350ºF (177ºC) for 10 minutes. Use a meat thermometer to ensure the scallops have an internal temperature of 135ºF (57ºC).

Steamed Tuna with Lemongrass

Prep time: 10 minutes | Cook time: 10 minutes | Serves 4

- 4 small tuna steaks
- 2 tablespoons low-sodium soy sauce
- 2 teaspoons sesame oil
- 2 teaspoons rice wine vinegar
- 1 teaspoon grated peeled
- fresh ginger
- ⅛ teaspoon freshly ground black pepper
- 1 stalk lemongrass, bent in half
- 3 tablespoons freshly squeezed lemon juice

1. Place the tuna steaks on a plate. 2. In a small bowl, whisk the soy sauce, sesame oil, vinegar, and ginger until combined. Pour this mixture over the tuna and gently rub it into both sides. Sprinkle the fish with the pepper. Let marinate for 10 minutes. 3. Insert the crisper plate into the basket and the basket into the unit. Preheat the unit by selecting BAKE, setting the temperature to 390ºF (199ºC), and setting the time to 3 minutes. Select START/STOP to begin. 4. Once the unit is preheated, place the lemongrass into the basket and top it with the tuna steaks. Drizzle the tuna with the lemon juice and 1 tablespoon of water. 5. Select BAKE, set the temperature to 390ºF (199ºC), and set the time to 10 minutes. Select START/STOP to begin. 6. When the cooking is complete, a food thermometer inserted into the tuna should register at least 145ºF (63ºC). Discard the lemongrass and serve the tuna.

Cilantro Lime Baked Salmon

Prep time: 10 minutes | Cook time: 12 minutes | Serves 2

- 2 (3-ounce / 85-g) salmon fillets, skin removed
- 1 tablespoon salted butter, melted
- 1 teaspoon chili powder
- ½ teaspoon finely minced garlic
- ¼ cup sliced pickled jalapeños
- ½ medium lime, juiced
- 2 tablespoons chopped cilantro

1. Place salmon fillets into a round baking pan. Brush each with butter and sprinkle with chili powder and garlic. 2. Place jalapeño slices on top and around salmon. Pour half of the lime juice over the salmon and cover with foil. Place pan into the air fryer basket. 3. Adjust the temperature to 370ºF (188ºC) and bake for 12 minutes. 4. When fully cooked, salmon should flake easily with a fork and reach an internal temperature of at least 145ºF (63ºC). 5. To serve, spritz with remaining lime juice and garnish with cilantro.

Snapper with Shallot and Tomato

Prep time: 20 minutes | Cook time: 15 minutes | Serves 2

- 2 snapper fillets
- 1 shallot, peeled and sliced
- 2 garlic cloves, halved
- 1 bell pepper, sliced
- 1 small-sized serrano pepper, sliced
- 1 tomato, sliced
- 1 tablespoon olive oil
- ¼ teaspoon freshly ground black pepper
- ½ teaspoon paprika
- Sea salt, to taste
- 2 bay leaves

1. Place two parchment sheets on a working surface. Place the fish in the center of one side of the parchment paper. 2. Top with the shallot, garlic, peppers, and tomato. Drizzle olive oil over the fish and vegetables. Season with black pepper, paprika, and salt. Add the bay leaves. 3. Fold over the other half of the parchment. Now, fold the paper around the edges tightly and create a half moon shape, sealing the fish inside. 4. Cook in the preheated air fryer at 390ºF (199ºC) for 15 minutes. Serve warm.

Air Fried Crab Bun

Prep time: 15 minutes | Cook time: 20 minutes | Serves 2

- 5 ounces (142 g) crab meat, chopped
- 2 eggs, beaten
- 2 tablespoons coconut flour
- ¼ teaspoon baking powder
- ½ teaspoon coconut aminos
- ½ teaspoon ground black pepper
- 1 tablespoon coconut oil, softened

1. In the mixing bowl, mix crab meat with eggs, coconut flour, baking powder, coconut aminos, ground black pepper, and coconut oil. 2. Knead the smooth dough and cut it into pieces. 3. Make the buns from the crab mixture and put them in the air fryer basket. 4. Cook the crab buns at 365ºF (185ºC) for 20 minutes.

Classic Shrimp Empanadas

Prep time: 10 minutes | Cook time: 8 minutes | Serves 5

- ½ pound (227g) raw shrimp, peeled, deveined and chopped
- ¼ cup chopped red onion
- 1 scallion, chopped
- 2 garlic cloves, minced
- 2 tablespoons minced red bell pepper
- 2 tablespoons chopped fresh cilantro
- ½ tablespoon fresh lime juice
- ¼ teaspoon sweet paprika
- ⅛ teaspoon kosher salt
- ⅛ teaspoon crushed red pepper flakes (optional)
- 1 large egg, beaten
- 10 frozen Goya Empanada Discos, thawed
- Cooking spray

1. In a medium bowl, combine the shrimp, red onion, scallion, garlic, bell pepper, cilantro, lime juice, paprika, salt, and pepper flakes (if using). 2. In a small bowl, beat the egg with 1 teaspoon water until smooth. 3. Place an empanada disc on a work surface and put 2 tablespoons of the shrimp mixture in the center. Brush the outer edges of the disc with the egg wash. Fold the disc over and gently press the edges to seal. Use a fork and press around the edges to crimp and seal completely. Brush the tops of the empanadas with the egg wash. 4. Preheat the air fryer to 380ºF (193ºC). 5. Spray the bottom of the air fryer basket with cooking spray to prevent sticking. Working in batches, arrange a single layer of the empanadas in the air fryer basket and air fry for about 8 minutes, flipping halfway, until golden brown and crispy. 6. Serve hot.

Lemon Pepper Shrimp

Prep time: 15 minutes | Cook time: 8 minutes | Serves 2

- Oil, for spraying
- 12 ounces (340 g) medium raw shrimp, peeled and deveined
- 3 tablespoons lemon juice
- 1 tablespoon olive oil
- 1 teaspoon lemon pepper
- ¼ teaspoon paprika
- ¼ teaspoon granulated garlic

1. Preheat the air fryer to 400ºF (204ºC). Line the air fryer basket with parchment and spray lightly with oil. 2. In a medium bowl, toss together the shrimp, lemon juice, olive oil, lemon pepper, paprika, and garlic until evenly coated. 3. Place the shrimp in the prepared basket. 4. Cook for 6 to 8 minutes, or until pink and firm. Serve immediately.

Cajun and Lemon Pepper Cod

Prep time: 5 minutes | Cook time: 12 minutes | Makes 2 cod fillets

- 1 tablespoon Cajun seasoning
- 1 teaspoon salt
- ½ teaspoon lemon pepper
- ½ teaspoon freshly ground black pepper
- 2 (8 ounces / 227 g) cod fillets, cut to fit into the air fryer basket
- Cooking spray
- 2 tablespoons unsalted butter, melted
- 1 lemon, cut into 4 wedges

1. Preheat the air fryer to 360ºF (182ºC). Spritz the air fryer basket with cooking spray. 2. Thoroughly combine the Cajun seasoning, salt, lemon pepper, and black pepper in a small bowl. Rub this mixture all over the cod fillets until completely coated. 3. Put the fillets in the air fryer basket and brush the melted butter over both sides of each fillet. 4. Bake in the preheated air fryer for 12 minutes, flipping the fillets halfway through, or until the fish flakes easily with a fork. 5. Remove the fillets from the basket and serve with fresh lemon wedges.

Chinese Ginger-Scallion Fish

Prep time: 15 minutes | Cook time: 15 minutes | Serves 2

Bean Sauce:
- 2 tablespoons soy sauce
- 1 tablespoon rice wine
- 1 tablespoon doubanjiang (Chinese black bean paste)
- 1 teaspoon minced fresh ginger
- 1 clove garlic, minced

Vegetables and Fish:
- 1 tablespoon peanut oil
- ¼ cup julienned green onions (white and green parts)
- ¼ cup chopped fresh cilantro
- 2 tablespoons julienned fresh ginger
- 2 (6 ounces / 170 g) white fish fillets, such as tilapia
-

1. For the sauce: In a small bowl, combine all the ingredients and stir until well combined; set aside. 2. For the vegetables and fish: In a medium bowl, combine the peanut oil, green onions, cilantro, and ginger. Toss to combine. 3. Cut two squares of parchment large enough to hold one fillet and half of the vegetables. Place one fillet on each parchment square, top with the vegetables, and pour over the sauce. Fold over the parchment paper and crimp the sides in small, tight folds to hold the fish, vegetables, and sauce securely inside the packet. 4. Place the packets in a single layer in the air fryer basket. Set fryer to 350ºF (177ºC) for 15 minutes. 5. Transfer each packet to a dinner plate. Cut open with scissors just before serving.

Dukkah-Crusted Halibut

Prep time: 15 minutes | Cook time: 17 minutes | Serves 2

Dukkah:
- 1 tablespoon coriander seeds
- 1 tablespoon sesame seeds
- 1½ teaspoons cumin seeds
- ⅓ cup roasted mixed nuts
- ¼ teaspoon kosher salt
- ¼ teaspoon black pepper

Fish:
- 2 (5 ounces / 142 g) halibut fillets
- 2 tablespoons mayonnaise
- Vegetable oil spray
- Lemon wedges, for serving

1. For the dukkah: Combine the coriander, sesame seeds, and cumin in a small baking pan. Place the pan in the air fryer basket. Set the air fryer to 400ºF (204ºC) for 5 minutes. Toward the end of the cooking time, you will hear the seeds popping. Transfer to a plate and let cool for 5 minutes. 2. Transfer the toasted seeds to a food processor or spice grinder and add the mixed nuts. Pulse until coarsely chopped. Add the salt and pepper and stir well. 3. For the fish: Spread each fillet with 1 tablespoon of the mayonnaise. Press a heaping tablespoon of the dukkah into the mayonnaise on each fillet, pressing lightly to adhere. 4. Spray the air fryer basket with vegetable oil spray. Place the fish in the basket. Set the air fryer to 400ºF (204ºC) for 12 minutes, or until the fish flakes easily with a fork. 5. Serve the fish with lemon wedges.

Baked Monkfish

Prep time: 20 minutes | Cook time: 12 minutes | Serves 2

- 2 teaspoons olive oil
- 1 cup celery, sliced
- 2 bell peppers, sliced
- 1 teaspoon dried thyme
- ½ teaspoon dried marjoram
- ½ teaspoon dried rosemary
- 2 monkfish fillets
- 1 tablespoon coconut
- aminos
- 2 tablespoons lime juice
- Coarse salt and ground black pepper, to taste
- 1 teaspoon cayenne pepper
- ½ cup Kalamata olives, pitted and sliced

1. In a nonstick skillet, heat the olive oil for 1 minute. Once hot, sauté the celery and peppers until tender, about 4 minutes. Sprinkle with thyme, marjoram, and rosemary and set aside. 2. Toss the fish fillets with the coconut aminos, lime juice, salt, black pepper, and cayenne pepper. Place the fish fillets in the lightly greased air fryer basket and bake at 390ºF (199ºC) for 8 minutes. 3. Turn them over, add the olives, and cook an additional 4 minutes. Serve with the sautéed vegetables on the side. Bon appétit!

Mustard-Crusted Fish Fillets

Prep time: 5 minutes | Cook time: 8 to 11 minutes | Serves 4

- 5 teaspoons low-sodium yellow mustard
- 1 tablespoon freshly squeezed lemon juice
- 4 (3½-ounce / 99-g) sole fillets
- ½ teaspoon dried thyme
- ½ teaspoon dried marjoram
- ⅛ teaspoon freshly ground black pepper
- 1 slice low-sodium whole-wheat bread, crumbled
- 2 teaspoons olive oil

1. In a small bowl, mix the mustard and lemon juice. Spread this evenly over the fillets. Place them in the air fryer basket. 2. In another small bowl, mix the thyme, marjoram, pepper, bread crumbs, and olive oil. Mix until combined. 3. Gently but firmly press the spice mixture onto the top of each fish fillet. 4. Bake at 320°F (160°C) for 8 to 11 minutes, or until the fish reaches an internal temperature of at least 145°F (63°C) on a meat thermometer and the topping is browned and crisp. Serve immediately.

Sea Bass with Roasted Root Vegetables

Prep time: 10 minutes | Cook time: 15 minutes | Serves 4

- 1 carrot, diced small
- 1 parsnip, diced small
- 1 rutabaga, diced small
- ¼ cup olive oil
- 1 teaspoon salt, divided
- 4 sea bass fillets
- ½ teaspoon onion powder
- 2 garlic cloves, minced
- 1 lemon, sliced, plus additional wedges for serving

1. Preheat the air fryer to 380°F(193°C). 2. In a small bowl, toss the carrot, parsnip, and rutabaga with olive oil and 1 teaspoon salt. 3. Lightly season the sea bass with the remaining 1 teaspoon of salt and the onion powder, then place it into the air fryer basket in a single layer. 4. Spread the garlic over the top of each fillet, then cover with lemon slices. 5. Pour the prepared vegetables into the basket around and on top of the fish. Roast for 15 minutes. 6. Serve with additional lemon wedges if desired.

Chapter 7
Snacks and Appetizers

Roasted Grape Dip

Prep time: 10 minutes | Cook time: 8 to 12 minutes | Serves 6

- 2 cups seedless red grapes, rinsed and patted dry
- 1 tablespoon apple cider vinegar
- 1 tablespoon honey
- 1 cup low-fat Greek yogurt
- 2 tablespoons 2% milk
- 2 tablespoons minced fresh basil

1. In the air fryer basket, sprinkle the grapes with the cider vinegar and drizzle with the honey. Toss to coat. Roast the grapes at 380ºF (193ºC) for 8 to 12 minutes, or until shriveled but still soft. Remove from the air fryer. 2. In a medium bowl, stir together the yogurt and milk. 3. Gently blend in the grapes and basil. Serve immediately, or cover and chill for 1 to 2 hours.

Cinnamon Apple Chips

Prep time: 5 minutes | Cook time: 7 to 8 hours | Serves 4

- 4 medium apples, any type, cored and cut into ⅓-inch-thick slices (thin slices yield crunchy chips)
- ¼ teaspoon ground cinnamon
- ¼ teaspoon ground nutmeg

1. Place the apple slices in a large bowl. Sprinkle the cinnamon and nutmeg onto the apple slices and toss to coat. 2. Insert the crisper plate into the basket and the basket into the unit. Preheat the unit by selecting DEHYDRATE, setting the temperature to 135ºF (57ºC), and setting the time to 3 minutes. Select START/STOP to begin. 3. Once the unit is preheated, place the apple chips into the basket. It is okay to stack them. 4. Select DEHYDRATE, set the temperature to 135ºF (57ºC), and set the time to 7 or 8 hours. Select START/STOP to begin. 5. When the cooking is complete, cool the apple chips. Serve or store at room temperature in an airtight container for up to 1 week.

Roasted Chickpeas

Prep time: 5 minutes | Cook time: 15 minutes | Makes about 1 cup

- 1 (15-ounce / 425-g) can chickpeas, drained
- 2 teaspoons curry powder
- ¼ teaspoon salt
- 1 tablespoon olive oil

1. Drain chickpeas thoroughly and spread in a single layer on paper towels. Cover with another paper towel and press gently to remove extra moisture. Don't press too hard or you'll crush the chickpeas. 2. Mix curry powder and salt together. 3. Place chickpeas in a medium bowl and sprinkle with seasonings. Stir well to coat. 4. Add olive oil and stir again to distribute oil. 5. Air fry at 390ºF (199ºC) for 15 minutes, stopping to shake basket about halfway through cooking time. 6. Cool completely and store in airtight container.

Parmesan French Fries

Prep time: 10 minutes | Cook time: 25 minutes | Serves 2 to 3

- 2 to 3 large russet potatoes, peeled and cut into ½-inch sticks
- 2 teaspoons vegetable or canola oil
- ¾ cup grated Parmesan
- cheese
- ½ teaspoon salt
- Freshly ground black pepper, to taste
- 1 teaspoon fresh chopped parsley

1. Bring a large saucepan of salted water to a boil on the stovetop while you peel and cut the potatoes. Blanch the potatoes in the boiling salted water for 4 minutes while you preheat the air fryer to 400ºF (204ºC). Strain the potatoes and rinse them with cold water. Dry them well with a clean kitchen towel. 2. Toss the dried potato sticks gently with the oil and place them in the air fryer basket. Air fry for 25 minutes, shaking the basket a few times while the fries cook to help them brown evenly. 3. Combine the Parmesan cheese, salt and pepper. With 2 minutes left on the air fryer cooking time, sprinkle the fries with the Parmesan cheese mixture. Toss the fries to coat them evenly with the cheese mixture and continue to air fry for the final 2 minutes, until the cheese has melted and just starts to brown. Sprinkle the finished fries with chopped parsley, a little more grated Parmesan cheese if you like, and serve.

Buffalo Bites

Prep time: 15 minutes | Cook time: 11 to 12 minutes per batch | Makes 16 meatballs

- 1½ cups cooked jasmine or sushi rice
- ¼ teaspoon salt
- 1 pound (454 g) ground chicken
- 8 tablespoons buffalo wing sauce
- 2 ounces (57 g) Gruyère cheese, cut into 16 cubes
- 1 tablespoon maple syrup

1. Mix 4 tablespoons buffalo wing sauce into all the ground chicken. 2. Shape chicken into a log and divide into 16 equal portions. 3. With slightly damp hands, mold each chicken portion around a cube of cheese and shape into a firm ball. When you have shaped 8 meatballs, place them in air fryer basket. 4. Air fry at 390ºF (199ºC) for approximately 5 minutes. Shake basket, reduce temperature to 360ºF (182ºC), and cook for 5 to 6 minutes longer. 5. While the first batch is cooking, shape remaining chicken and cheese into 8 more meatballs. 6. Repeat step 4 to cook second batch of meatballs. 7. In a medium bowl, mix the remaining 4 tablespoons of buffalo wing sauce with the maple syrup. Add all the cooked meatballs and toss to coat. 8. Place meatballs back into air fryer basket and air fry at 390ºF (199ºC) for 2 to 3 minutes to set the glaze. Skewer each with a toothpick and serve.

Kale Chips with Tex-Mex Dip

Prep time: 10 minutes | Cook time: 5 to 6 minutes | Serves 8

- 1 cup Greek yogurt
- 1 tablespoon chili powder
- ⅓ cup low-sodium salsa, well drained
- 1 bunch curly kale
- 1 teaspoon olive oil
- ¼ teaspoon coarse sea salt

1. In a small bowl, combine the yogurt, chili powder, and drained salsa; refrigerate. 2. Rinse the kale thoroughly, and pat dry. Remove the stems and ribs from the kale, using a sharp knife. Cut or tear the leaves into 3-inch pieces. 3. Toss the kale with the olive oil in a large bowl. 4. Air fry the kale in small batches at 390°F (199°C) until the leaves are crisp. This should take 5 to 6 minutes. Shake the basket once during cooking time. 5. As you remove the kale chips, sprinkle them with a bit of the sea salt. 6. When all of the kale chips are done, serve with the dip.

Lemony Pear Chips

Prep time: 15 minutes | Cook time: 9 to 13 minutes | Serves 4

- 2 firm Bosc pears, cut crosswise into ⅛-inch-thick slices
- 1 tablespoon freshly squeezed lemon juice
- ½ teaspoon ground cinnamon
- ⅛ teaspoon ground cardamom

1. Preheat the air fryer to 380°F (193°C). 2. Separate the smaller stem-end pear rounds from the larger rounds with seeds. Remove the core and seeds from the larger slices. Sprinkle all slices with lemon juice, cinnamon, and cardamom. 3. Put the smaller chips into the air fryer basket. Air fry for 3 to 5 minutes, or until light golden brown, shaking the basket once during cooking. Remove from the air fryer. 4. Repeat with the larger slices, air frying for 6 to 8 minutes, or until light golden brown, shaking the basket once during cooking. 5. Remove the chips from the air fryer. Cool and serve or store in an airtight container at room temperature up for to 2 days.

Sausage Balls with Cheese

Prep time: 10 minutes | Cook time: 10 to 11 minutes | Serves 8

- 12 ounces (340 g) mild ground sausage
- 1½ cups baking mix
- 1 cup shredded mild Cheddar cheese
- 3 ounces (85 g) cream cheese, at room temperature
- 1 to 2 tablespoons olive oil

1. Preheat the air fryer to 325°F (163°C). Line the air fryer basket with parchment paper. 2. Mix together the ground sausage, baking mix, Cheddar cheese, and cream cheese in a large bowl and stir to incorporate. 3. Divide the sausage mixture into 16 equal portions and roll them into 1-inch balls with your hands. 4. Arrange the sausage balls on the parchment, leaving space between each ball. You may need to work in batches to avoid overcrowding. 5. Brush the sausage balls with the olive oil. Bake for 10 to 11 minutes, shaking the basket halfway through, or until the balls are firm and lightly browned on both sides. 6. Remove from the basket to a plate and repeat with the remaining balls. 7. Serve warm.

Tortellini with Spicy Dipping Sauce

Prep time: 5 minutes | Cook time: 20 minutes | Serves 4

- ¾ cup mayonnaise
- 2 tablespoons mustard
- 1 egg
- ½ cup flour
- ½ teaspoon dried oregano
- 1½ cups bread crumbs
- 2 tablespoons olive oil
- 2 cups frozen cheese tortellini

1. Preheat the air fryer to 380°F (193°C). 2. In a small bowl, combine the mayonnaise and mustard and mix well. Set aside. 3. In a shallow bowl, beat the egg. In a separate bowl, combine the flour and oregano. In another bowl, combine the bread crumbs and olive oil, and mix well. 4. Drop the tortellini, a few at a time, into the egg, then into the flour, then into the egg again, and then into the bread crumbs to coat. Put into the air fryer basket, cooking in batches. 5. Air fry for about 10 minutes, shaking halfway through the cooking time, or until the tortellini are crisp and golden brown on the outside. Serve with the mayonnaise mixture.

Beef and Mango Skewers

Prep time: 10 minutes | Cook time: 4 to 7 minutes | Serves 4

- ¾ pound (340 g) beef sirloin tip, cut into 1-inch cubes
- 2 tablespoons balsamic vinegar
- 1 tablespoon olive oil
- 1 tablespoon honey
- ½ teaspoon dried marjoram
- Pinch of salt
- Freshly ground black pepper, to taste
- 1 mango

1. Preheat the air fryer to 390°F (199°C). 2. Put the beef cubes in a medium bowl and add the balsamic vinegar, olive oil, honey, marjoram, salt, and pepper. Mix well, then massage the marinade into the beef with your hands. Set aside. 3. To prepare the mango, stand it on end and cut the skin off, using a sharp knife. Then carefully cut around the oval pit to remove the flesh. Cut the mango into 1-inch cubes. 4. Thread metal skewers alternating with three beef cubes and two mango cubes. 5. Roast the skewers in the air fryer basket for 4 to 7 minutes, or until the beef is browned and at least 145°F (63°C). 6. Serve hot.

Five-Ingredient Falafel with Garlic-Yogurt Sauce

Prep time: 5 minutes | Cook time: 15 minutes | Serves 4

Falafel:
- 1 (15-ounce / 425-g) can chickpeas, drained and rinsed
- ½ cup fresh parsley
- 2 garlic cloves, minced
- ½ tablespoon ground cumin
- 1 tablespoon whole wheat flour
- Salt

Garlic-Yogurt Sauce:
- 1 cup nonfat plain Greek yogurt
- 1 garlic clove, minced
- 1 tablespoon chopped fresh dill
- 2 tablespoons lemon juice

Make the Falafel: 1. Preheat the air fryer to 360°F(182°C). 2. Put the chickpeas into a food processor. Pulse until mostly chopped, then add the parsley, garlic, and cumin and pulse for another 1 to 2 minutes, or until the ingredients are combined and turning into a dough. 3. Add the flour. Pulse a few more times until combined. The dough will have texture, but the chickpeas should be pulsed into small bits. 4. Using clean hands, roll the dough into 8 balls of equal size, then pat the balls down a bit so they are about ½-thick disks. 5. Spray the basket of the air fryer with olive oil cooking spray, then place the falafel patties in the basket in a single layer, making sure they don't touch each other. 6. Fry in the air fryer for 15 minutes. Make the garlic-yogurt sauce 7. In a small bowl, combine the yogurt, garlic, dill, and lemon juice. 8. Once the falafel are done cooking and nicely browned on all sides, remove them from the air fryer and season with salt. 9. Serve hot with a side of dipping sauce.

Lemon Shrimp with Garlic Olive Oil

Prep time: 5 minutes | Cook time: 6 minutes | Serves 4

- 1 pound (454 g) medium shrimp, cleaned and deveined
- ¼ cup plus 2 tablespoons olive oil, divided
- Juice of ½ lemon
- 3 garlic cloves, minced and
- divided
- ½ teaspoon salt
- ¼ teaspoon red pepper flakes
- Lemon wedges, for serving (optional)
- Marinara sauce, for dipping (optional)

1. Preheat the air fryer to 380°F(193°C). 2. In a large bowl, combine the shrimp with 2 tablespoons of the olive oil, as well as the lemon juice, ⅓ of the minced garlic, salt, and red pepper flakes. Toss to coat the shrimp well. 3. In a small ramekin, combine the remaining ¼ cup of olive oil and the remaining minced garlic. 4. Tear off a 12-by-12-inch sheet of aluminum foil. Pour the shrimp into the center of the foil, then fold the sides up and crimp the edges so that it forms an aluminum foil bowl that is open on top. Place this packet into the air fryer basket. 5. Roast the shrimp for 4 minutes, then open the air fryer and place the ramekin with oil and garlic in the basket beside the shrimp packet. Cook for 2 more minutes. 6. Transfer the shrimp on a serving plate or platter with the ramekin of garlic olive oil on the side for dipping. You may also serve with lemon wedges and marinara sauce, if desired.

Cinnamon-Apple Chips

Prep time: 10 minutes | Cook time: 32 minutes | Serves 4

- Oil, for spraying
- 2 Red Delicious or Honeycrisp apples
- ¼ teaspoon ground cinnamon, divided

1. Line the air fryer basket with parchment and spray lightly with oil. 2. Trim the uneven ends off the apples. Using a mandoline on the thinnest setting or a sharp knife, cut the apples into very thin slices. Discard the cores. 3. Place half of the apple slices in a single layer in the prepared basket and sprinkle with half of the cinnamon. 4. Place a metal air fryer trivet on top of the apples to keep them from flying around while they are cooking. 5. Air fry at 300°F (149°C) for 16 minutes, flipping every 5 minutes to ensure even cooking. Repeat with the remaining apple slices and cinnamon. 6. Let cool to room temperature before serving. The chips will firm up as they cool.

Polenta Fries with Chili-Lime Mayo

Prep time: 10 minutes | Cook time: 28 minutes | Serves 4

Polenta Fries:
- 2 teaspoons vegetable or olive oil
- ¼ teaspoon paprika
- 1 pound (454 g) prepared polenta, cut into 3-inch × ½-inch strips

Chili-Lime Mayo:
- ½ cup mayonnaise
- 1 teaspoon chili powder
- 1 teaspoon chopped fresh cilantro
- ¼ teaspoon ground cumin
- Juice of ½ lime
- Salt and freshly ground black pepper, to taste

1. Preheat the air fryer to 400°F (204°C). 2. Mix the oil and paprika in a bowl. Add the polenta strips and toss until evenly coated. 3. Transfer the polenta strips to the air fry basket and air fry for 28 minutes until the fries are golden brown, shaking the basket once during cooking. Season as desired with salt and pepper. 4. Meanwhile, whisk together all the ingredients for the chili-lime mayo in a small bowl. 5. Remove the polenta fries from the air fryer to a plate and serve alongside the chili-lime mayo as a dipping sauce.

Spiralized Potato Nest with Tomato Ketchup

Prep time: 10 minutes | Cook time: 15 minutes | Serves 2

- 1 large russet potato (about 12 ounces / 340 g)
- 2 tablespoons vegetable oil
- 1 tablespoon hot smoked paprika
- ½ teaspoon garlic powder
- Kosher salt and freshly ground black pepper, to taste
- ½ cup canned crushed tomatoes
- 2 tablespoons apple cider vinegar
- 1 tablespoon dark brown sugar
- 1 tablespoon Worcestershire sauce
- 1 teaspoon mild hot sauce

1. Using a spiralizer, spiralize the potato, then place in a large colander. (If you don't have a spiralizer, cut the potato into thin ⅛-inch-thick matchsticks.) Rinse the potatoes under cold running water until the water runs clear. Spread the potatoes out on a double-thick layer of paper towels and pat completely dry. 2. In a large bowl, combine the potatoes, oil, paprika, and garlic powder. Season with salt and pepper and toss to combine. Transfer the potatoes to the air fryer and air fry at 400°F (204°C) until the potatoes are browned and crisp, 15 minutes, shaking the basket halfway through. 3. Meanwhile, in a small blender, purée the tomatoes, vinegar, brown sugar, Worcestershire, and hot sauce until smooth. Pour into a small saucepan or skillet and simmer over medium heat until reduced by half, 3 to 5 minutes. Pour the homemade ketchup into a bowl and let cool. 4. Remove the spiralized potato nest from the air fryer and serve hot with the ketchup.

Pork and Cabbage Egg Rolls

Prep time: 15 minutes | Cook time: 12 minutes | Makes 12 egg rolls

- Cooking oil spray
- 2 garlic cloves, minced
- 12 ounces (340 g) ground pork
- 1 teaspoon sesame oil
- ¼ cup soy sauce
- 2 teaspoons grated peeled
- fresh ginger
- 2 cups shredded green cabbage
- 4 scallions, green parts (white parts optional), chopped
- 24 egg roll wrappers

1. Spray a skillet with the cooking oil and place it over medium-high heat. Add the garlic and cook for 1 minute until fragrant. 2. Add the ground pork to the skillet. Using a spoon, break the pork into smaller chunks. 3. In a small bowl, whisk the sesame oil, soy sauce, and ginger until combined. Add the sauce to the skillet. Stir to combine and continue cooking for about 5 minutes until the pork is browned and thoroughly cooked. 4. Stir in the cabbage and scallions. Transfer the pork mixture to a large bowl. 5. Lay the egg roll wrappers on a flat surface. Dip a basting brush in water and glaze each egg roll wrapper along the edges with the wet brush. This will soften the dough and make it easier to roll. 6. Stack 2 egg roll wrappers (it works best if you double-wrap the egg rolls). Scoop 1 to 2 tablespoons of the pork mixture into the center of each wrapper stack. 7. Roll one long side of the wrappers up over the filling. Press firmly on the area with the filling, tucking it in lightly to secure it in place. Fold in the left and right sides. Continue rolling to close. Use the basting brush to wet the seam and seal the egg roll. Repeat with the remaining ingredients. 8. Insert the crisper plate into the basket and the basket into the unit. Preheat the unit by selecting AIR FRY, setting the temperature to 400°F (204°C), and setting the time to 3 minutes. Select START/STOP to begin. 9. Once the unit is preheated, spray the crisper plate with cooking oil. Place the egg rolls into the basket. It is okay to stack them. Spray them with cooking oil. 10. Select AIR FRY, set the temperature to 400°F (204°C), and set the time to 12 minutes. Insert the basket into the unit. Select START/STOP to begin. 11. After 8 minutes, use tongs to flip the egg rolls. Reinsert the basket to resume cooking. 12. When the cooking is complete, serve the egg rolls hot.

Crispy Chili Chickpeas

Prep time: 5 minutes | Cook time: 15 minutes | Serves 4

- 1 (15 ounces / 425 g) can cooked chickpeas, drained and rinsed
- 1 tablespoon olive oil
- ¼ teaspoon salt
- ⅛ teaspoon chili powder
- ⅛ teaspoon garlic powder
- ⅛ teaspoon paprika

1. Preheat the air fryer to 380°F(193°C). 2. In a medium bowl, toss all of the ingredients together until the chickpeas are well coated. 3. Pour the chickpeas into the air fryer and spread them out in a single layer. 4. Roast for 15 minutes, stirring once halfway through the cook time.

Black Bean Corn Dip

Prep time: 10 minutes | Cook time: 10 minutes | Serves 4

- ½ (15 ounces / 425 g) can black beans, drained and rinsed
- ½ (15 ounces / 425 g) can corn, drained and rinsed
- ¼ cup chunky salsa
- 2 ounces (57 g) reduced-fat
- cream cheese, softened
- ¼ cup shredded reduced-fat Cheddar cheese
- ½ teaspoon ground cumin
- ½ teaspoon paprika
- Salt and freshly ground black pepper, to taste

1. Preheat the air fryer to 325°F (163°C). 2. In a medium bowl, mix together the black beans, corn, salsa, cream cheese, Cheddar cheese, cumin, and paprika. Season with salt and pepper and stir until well combined. 3. Spoon the mixture into a baking dish. 4. Place baking dish in the air fryer basket and bake until heated through, about 10 minutes. 5. Serve hot.

Garlic-Roasted Tomatoes and Olives

Prep time: 5 minutes | Cook time: 20 minutes | Serves 6

- 2 cups cherry tomatoes
- 4 garlic cloves, roughly chopped
- ½ red onion, roughly chopped
- 1 cup black olives
- 1 cup green olives
- 1 tablespoon fresh basil, minced
- 1 tablespoon fresh oregano, minced
- 2 tablespoons olive oil
- ¼ to ½ teaspoon salt

1. Preheat the air fryer to 380°F(193°C). 2. In a large bowl, combine all of the ingredients and toss together so that the tomatoes and olives are coated well with the olive oil and herbs. 3. Pour the mixture into the air fryer basket, and roast for 10 minutes. Stir the mixture well, then continue roasting for an additional 10 minutes. 4. Remove from the air fryer, transfer to a serving bowl, and enjoy.

Golden Onion Rings

Prep time: 15 minutes | Cook time: 14 minutes per batch | Serves 4

- 1 large white onion, peeled and cut into ½ to ¾-inch-thick slices (about 2 cups)
- ½ cup 2% milk
- 1 cup whole-wheat pastry flour, or all-purpose flour
- 2 tablespoons cornstarch
- ¾ teaspoon sea salt, divided
- ½ teaspoon freshly ground black pepper, divided
- ¾ teaspoon granulated garlic, divided
- 1½ cups whole-grain bread crumbs, or gluten-free bread crumbs
- Cooking oil spray (coconut, sunflower, or safflower)
- Ketchup, for serving (optional)

1. Carefully separate the onion slices into rings—a gentle touch is important here. 2. Place the milk in a shallow bowl and set aside. 3. Make the first breading: In a medium bowl, stir together the flour, cornstarch, ¼ teaspoon of salt, ¼ teaspoon of pepper, and ¼ teaspoon of granulated garlic. Set aside. 4. Make the second breading: In a separate medium bowl, stir together the bread crumbs with the remaining ½ teaspoon of salt, the remaining ½ teaspoon of garlic, and the remaining ½ teaspoon of pepper. Set aside. 5. Insert the crisper plate into the basket and the basket into the unit. Preheat the unit by selecting AIR FRY, setting the temperature to 390°F (199°C), and setting the time to 3 minutes. Select START/STOP to begin. 6. Once the unit is preheated, spray the crisper plate and the basket with cooking oil. 7. To make the onion rings, dip one ring into the milk and into the first breading mixture. Dip the ring into the milk again and back into the first breading mixture, coating thoroughly. Dip the ring into the milk one last time and then into the second breading mixture, coating thoroughly. Gently lay the onion ring in the basket. Repeat with additional rings and, as you place them into the basket, do not overlap them too much. Once all the onion rings are in the basket, generously spray the tops with cooking oil. 8. Select AIR FRY, set the temperature to 390°F (199°C), and set the time to 14 minutes. Insert the basket into the unit. Select START/STOP to begin. 9. After 4 minutes, open the unit and spray the rings generously with cooking oil. Close the unit to resume cooking. After 3 minutes, remove the basket and spray the onion rings again. Remove the rings, turn them over, and place them back into the basket. Generously spray them again with oil. Reinsert the basket to resume cooking. After 4 minutes, generously spray the rings with oil one last time. Resume cooking for the remaining 3 minutes, or until the onion rings are very crunchy and brown. 10. When the cooking is complete, serve the hot rings with ketchup, or other sauce of choice.

Cheesy Zucchini Tots

Prep time: 15 minutes | Cook time: 6 minutes | Serves 8

- 2 medium zucchini (about 12 ounces / 340 g), shredded
- 1 large egg, whisked
- ½ cup grated pecorino romano cheese
- ½ cup panko bread crumbs
- ¼ teaspoon black pepper
- 1 clove garlic, minced
- Cooking spray

1. Using your hands, squeeze out as much liquid from the zucchini as possible. In a large bowl, mix the zucchini with the remaining ingredients except the oil until well incorporated. 2. Make the zucchini tots: Use a spoon or cookie scoop to place tablespoonfuls of the zucchini mixture onto a lightly floured cutting board and form into 1-inch logs. 3. Preheat air fryer to 375°F (191°C). Spritz the air fryer basket with cooking spray. 4. Place the tots in the basket. You may need to cook in batches to avoid overcrowding. 5. Air fry for 6 minutes until golden brown. 6. Remove from the basket to a serving plate and repeat with the remaining zucchini tots. 7. Serve immediately.

Roasted Mushrooms with Garlic

Prep time: 3 minutes | Cook time: 22 to 27 minutes | Serves 4

- 16 garlic cloves, peeled
- 2 teaspoons olive oil, divided
- 16 button mushrooms
- ½ teaspoon dried marjoram
- ⅛ teaspoon freshly ground black pepper
- 1 tablespoon white wine or low-sodium vegetable broth

1. In a baking pan, mix the garlic with 1 teaspoon of olive oil. Roast in the air fryer at 350°F (177°C) for 12 minutes. 2. Add the mushrooms, marjoram, and pepper. Stir to coat. Drizzle with the remaining 1 teaspoon of olive oil and the white wine. 3. Return to the air fryer and roast for 10 to 15 minutes more, or until the mushrooms and garlic cloves are tender. Serve.

Air Fryer Popcorn with Garlic Salt

Prep time: 3 minutes | Cook time: 10 minutes | Serves 2

- 2 tablespoons olive oil
- ¼ cup popcorn kernels
- 1 teaspoon garlic salt

1. Preheat the air fryer to 380°F(193ºC). 2. Tear a square of aluminum foil the size of the bottom of the air fryer and place into the air fryer. 3. Drizzle olive oil over the top of the foil, and then pour in the popcorn kernels. 4. Roast for 8 to 10 minutes, or until the popcorn stops popping. 5. Transfer the popcorn to a large bowl and sprinkle with garlic salt before serving.

Shrimp Egg Rolls

Prep time: 15 minutes | Cook time: 10 minutes per batch | Serves 4

- 1 tablespoon vegetable oil
- ½ head green or savoy cabbage, finely shredded
- 1 cup shredded carrots
- 1 cup canned bean sprouts, drained
- 1 tablespoon soy sauce
- ½ teaspoon sugar
- 1 teaspoon sesame oil
- ¼ cup hoisin sauce
- Freshly ground black pepper, to taste
- 1 pound (454 g) cooked shrimp, diced
- ¼ cup scallions
- 8 egg roll wrappers
- Vegetable oil
- Duck sauce

1. Preheat a large sauté pan over medium-high heat. Add the oil and cook the cabbage, carrots and bean sprouts until they start to wilt, about 3 minutes. Add the soy sauce, sugar, sesame oil, hoisin sauce and black pepper. Sauté for a few more minutes. Stir in the shrimp and scallions and cook until the vegetables are just tender. Transfer the mixture to a colander in a bowl to cool. Press or squeeze out any excess water from the filling so that you don't end up with soggy egg rolls. 2. Make the egg rolls: Place the egg roll wrappers on a flat surface with one of the points facing towards you so they look like diamonds. Dividing the filling evenly between the eight wrappers, spoon the mixture onto the center of the egg roll wrappers. Spread the filling across the center of the wrappers from the left corner to the right corner, but leave 2 inches from each corner empty. Brush the empty sides of the wrapper with a little water. Fold the bottom corner of the wrapper tightly up over the filling, trying to avoid making any air pockets. Fold the left corner in toward the center and then the right corner toward the center. It should now look like an envelope. Tightly roll the egg roll from the bottom to the top open corner. Press to seal the egg roll together, brushing with a little extra water if need be. Repeat this technique with all 8 egg rolls. 3. Preheat the air fryer to 370°F (188ºC). 4. Spray or brush all sides of the egg rolls with vegetable oil. Air fry four egg rolls at a time for 10 minutes, turning them over halfway through the cooking time. 5. Serve hot with duck sauce or your favorite dipping sauce.

Onion Pakoras

Prep time: 30 minutes | Cook time: 10 minutes per batch | Serves 2

- 2 medium yellow or white onions, sliced (2 cups)
- ½ cup chopped fresh cilantro
- 2 tablespoons vegetable oil
- 1 tablespoon chickpea flour
- 1 tablespoon rice flour, or 2
- tablespoons chickpea flour
- 1 teaspoon ground turmeric
- 1 teaspoon cumin seeds
- 1 teaspoon kosher salt
- ½ teaspoon cayenne pepper
- Vegetable oil spray

1. In a large bowl, combine the onions, cilantro, oil, chickpea flour, rice flour, turmeric, cumin seeds, salt, and cayenne. Stir to combine. Cover and let stand for 30 minutes or up to overnight. (This allows the onions to release moisture, creating a batter.) Mix well before using. 2. Spray the air fryer basket generously with vegetable oil spray. Drop half of the batter in 6 heaping tablespoons into the basket. Set the air fryer to 350ºF (177ºC) for 8 minutes. Carefully turn the pakoras over and spray with oil spray. Set the air fryer for 2 minutes, or until the batter is cooked through and crisp. 3. Repeat with remaining batter to make 6 more pakoras, checking at 6 minutes for doneness. Serve hot.

Cheese Drops

Prep time: 15 minutes | Cook time: 10 minutes per batch | Serves 8

- ¾ cup all-purpose flour
- ½ teaspoon kosher salt
- ¼ teaspoon cayenne pepper
- ¼ teaspoon smoked paprika
- ¼ teaspoon black pepper
- Dash garlic powder
- (optional)
- ¼ cup butter, softened
- 1 cup shredded sharp Cheddar cheese, at room temperature
- Olive oil spray

1. In a small bowl, combine the flour, salt, cayenne, paprika, pepper, and garlic powder, if using. 2. Using a food processor, cream the butter and cheese until smooth. Gently add the seasoned flour and process until the dough is well combined, smooth, and no longer sticky. (Or make the dough in a stand mixer fitted with the paddle attachment: Cream the butter and cheese on medium speed until smooth, then add the seasoned flour and beat at low speed until smooth.) 3. Divide the dough into 32 equal-size pieces. On a lightly floured surface, roll each piece into a small ball. 4. Spray the air fryer basket with oil spray. Arrange 16 cheese drops in the basket. Set the air fryer to 325ºF (163ºC) for 10 minutes, or until drops are just starting to brown. Transfer to a wire rack. Repeat with remaining dough, checking for doneness at 8 minutes. 5. Cool the cheese drops completely on the wire rack. Store in an airtight container until ready to serve, or up to 1 or 2 days.

Roasted Pearl Onion Dip

Prep time: 5 minutes | Cook time: 12 minutes | Serves 4

- 2 cups peeled pearl onions
- 3 garlic cloves
- 3 tablespoons olive oil, divided
- ½ teaspoon salt
- 1 cup nonfat plain Greek yogurt
- 1 tablespoon lemon juice
- ¼ teaspoon black pepper
- ⅛ teaspoon red pepper flakes
- Pita chips, vegetables, or toasted bread for serving (optional)

1. Preheat the air fryer to 360°F(182°C). 2. In a large bowl, combine the pearl onions and garlic with 2 tablespoons of the olive oil until the onions are well coated. 3. Pour the garlic-and-onion mixture into the air fryer basket and roast for 12 minutes. 4. Transfer the garlic and onions to a food processor. Pulse the vegetables several times, until the onions are minced but still have some chunks. 5. In a large bowl, combine the garlic and onions and the remaining 1 tablespoon of olive oil, along with the salt, yogurt, lemon juice, black pepper, and red pepper flakes. 6. Cover and chill for 1 hour before serving with pita chips, vegetables, or toasted bread.

Authentic Scotch Eggs

Prep time: 15 minutes | Cook time: 11 to 13 minutes | Serves 6

- 1½ pounds (680 g) bulk lean chicken or turkey sausage
- 3 raw eggs, divided
- 1½ cups dried bread
- crumbs, divided
- ½ cup all-purpose flour
- 6 hardboiled eggs, peeled
- Cooking oil spray

1. In a large bowl, combine the chicken sausage, 1 raw egg, and ½ cup of bread crumbs and mix well. Divide the mixture into 6 pieces and flatten each into a long oval. 2. In a shallow bowl, beat the remaining 2 raw eggs. 3. Place the flour in a small bowl. 4. Place the remaining 1 cup of bread crumbs in a second small bowl. 5. Roll each hardboiled egg in the flour and wrap one of the chicken sausage pieces around each egg to encircle it completely. 6. One at a time, roll the encased eggs in the flour, dip in the beaten eggs, and finally dip in the bread crumbs to coat. 7. Insert the crisper plate into the basket and the basket into the unit. Preheat the unit by selecting AIR FRY, setting the temperature to 375°F (191°C), and setting the time to 3 minutes. Select START/STOP to begin. 8. Once the unit is preheated, spray the crisper plate with cooking oil. Place the eggs in a single layer into the basket and spray them with oil. 9. Select AIR FRY, set the temperature to 375°F (191°C), and set the time to 13 minutes. Select START/STOP to begin. 10. After about 6 minutes, use tongs to turn the eggs and spray them with more oil. Resume cooking for 5 to 7 minutes more, or until the chicken is thoroughly cooked and the Scotch eggs

are browned. 11. When the cooking is complete, serve warm.

Italian Rice Balls

Prep time: 20 minutes | Cook time: 10 minutes | Makes 8 rice balls

- 1½ cups cooked sticky rice
- ½ teaspoon Italian seasoning blend
- ¾ teaspoon salt, divided
- 8 black olives, pitted
- 1 ounce (28 g) Mozzarella cheese, cut into tiny pieces
- (small enough to stuff into olives)
- 2 eggs
- ⅓ cup Italian bread crumbs
- ¾ cup panko bread crumbs
- Cooking spray

1. Preheat air fryer to 390°F (199°C). 2. Stuff each black olive with a piece of Mozzarella cheese. Set aside. 3. In a bowl, combine the cooked sticky rice, Italian seasoning blend, and ½ teaspoon of salt and stir to mix well. Form the rice mixture into a log with your hands and divide it into 8 equal portions. Mold each portion around a black olive and roll into a ball. 4. Transfer to the freezer to chill for 10 to 15 minutes until firm. 5. In a shallow dish, place the Italian bread crumbs. In a separate shallow dish, whisk the eggs. In a third shallow dish, combine the panko bread crumbs and remaining salt. 6. One by one, roll the rice balls in the Italian bread crumbs, then dip in the whisked eggs, finally coat them with the panko bread crumbs. 7. Arrange the rice balls in the air fryer basket and spritz both sides with cooking spray. 8. Air fry for 10 minutes until the rice balls are golden brown. Flip the balls halfway through the cooking time. 9. Serve warm.

Baked Ricotta

Prep time: 10 minutes | Cook time: 15 minutes | Makes 2 cups

- 1 (15 ounces / 425 g) container whole milk Ricotta cheese
- 3 tablespoons grated Parmesan cheese, divided
- 2 tablespoons extra-virgin olive oil
- 1 teaspoon chopped fresh
- thyme leaves
- 1 teaspoon grated lemon zest
- 1 clove garlic, crushed with press
- ¼ teaspoon salt
- ¼ teaspoon pepper
- Toasted baguette slices or crackers, for serving

1. Preheat the air fryer to 380°F (193°C). 2. To get the baking dish in and out of the air fryer, create a sling using a 24-inch length of foil, folded lengthwise into thirds. 3. Whisk together the Ricotta, 2 tablespoons of the Parmesan, oil, thyme, lemon zest, garlic, salt, and pepper. Pour into a baking dish. Cover the dish tightly with foil. 4. Place the sling under dish and lift by the ends into the air fryer, tucking the ends of the sling around the dish. Bake for 10 minutes. Remove the foil cover and sprinkle with the remaining 1 tablespoon of the Parmesan. Air fry for 5 more minutes, or until bubbly at edges and the top is browned. 5. Serve warm with toasted baguette slices or crackers.

Greek Potato Skins with Olives and Feta

Prep time: 5 minutes | Cook time: 45 minutes | Serves 4

- 2 russet potatoes
- 3 tablespoons olive oil, divided, plus more for drizzling (optional)
- 1 teaspoon kosher salt, divided
- ¼ teaspoon black pepper
- 2 tablespoons fresh

- cilantro, chopped, plus more for serving
- ¼ cup Kalamata olives, diced
- ¼ cup crumbled feta
- Chopped fresh parsley, for garnish (optional)

1. Preheat the air fryer to 380°F(193°C). 2. Using a fork, poke 2 to 3 holes in the potatoes, then coat each with about ½ tablespoon olive oil and ½ teaspoon salt. 3. Place the potatoes into the air fryer basket and bake for 30 minutes. 4. Remove the potatoes from the air fryer, and slice in half. Using a spoon, scoop out the flesh of the potatoes, leaving a ½-inch layer of potato inside the skins, and set the skins aside. 5. In a medium bowl, combine the scooped potato middles with the remaining 2 tablespoons of olive oil, ½ teaspoon of salt, black pepper, and cilantro. Mix until well combined. 6. Divide the potato filling into the now-empty potato skins, spreading it evenly over them. Top each potato with a tablespoon each of the olives and feta. 7. Place the loaded potato skins back into the air fryer and bake for 15 minutes. 8. Serve with additional chopped cilantro or parsley and a drizzle of olive oil, if desired.

Garlicky and Cheesy French Fries

Prep time: 5 minutes | Cook time: 20 to 25 minutes | Serves 4

- 3 medium russet potatoes, rinsed, dried, and cut into thin wedges or classic fry shapes
- 2 tablespoons extra-virgin olive oil
- 1 tablespoon granulated garlic
- ⅓ cup grated Parmesan

- cheese
- ½ teaspoon salt
- ¼ teaspoon freshly ground black pepper
- Cooking oil spray
- 2 tablespoons finely chopped fresh parsley (optional)

1. In a large bowl combine the potato wedges or fries and the olive oil. Toss to coat. 2. Sprinkle the potatoes with the granulated garlic, Parmesan cheese, salt, and pepper, and toss again. 3. Insert the crisper plate into the basket and the basket into the unit. Preheat the unit by selecting AIR FRY, setting the temperature to 400°F (204°C), and setting the time to 3 minutes. Select START/STOP to begin. 4. Once the unit is preheated, spray the crisper plate with cooking oil. Place the

potatoes into the basket. 5. Select AIR FRY, set the temperature to 400°F (204°C), and set the time to 20 to 25 minutes. Select START/STOP to begin. 6. After about 10 minutes, remove the basket and shake it so the fries at the bottom come up to the top. Reinsert the basket to resume cooking. 7. When the cooking is complete, top the fries with the parsley (if using) and serve hot.

Peppery Chicken Meatballs

Prep time: 5 minutes | Cook time: 13 to 20 minutes | Makes 16 meatballs

- 2 teaspoons olive oil
- ¼ cup minced onion
- ¼ cup minced red bell pepper
- 2 vanilla wafers, crushed

- 1 egg white
- ½ teaspoon dried thyme
- ½ pound (227 g) ground chicken breast

1. Preheat the air fryer to 370°F (188°C). 2. In a baking pan, mix the olive oil, onion, and red bell pepper. Put the pan in the air fryer. Air fry for 3 to 5 minutes, or until the vegetables are tender. 3. In a medium bowl, mix the cooked vegetables, crushed wafers, egg white, and thyme until well combined 4. Mix in the chicken, gently but thoroughly, until everything is combined. 5. Form the mixture into 16 meatballs and place them in the air fryer basket. Air fry for 10 to 15 minutes, or until the meatballs reach an internal temperature of 165°F (74°C) on a meat thermometer. 6. Serve immediately.

Corn Dog Muffins

Prep time: 10 minutes | Cook time: 8 to 10 minutes per batch | Makes 8 muffins

- 1¼ cups sliced kosher hotdogs (3 or 4, depending on size)
- ½ cup flour
- ½ cup yellow cornmeal
- 2 teaspoons baking powder
- ½ cup skim milk

- 1 egg
- 2 tablespoons canola oil
- 8 foil muffin cups, paper liners removed
- Cooking spray
- Mustard or your favorite dipping sauce

1. Slice each hotdog in half lengthwise, then cut in ¼-inch half-moon slices. Set aside. 2. Preheat the air fryer to 390°F (199°C). 3. In a large bowl, stir together flour, cornmeal, and baking powder. 4. In a small bowl, beat together the milk, egg, and oil until just blended. 5. Pour egg mixture into dry ingredients and stir with a spoon to mix well. 6. Stir in sliced hot dogs. 7. Spray the foil cups lightly with cooking spray. 8. Divide mixture evenly into muffin cups. 9. Place 4 muffin cups in the air fryer basket and cook for 5 minutes. 10. Reduce temperature to 360°F (182°C) and cook 3 to 5 minutes or until toothpick inserted in center of muffin comes out clean. 11. Repeat steps 9 and 10 to bake remaining corn dog muffins. 12. Serve with mustard or other sauces for dipping.

Shrimp Toasts with Sesame Seeds

Prep time: 15 minutes | Cook time: 6 to 8 minutes | Serves 4 to 6

- ½ pound (227 g) raw shrimp, peeled and deveined
- 1 egg, beaten
- 2 scallions, chopped, plus more for garnish
- 2 tablespoons chopped fresh cilantro
- 2 teaspoons grated fresh ginger
- 1 to 2 teaspoons sriracha sauce
- 1 teaspoon soy sauce
- ½ teaspoon toasted sesame oil
- 6 slices thinly sliced white sandwich bread
- ½ cup sesame seeds
- Cooking spray
- Thai chili sauce, for serving

1. Preheat the air fryer to 400°F (204°C). Spritz the air fryer basket with cooking spray. 2. In a food processor, add the shrimp, egg, scallions, cilantro, ginger, sriracha sauce, soy sauce and sesame oil, and pulse until chopped finely. You'll need to stop the food processor occasionally to scrape down the sides. Transfer the shrimp mixture to a bowl. 3. On a clean work surface, cut the crusts off the sandwich bread. Using a brush, generously brush one side of each slice of bread with shrimp mixture. 4. Place the sesame seeds on a plate. Press bread slices, shrimp-side down, into sesame seeds to coat evenly. Cut each slice diagonally into quarters. 5. Spread the coated slices in a single layer in the air fryer basket. 6. Air fry in batches for 6 to 8 minutes, or until golden and crispy. Flip the bread slices halfway through. Repeat with the remaining bread slices. 7. Transfer to a plate and let cool for 5 minutes. Top with the chopped scallions and serve warm with Thai chili sauce.

Mushroom Tarts

Prep time: 15 minutes | Cook time: 38 minutes | Makes 15 tarts

- 2 tablespoons extra-virgin olive oil, divided
- 1 small white onion, sliced
- 8 ounces (227 g) shiitake mushrooms, sliced
- ¼ teaspoon sea salt
- ¼ teaspoon freshly ground black pepper
- ¼ cup dry white wine
- 1 sheet frozen puff pastry, thawed
- 1 cup shredded Gruyère cheese
- Cooking oil spray
- 1 tablespoon thinly sliced fresh chives

1. Insert the crisper plate into the basket and the basket into the unit. Preheat the unit by selecting BAKE, setting the temperature to 300°F (149°C), and setting the time to 3 minutes. Select START/STOP to begin. 2. In a heatproof bowl that fits into the basket, stir together 1 tablespoon of olive oil, the onion, and the mushrooms. 3. Once the unit is preheated, place the bowl into the basket. 4. Select BAKE, set the temperature to 300°F (149°C), and set the time to 7 minutes. Select START/STOP to begin. 5. After about 2½ minutes, stir the vegetables. Resume cooking. After another 2½ minutes, the vegetables should be browned and tender. Season with the salt and pepper and add the wine. Resume cooking until the liquid evaporates, about 2 minutes. 6. When the cooking is complete, place the bowl on a heatproof surface. 7. Increase the air fryer temperature to 390°F (199°C) and set the time to 3 minutes. Select START/STOP to begin. 8. Unfold the puff pastry and cut it into 15 (3-by-3-inch) squares. Using a fork, pierce the dough and brush both sides with the remaining 1 tablespoon of olive oil. 9. Evenly distribute half the cheese among the puff pastry squares, leaving a ½-inch border around the edges. Divide the mushroom-onion mixture among the pastry squares and top with the remaining cheese. 10. Once the unit is preheated, spray the crisper plate with cooking oil. Working in batches, place 5 tarts into the basket; do not stack or overlap. 11. Select BAKE, set the temperature to 390°F (199°C), and set the time to 8 minutes. Select START/STOP to begin. 12. After 6 minutes, check the tarts; if not yet golden brown, resume cooking for about 2 minutes more. 13. When the cooking is complete, remove the tarts and transfer to a wire rack to cool. Repeat steps 10, 11, and 12 with the remaining tarts. 14. Serve garnished with the chives.

Hush Puppies

Prep time: 45 minutes | Cook time: 10 minutes | Serves 12

- 1 cup self-rising yellow cornmeal
- ½ cup all-purpose flour
- 1 teaspoon sugar
- 1 teaspoon salt
- 1 teaspoon freshly ground black pepper
- 1 large egg
- ⅓ cup canned creamed corn
- 1 cup minced onion
- 2 teaspoons minced jalapeño pepper
- 2 tablespoons olive oil, divided

1. Thoroughly combine the cornmeal, flour, sugar, salt, and pepper in a large bowl. 2. Whisk together the egg and corn in a small bowl. Pour the egg mixture into the bowl of cornmeal mixture and stir to combine. Stir in the minced onion and jalapeño. Cover the bowl with plastic wrap and place in the refrigerator for 30 minutes. 3. Preheat the air fryer to 375°F (191°C). Line the air fryer basket with parchment paper and lightly brush it with 1 tablespoon of olive oil. 4. Scoop out the cornmeal mixture and form into 24 balls, about 1 inch. 5. Arrange the balls in the parchment paper-lined basket, leaving space between each ball. 6. Air fry in batches for 5 minutes. Shake the basket and brush the balls with the remaining 1 tablespoon of olive oil. Continue cooking for 5 minutes until golden brown. 7. Remove the balls (hush puppies) from the basket and serve on a plate.

Chile-Brined Fried Calamari

Prep time: 20 minutes | Cook time: 8 minutes | Serves 2

- 1 (8 ounces / 227 g) jar sweet or hot pickled cherry peppers
- ½ pound (227 g) calamari bodies and tentacles, bodies cut into ½-inch-wide rings
- 1 lemon
- 2 cups all-purpose flour
- Kosher salt and freshly ground black pepper, to taste
- 3 large eggs, lightly beaten
- Cooking spray
- ½ cup mayonnaise
- 1 teaspoon finely chopped rosemary
- 1 garlic clove, minced

1. Drain the pickled pepper brine into a large bowl and tear the peppers into bite-size strips. Add the pepper strips and calamari to the brine and let stand in the refrigerator for 20 minutes or up to 2 hours. 2. Grate the lemon zest into a large bowl then whisk in the flour and season with salt and pepper. Dip the calamari and pepper strips in the egg, then toss them in the flour mixture until fully coated. Spray the calamari and peppers liberally with cooking spray, then transfer half to the air fryer. Air fry at 400°F (204°C), shaking the basket halfway into cooking, until the calamari is cooked through and golden brown, about 8 minutes. Transfer to a plate and repeat with the remaining pieces. 3. In a small bowl, whisk together the mayonnaise, rosemary, and garlic. Squeeze half the zested lemon to get 1 tablespoon of juice and stir it into the sauce. Season with salt and pepper. Cut the remaining zested lemon half into 4 small wedges and serve alongside the calamari, peppers, and sauce.

Crispy Green Bean Fries with Lemon-Yogurt Sauce

Prep time: 5 minutes | Cook time: 5 minutes | Serves 4

Green Beans:
- 1 egg
- 2 tablespoons water
- 1 tablespoon whole wheat flour
- ¼ teaspoon paprika

Lemon-Yogurt Sauce:
- ½ cup nonfat plain Greek yogurt
- 1 tablespoon lemon juice
- ¼ teaspoon salt

- ½ teaspoon garlic powder
- ½ teaspoon salt
- ¼ cup whole wheat bread crumbs
- ½ pound (227 g) whole green beans

- ⅛ teaspoon cayenne pepper
- ⅛ teaspoon cayenne pepper

Make the Green Beans: 1. Preheat the air fryer to 380°F(193°C). 2. In a medium shallow bowl, beat together the egg and water until frothy. 3. In a separate medium shallow bowl, whisk together the flour, paprika, garlic powder, and salt, then mix in the bread crumbs. 4. Spray the bottom of the air fryer with cooking spray. 5. Dip each green bean into the egg mixture, then into the bread crumb mixture, coating the outside with the crumbs. Place the green beans in a single layer in the bottom of the air fryer basket. 6. Fry in the air fryer for 5 minutes, or until the breading is golden brown. Make the Lemon-Yogurt Sauce: 7. In a small bowl, combine the yogurt, lemon juice, salt, and cayenne. 8. Serve the green bean fries alongside the lemon-yogurt sauce as a snack or appetizer.

Rumaki

Prep time: 30 minutes | Cook time: 10 to 12 minutes per batch | Makes about 24 rumaki

- 10 ounces (283 g) raw chicken livers
- 1 can sliced water chestnuts, drained
- ¼ cup low-sodium teriyaki sauce
- 12 slices turkey bacon

1. Cut livers into 1½-inch pieces, trimming out tough veins as you slice. 2. Place livers, water chestnuts, and teriyaki sauce in small container with lid. If needed, add another tablespoon of teriyaki sauce to make sure livers are covered. Refrigerate for 1 hour. 3. When ready to cook, cut bacon slices in half crosswise. 4. Wrap 1 piece of liver and 1 slice of water chestnut in each bacon strip. Secure with toothpick. 5. When you have wrapped half of the livers, place them in the air fryer basket in a single layer. 6. Air fry at 390°F (199°C) for 10 to 12 minutes, until liver is done and bacon is crispy. 7. While first batch cooks, wrap the remaining livers. Repeat step 6 to cook your second batch.

Chapter ⑧

Vegetables and Sides

Sesame Taj Tofu

Prep time: 5 minutes | Cook time: 25 minutes | Serves 4

- 1 block firm tofu, pressed and cut into 1-inch thick cubes
- 2 tablespoons soy sauce
- 2 teaspoons toasted sesame seeds
- 1 teaspoon rice vinegar
- 1 tablespoon cornstarch

1. Preheat the air fryer to 400ºF (204ºC). 2. Add the tofu, soy sauce, sesame seeds, and rice vinegar in a bowl together and mix well to coat the tofu cubes. Then cover the tofu in cornstarch and put it in the air fryer basket. 3. Air fry for 25 minutes, giving the basket a shake at five-minute intervals to ensure the tofu cooks evenly. 4. Serve immediately.

Ricotta Potatoes

Prep time: 15 minutes | Cook time: 15 minutes | Serves 4

- 4 potatoes
- 2 tablespoons olive oil
- ½ cup Ricotta cheese, at room temperature
- 2 tablespoons chopped scallions
- 1 tablespoon roughly chopped fresh parsley
- 1 tablespoon minced coriander
- 2 ounces (57 g) Cheddar cheese, preferably freshly grated
- 1 teaspoon celery seeds
- ½ teaspoon salt
- ½ teaspoon garlic pepper

1. Preheat the air fryer to 350ºF (177ºC). 2. Pierce the skin of the potatoes with a knife. 3. Air fry in the air fryer basket for 13 minutes. If they are not cooked through by this time, leave for 2 to 3 minutes longer. 4. In the meantime, make the stuffing by combining all the other ingredients. 5. Cut halfway into the cooked potatoes to open them. 6. Spoon equal amounts of the stuffing into each potato and serve hot.

Sweet-and-Sour Brussels Sprouts

Prep time: 10 minutes | Cook time: 20 minutes | Serves 2

- ¼ cup Thai sweet chili sauce
- 2 tablespoons black vinegar or balsamic vinegar
- ½ teaspoon hot sauce, such as Tabasco
- 8 ounces (227 g) Brussels sprouts, trimmed (large
- sprouts halved)
- 2 small shallots, cut into ¼-inch-thick slices
- Kosher salt and freshly ground black pepper, to taste
- 2 teaspoons lightly packed fresh cilantro leaves

1. In a large bowl, whisk together the chili sauce, vinegar, and hot sauce. Add the Brussels sprouts and shallots, season with salt and pepper, and toss to combine. Scrape the Brussels sprouts and sauce into a cake pan. 2. Place the pan in the air fryer and roast at 375ºF (191ºC), stirring every 5 minutes, until the Brussels sprouts are tender and the sauce is reduced to a sticky glaze, about 20 minutes. 3. Remove the pan from the air fryer and transfer the Brussels sprouts to plates. Sprinkle with the cilantro and serve warm.

"Faux-Tato" Hash

Prep time: 10 minutes | Cook time: 12 minutes | Serves 4

- 1 pound (454 g) radishes, ends removed, quartered
- ¼ medium yellow onion, peeled and diced
- ½ medium green bell pepper, seeded and chopped
- 2 tablespoons salted butter, melted
- ½ teaspoon garlic powder
- ¼ teaspoon ground black pepper

1. In a large bowl, combine radishes, onion, and bell pepper. Toss with butter. 2. Sprinkle garlic powder and black pepper over mixture in bowl, then spoon into ungreased air fryer basket. 3. Adjust the temperature to 320ºF (160ºC) and air fry for 12 minutes. Shake basket halfway through cooking. Radishes will be tender when done. Serve warm.

Broccoli-Cheddar Twice-Baked Potatoes

Prep time: 10 minutes | Cook time: 46 minutes | Serves 4

- Oil, for spraying
- 2 medium russet potatoes
- 1 tablespoon olive oil
- ¼ cup broccoli florets
- 1 tablespoon sour cream
- 1 teaspoon granulated garlic
- 1 teaspoon onion powder
- ½ cup shredded Cheddar cheese

1. Line the air fryer basket with parchment and spray lightly with oil. 2. Rinse the potatoes and pat dry with paper towels. Rub the outside of the potatoes with the olive oil and place them in the prepared basket. 3. Air fry at 400ºF (204ºC) for 40 minutes, or until easily pierced with a fork. Let cool just enough to handle, then cut the potatoes in half lengthwise. 4. Meanwhile, place the broccoli in a microwave-safe bowl, cover with water, and microwave on high for 5 to 8 minutes. Drain and set aside. 5. Scoop out most of the potato flesh and transfer to a medium bowl. 6. Add the sour cream, garlic, and onion powder and stir until the potatoes are mashed. 7. Spoon the potato mixture back into the hollowed potato skins, mounding it to fit, if necessary. Top with the broccoli and cheese. Return the potatoes to the basket. You may need to work in batches, depending on the size of your air fryer. 8. Air fry at 400ºF (204ºC) for 3 to 6 minutes, or until the cheese has melted. Serve immediately.

Glazed Carrots

Prep time: 10 minutes | Cook time: 8 to 10 minutes | Serves 4

- 2 teaspoons honey
- 1 teaspoon orange juice
- ½ teaspoon grated orange rind
- ⅛ teaspoon ginger
- 1 pound (454 g) baby carrots
- 2 teaspoons olive oil
- ¼ teaspoon salt

1. Combine honey, orange juice, grated rind, and ginger in a small bowl and set aside. 2. Toss the carrots, oil, and salt together to coat well and pour them into the air fryer basket. 3. Roast at 390°F (199°C) for 5 minutes. Shake basket to stir a little and cook for 2 to 4 minutes more, until carrots are barely tender. 4. Pour carrots into a baking pan. 5. Stir the honey mixture to combine well, pour glaze over carrots, and stir to coat. 6. Roast at 360°F (182°C) for 1 minute or just until heated through.

Chiles Rellenos with Red Chile Sauce

Prep time: 20 minutes | Cook time: 20 minutes | Serves 2

Peppers:

- 2 poblano peppers, rinsed and dried
- ⅔ cup thawed frozen or drained canned corn kernels
- 1 scallion, sliced

Sauce:

- 3 tablespoons extra-virgin olive oil
- ½ cup finely chopped yellow onion
- 2 teaspoons minced garlic
- 1 (6-ounce / 170-g) can tomato paste
- 2 tablespoons ancho chile powder
- 2 tablespoons chopped fresh cilantro
- ½ teaspoon kosher salt
- ¼ teaspoon black pepper
- ⅔ cup grated Monterey Jack cheese

- 1 teaspoon dried oregano
- 1 teaspoon ground cumin
- ½ teaspoon kosher salt
- 2 cups chicken broth
- 2 tablespoons fresh lemon juice
- Mexican crema or sour cream, for serving

1. For the peppers: Place the peppers in the air fryer basket. Set the air fryer to 400°F (204°C) for 10 minutes, turning the peppers halfway through the cooking time, until their skins are charred. Transfer the peppers to a resealable plastic bag, seal, and set aside to steam for 5 minutes. Peel the peppers and discard the skins. Cut a slit down the center of each pepper, starting at the stem and continuing to the tip. Remove the seeds, being careful not to tear the chile. 2. In a medium bowl, combine the corn, scallion, cilantro, salt, black pepper, and cheese; set aside. 3. Meanwhile, for the sauce: In a large skillet, heat the olive oil over medium-high heat. Add the onion and cook, stirring, until tender, about 5 minutes. Add the garlic and cook, stirring, for 30 seconds. Stir in the tomato paste, chile powder, oregano, and cumin, and salt. Cook, stirring, for 1 minute. Whisk in the broth and lemon juice. Bring to a simmer and cook, stirring occasionally, while the stuffed peppers finish cooking. 4. Cut a slit down the center of each poblano pepper, starting at the stem and continuing to the tip. Remove the seeds, being careful not to tear the chile. 5. Carefully stuff each pepper with half the corn mixture. Place the stuffed peppers in a baking pan. Place the pan in the air fryer basket. Set the air fryer to 400°F (204°C) for 10 minutes, or until the cheese has melted. 6. Transfer the stuffed peppers to a serving platter and drizzle with the sauce and some crema.

Mediterranean Zucchini Boats

Prep time: 5 minutes | Cook time: 10 minutes | Serves 4

- 1 large zucchini, ends removed, halved lengthwise
- 6 grape tomatoes, quartered
- ¼ teaspoon salt
- ¼ cup feta cheese
- 1 tablespoon balsamic vinegar
- 1 tablespoon olive oil

1. Use a spoon to scoop out 2 tablespoons from center of each zucchini half, making just enough space to fill with tomatoes and feta. 2. Place tomatoes evenly in centers of zucchini halves and sprinkle with salt. Place into ungreased air fryer basket. Adjust the temperature to 350°F (177°C) and roast for 10 minutes. When done, zucchini will be tender. 3. Transfer boats to a serving tray and sprinkle with feta, then drizzle with vinegar and olive oil. Serve warm.

Fried Zucchini Salad

Prep time: 10 minutes | Cook time: 5 to 7 minutes | Serves 4

- 2 medium zucchini, thinly sliced
- 5 tablespoons olive oil, divided
- ¼ cup chopped fresh parsley
- 2 tablespoons chopped
- fresh mint
- Zest and juice of ½ lemon
- 1 clove garlic, minced
- ¼ cup crumbled feta cheese
- Freshly ground black pepper, to taste

1. Preheat the air fryer to 400°F (204°C). 2. In a large bowl, toss the zucchini slices with 1 tablespoon of the olive oil. 3. Working in batches if necessary, arrange the zucchini slices in an even layer in the air fryer basket. Pausing halfway through the cooking time to shake the basket, air fry for 5 to 7 minutes until soft and lightly browned on each side. 4. Meanwhile, in a small bowl, combine the remaining 4 tablespoons olive oil, parsley, mint, lemon zest, lemon juice, and garlic. 5. Arrange the zucchini on a plate and drizzle with the dressing. Sprinkle the feta and black pepper on top. Serve warm or at room temperature.

Corn and Cilantro Salad

Prep time: 10 minutes | Cook time: 10 minutes | Serves 2

- 2 ears of corn, shucked (halved crosswise if too large to fit in your air fryer)
- 1 tablespoon unsalted butter, at room temperature
- 1 teaspoon chili powder
- ¼ teaspoon garlic powder
- Kosher salt and freshly ground black pepper, to taste
- 1 cup lightly packed fresh cilantro leaves
- 1 tablespoon sour cream
- 1 tablespoon mayonnaise
- 1 teaspoon adobo sauce (from a can of chipotle peppers in adobo sauce)
- 2 tablespoons crumbled queso fresco
- Lime wedges, for serving

1. Brush the corn all over with the butter, then sprinkle with the chili powder and garlic powder, and season with salt and pepper. Place the corn in the air fryer and air fry at 400°F (204°C), turning over halfway through, until the kernels are lightly charred and tender, about 10 minutes. 2. Transfer the ears to a cutting board, let stand 1 minute, then carefully cut the kernels off the cobs and move them to a bowl. Add the cilantro leaves and toss to combine (the cilantro leaves will wilt slightly). 3. In a small bowl, stir together the sour cream, mayonnaise, and adobo sauce. Divide the corn and cilantro among plates and spoon the adobo dressing over the top. Sprinkle with the queso fresco and serve with lime wedges on the side.

Super Cheesy Gold Eggplant

Prep time: 15 minutes | Cook time: 30 minutes | Serves 4

- 1 medium eggplant, peeled and cut into ½-inch-thick rounds
- 1 teaspoon salt, plus more for seasoning
- ½ cup all-purpose flour
- 2 eggs
- ¾ cup Italian bread crumbs
- 2 tablespoons grated
- Parmesan cheese
- Freshly ground black pepper, to taste
- Cooking oil spray
- ¾ cup marinara sauce
- ½ cup shredded Parmesan cheese, divided
- ½ cup shredded Mozzarella cheese, divided

1. Blot the eggplant with paper towels to dry completely. You can also sprinkle with 1 teaspoon of salt to sweat out the moisture; if you do this, rinse the eggplant slices and blot dry again. 2. Place the flour in a shallow bowl. 3. In another shallow bowl, beat the eggs. 4. In a third shallow bowl, stir together the bread crumbs and grated Parmesan cheese and season with salt and pepper. 5. Dip each eggplant round in the flour, in the eggs, and into the bread crumbs to coat. 6. Insert the crisper plate into the basket and the basket into the unit. Preheat the unit by selecting AIR FRY, setting the temperature to 400°F (204°C), and setting the time to 3 minutes. Select START/STOP to begin. 7. Once the unit is preheated, spray the crisper plate and the basket with cooking oil. Working in batches, place the eggplant rounds into the basket. Do not stack them. Spray the eggplant with the cooking oil. 8. Select AIR FRY, set the temperature to 400°F (204°C), and set the time to 10 minutes. Select START/STOP to begin. 9. After 7 minutes, open the unit and top each round with 1 teaspoon of marinara sauce and ½ tablespoon each of shredded Parmesan and Mozzarella cheese. Resume cooking for 2 to 3 minutes until the cheese melts. 10. Repeat steps 5, 6, 7, 8, and 9 with the remaining eggplant. 11. When the cooking is complete, serve immediately.

Parmesan-Thyme Butternut Squash

Prep time: 15 minutes | Cook time: 20 minutes | Serves 4

- 2½ cups butternut squash, cubed into 1-inch pieces (approximately 1 medium)
- 2 tablespoons olive oil
- ¼ teaspoon salt
- ¼ teaspoon garlic powder
- ¼ teaspoon black pepper
- 1 tablespoon fresh thyme
- ¼ cup grated Parmesan

1. Preheat the air fryer to 360°F(182°C). 2. In a large bowl, combine the cubed squash with the olive oil, salt, garlic powder, pepper, and thyme until the squash is well coated. 3. Pour this mixture into the air fryer basket, and roast for 10 minutes. Stir and roast another 8 to 10 minutes more. 4. Remove the squash from the air fryer and toss with freshly grated Parmesan before serving.

Sausage-Stuffed Mushroom Caps

Prep time: 10 minutes | Cook time: 8 minutes | Serves 2

- 6 large portobello mushroom caps
- ½ pound (227 g) Italian sausage
- ¼ cup chopped onion
- 2 tablespoons blanched
- finely ground almond flour
- ¼ cup grated Parmesan cheese
- 1 teaspoon minced fresh garlic

1. Use a spoon to hollow out each mushroom cap, reserving scrapings. 2. In a medium skillet over medium heat, brown the sausage about 10 minutes or until fully cooked and no pink remains. Drain and then add reserved mushroom scrapings, onion, almond flour, Parmesan, and garlic. Gently fold ingredients together and continue cooking an additional minute, then remove from heat. 3. Evenly spoon the mixture into mushroom caps and place the caps into a 6-inch round pan. Place pan into the air fryer basket. 4. Adjust the temperature to 375°F (191°C) and set the timer for 8 minutes. 5. When finished cooking, the tops will be browned and bubbling. Serve warm.

Tingly Chili-Roasted Broccoli

Prep time: 5 minutes | Cook time: 10 minutes | Serves 2

- 12 ounces (340 g) broccoli florets
- 2 tablespoons Asian hot chili oil
- 1 teaspoon ground Sichuan peppercorns (or black pepper)
- 2 garlic cloves, finely
- chopped
- 1 (2-inch) piece fresh ginger, peeled and finely chopped
- Kosher salt and freshly ground black pepper, to taste

1. In a bowl, toss together the broccoli, chili oil, Sichuan peppercorns, garlic, ginger, and salt and black pepper to taste. 2. Transfer to the air fryer and roast at 375°F (191°C), shaking the basket halfway through, until lightly charred and tender, about 10 minutes. Remove from the air fryer and serve warm.

Cheese-Walnut Stuffed Mushrooms

Prep time: 5 minutes | Cook time: 10 minutes | Serves 4

- 4 large portobello mushrooms
- 1 tablespoon canola oil
- ½ cup shredded Mozzarella cheese
- ⅓ cup minced walnuts
- 2 tablespoons chopped fresh parsley
- Cooking spray

1. Preheat the air fryer to 350°F (177°C). Spritz the air fryer basket with cooking spray. 2. On a clean work surface, remove the mushroom stems. Scoop out the gills with a spoon and discard. Coat the mushrooms with canola oil. Top each mushroom evenly with the shredded Mozzarella cheese, followed by the minced walnuts. 3. Arrange the mushrooms in the air fryer and roast for 10 minutes until golden brown. 4. Transfer the mushrooms to a plate and sprinkle the parsley on top for garnish before serving.

Citrus-Roasted Broccoli Florets

Prep time: 5 minutes | Cook time: 12 minutes | Serves 6

- 4 cups broccoli florets (approximately 1 large head)
- 2 tablespoons olive oil
- ½ teaspoon salt
- ½ cup orange juice
- 1 tablespoon raw honey
- Orange wedges, for serving (optional)

1. Preheat the air fryer to 360°F(182°C). 2. In a large bowl, combine the broccoli, olive oil, salt, orange juice, and honey. Toss the broccoli in the liquid until well coated. 3. Pour the broccoli mixture into the air fryer basket and roast for 6 minutes. Stir and roast for 6 minutes more. 4. Serve alone or with orange wedges for additional citrus flavor, if desired.

Spinach and Cheese Stuffed Tomatoes

Prep time: 20 minutes | Cook time: 15 minutes | Serves 2

- 4 ripe beefsteak tomatoes
- ¾ teaspoon black pepper
- ½ teaspoon kosher salt
- 1 (10-ounce / 283-g) package frozen chopped spinach, thawed and squeezed dry
- 1 (5.2-ounce / 147-g) package garlic-and-herb Boursin cheese
- 3 tablespoons sour cream
- ½ cup finely grated Parmesan cheese

1. Cut the tops off the tomatoes. Using a small spoon, carefully remove and discard the pulp. Season the insides with ½ teaspoon of the black pepper and ¼ teaspoon of the salt. Invert the tomatoes onto paper towels and allow to drain while you make the filling. 2. Meanwhile, in a medium bowl, combine the spinach, Boursin cheese, sour cream, ¼ cup of the Parmesan, and the remaining ¼ teaspoon salt and ¼ teaspoon pepper. Stir until ingredients are well combined. Divide the filling among the tomatoes. Top with the remaining ¼ cup Parmesan. 3. Place the tomatoes in the air fryer basket. Set the air fryer to 350°F (177°C) for 15 minutes, or until the filling is hot.

Breaded Green Tomatoes

Prep time: 15 minutes | Cook time: 30 minutes | Serves 4

- ½ cup all-purpose flour
- 2 eggs
- ½ cup yellow cornmeal
- ½ cup panko bread crumbs
- 1 teaspoon garlic powder
- Salt and freshly ground black pepper, to taste
- 2 green tomatoes, cut into ½-inch-thick rounds
- Cooking oil spray

1. Place the flour in a small bowl. 2. In another small bowl, beat the eggs. 3. In a third small bowl, stir together the cornmeal, panko, and garlic powder. Season with salt and pepper. 4. Dip each tomato slice into the flour, the egg, and finally the cornmeal mixture to coat. 5. Insert the crisper plate into the basket and the basket into the unit. Preheat the unit by selecting AIR FRY, setting the temperature to 400°F (204°C), and setting the time to 3 minutes. Select START/STOP to begin. 6. Once the unit is preheated, spray the crisper plate and the basket with cooking oil. Working in batches, place the tomato slices in the air fryer in a single layer. Do not stack them. Spray the tomato slices with the cooking oil. 7. Select AIR FRY, set the temperature to 400°F (204°C), and set the time to 10 minutes. Select START/STOP to begin. 8. After 5 minutes, use tongs to flip the tomatoes. Resume cooking for 4 to 5 minutes, or until crisp. 9. When the cooking is complete, transfer the fried green tomatoes to a plate. Repeat steps 6, 7, and 8 for the remaining tomatoes.

Gorgonzola Mushrooms with Horseradish Mayo

Prep time: 15 minutes | Cook time: 10 minutes | Serves 5

- ½ cup bread crumbs
- 2 cloves garlic, pressed
- 2 tablespoons chopped fresh coriander
- ⅓ teaspoon kosher salt
- ½ teaspoon crushed red pepper flakes
- 1½ tablespoons olive oil
- 20 medium mushrooms,
- stems removed
- ½ cup grated Gorgonzola cheese
- ¼ cup low-fat mayonnaise
- 1 teaspoon prepared horseradish, well-drained
- 1 tablespoon finely chopped fresh parsley

1. Preheat the air fryer to 380ºF (193ºC). 2. Combine the bread crumbs together with the garlic, coriander, salt, red pepper, and olive oil. 3. Take equal-sized amounts of the bread crumb mixture and use them to stuff the mushroom caps. Add the grated Gorgonzola on top of each. 4. Put the mushrooms in a baking pan and transfer to the air fryer. 5. Air fry for 10 minutes, ensuring the stuffing is warm throughout. 6. In the meantime, prepare the horseradish mayo. Mix the mayonnaise, horseradish and parsley. 7. When the mushrooms are ready, serve with the mayo.

Garlic Cauliflower with Tahini

Prep time: 10 minutes | Cook time: 20 minutes | Serves 4

Cauliflower:
- 5 cups cauliflower florets (about 1 large head)
- 6 garlic cloves, smashed and cut into thirds
- 3 tablespoons vegetable oil

Sauce:
- 2 tablespoons tahini (sesame paste)
- 2 tablespoons hot water
- 1 tablespoon fresh lemon

- ½ teaspoon ground cumin
- ½ teaspoon ground coriander
- ½ teaspoon kosher salt

- juice
- 1 teaspoon minced garlic
- ½ teaspoon kosher salt

1. For the cauliflower: In a large bowl, combine the cauliflower florets and garlic. Drizzle with the vegetable oil. Sprinkle with the cumin, coriander, and salt. Toss until well coated. 2. Place the cauliflower in the air fryer basket. Set the air fryer to 400ºF (204ºC) for 20 minutes, turning the cauliflower halfway through the cooking time. 3. Meanwhile, for the sauce: In a small bowl, combine the tahini, water, lemon juice, garlic, and salt. (The sauce will appear curdled at first, but keep stirring until you have a thick, creamy, smooth mixture.) 4. Transfer the cauliflower to a large serving bowl. Pour the sauce over and toss gently to coat. Serve immediately.

Blackened Zucchini with Kimchi-Herb Sauce

Prep time: 10 minutes | Cook time: 15 minutes | Serves 2

- 2 medium zucchini, ends trimmed (about 6 ounces / 170 g each)
- 2 tablespoons olive oil
- ½ cup kimchi, finely chopped
- ¼ cup finely chopped fresh cilantro
- ¼ cup finely chopped fresh flat-leaf parsley, plus more
- for garnish
- 2 tablespoons rice vinegar
- 2 teaspoons Asian chili-garlic sauce
- 1 teaspoon grated fresh ginger
- Kosher salt and freshly ground black pepper, to taste

1. Brush the zucchini with half of the olive oil, place in the air fryer, and air fry at 400ºF (204ºC), turning halfway through, until lightly charred on the outside and tender, about 15 minutes. 2. Meanwhile, in a small bowl, combine the remaining 1 tablespoon olive oil, the kimchi, cilantro, parsley, vinegar, chili-garlic sauce, and ginger. 3. Once the zucchini is finished cooking, transfer it to a colander and let it cool for 5 minutes. Using your fingers, pinch and break the zucchini into bite-size pieces, letting them fall back into the colander. Season the zucchini with salt and pepper, toss to combine, then let sit a further 5 minutes to allow some of its liquid to drain. Pile the zucchini atop the kimchi sauce on a plate and sprinkle with more parsley to serve.

Blistered Shishito Peppers with Lime Juice

Prep time: 5 minutes | Cook time: 9 minutes | Serves 3

- ½ pound (227 g) shishito peppers, rinsed
- Cooking spray

Sauce:
- 1 tablespoon tamari or shoyu
- 2 teaspoons fresh lime juice
- 2 large garlic cloves, minced

1. Preheat the air fryer to 392ºF (200ºC). Spritz the air fryer basket with cooking spray. 2. Place the shishito peppers in the basket and spritz them with cooking spray. Roast for 3 minutes. 3. Meanwhile, whisk together all the ingredients for the sauce in a large bowl. Set aside. 4. Shake the basket and spritz them with cooking spray again, then roast for an additional 3 minutes. 5. Shake the basket one more time and spray the peppers with cooking spray. Continue roasting for 3 minutes until the peppers are blistered and nicely browned. 6. Remove the peppers from the basket to the bowl of sauce. Toss to coat well and serve immediately.

Lebanese Baba Ghanoush

Prep time: 15 minutes | Cook time: 20 minutes | Serves 4

- 1 medium eggplant
- 2 tablespoons vegetable oil
- 2 tablespoons tahini (sesame paste)
- 2 tablespoons fresh lemon juice
- ½ teaspoon kosher salt
- 1 tablespoon extra-virgin olive oil
- ½ teaspoon smoked paprika
- 2 tablespoons chopped fresh parsley

1. Rub the eggplant all over with the vegetable oil. Place the eggplant in the air fryer basket. Set the air fryer to 400°F (204°C) for 20 minutes, or until the eggplant skin is blistered and charred. 2. Transfer the eggplant to a resealable plastic bag, seal, and set aside for 15 minutes (the eggplant will finish cooking in the residual heat trapped in the bag). 3. Transfer the eggplant to a large bowl. Peel off and discard the charred skin. Roughly mash the eggplant flesh. Add the tahini, lemon juice, and salt. Stir to combine. 4. Transfer the mixture to a serving bowl. Drizzle with the olive oil. Sprinkle with the paprika and parsley and serve.

Fried Brussels Sprouts

Prep time: 10 minutes | Cook time: 18 minutes | Serves 4

- 1 teaspoon plus 1 tablespoon extra-virgin olive oil, divided
- 2 teaspoons minced garlic
- 2 tablespoons honey
- 1 tablespoon sugar
- 2 tablespoons freshly squeezed lemon juice
- 2 tablespoons rice vinegar
- 2 tablespoons sriracha
- 1 pound (454 g) Brussels sprouts, stems trimmed and any tough leaves removed, rinsed, halved lengthwise, and dried
- ½ teaspoon salt
- Cooking oil spray

1. In a small saucepan over low heat, combine 1 teaspoon of olive oil, the garlic, honey, sugar, lemon juice, vinegar, and sriracha. Cook for 2 to 3 minutes, or until slightly thickened. Remove the pan from the heat, cover, and set aside. 2. Place the Brussels sprouts in a resealable bag or small bowl. Add the remaining olive oil and the salt, and toss to coat. 3. Insert the crisper plate into the basket and the basket into the unit. Preheat the unit by selecting AIR FRY, setting the temperature to 390°F (199°C), and setting the time to 3 minutes. Select START/STOP to begin. 4. Once the unit is preheated, spray the crisper plate with cooking oil. Add the Brussels sprouts to the basket. 5. Select AIR FRY, set the temperature to 390°F (199°C), and set the time to 15 minutes. Select START/STOP to begin. 6. After 7 or 8 minutes, remove the basket and shake it to toss the sprouts. Reinsert the basket to resume cooking. 7. When the cooking is complete, the leaves should be crispy and light brown and the sprout centers tender. 8. Place the sprouts

in a medium serving bowl and drizzle the sauce over the top. Toss to coat, and serve immediately.

Crispy Zucchini Sticks

Prep time: 5 minutes | Cook time: 14 minutes | Serves 4

- 2 small zucchini, cut into 2-inch × ½-inch sticks
- 3 tablespoons chickpea flour
- 2 teaspoons arrowroot (or cornstarch)
- ½ teaspoon garlic granules
- ¼ teaspoon sea salt
- ⅛ teaspoon freshly ground black pepper
- 1 tablespoon water
- Cooking spray

1. Preheat the air fryer to 392°F (200°C). 2. Combine the zucchini sticks with the chickpea flour, arrowroot, garlic granules, salt, and pepper in a medium bowl and toss to coat. Add the water and stir to mix well. 3. Spritz the air fryer basket with cooking spray and spread out the zucchini sticks in the basket. Mist the zucchini sticks with cooking spray. 4. Air fry for 14 minutes, shaking the basket halfway through, or until the zucchini sticks are crispy and nicely browned. 5. Serve warm.

Curried Fruit

Prep time: 10 minutes | Cook time: 20 minutes | Serves 6 to 8

- 1 cup cubed fresh pineapple
- 1 cup cubed fresh pear (firm, not overly ripe)
- 8 ounces (227 g) frozen peaches, thawed
- 1 (15-ounce / 425-g) can dark, sweet, pitted cherries with juice
- 2 tablespoons brown sugar
- 1 teaspoon curry powder

1. Combine all ingredients in large bowl. Stir gently to mix in the sugar and curry. 2. Pour into a baking pan and bake at 360°F (182°C) for 10 minutes. 3. Stir fruit and cook 10 more minutes. 4. Serve hot.

Zesty Fried Asparagus

Prep time: 3 minutes | Cook time: 10 minutes | Serves 4

- Oil, for spraying
- 10 to 12 spears asparagus, trimmed
- 2 tablespoons olive oil
- 1 tablespoon granulated
- garlic
- 1 teaspoon chili powder
- ½ teaspoon ground cumin
- ¼ teaspoon salt

1. Line the air fryer basket with parchment and spray lightly with oil. 2. If the asparagus are too long to fit easily in the air fryer, cut them in half. 3. Place the asparagus, olive oil, garlic, chili powder, cumin, and salt in a zip-top plastic bag, seal, and toss until evenly coated. 4. Place the asparagus in the prepared basket. 5. Roast at 390°F (199°C) for 5 minutes, flip, and cook for another 5 minutes, or until bright green and firm but tender.

Chili Fingerling Potatoes

Prep time: 10 minutes | Cook time: 16 minutes | Serves 4

- 1 pound (454 g) fingerling potatoes, rinsed and cut into wedges
- 1 teaspoon olive oil
- 1 teaspoon salt
- 1 teaspoon black pepper
- 1 teaspoon cayenne pepper
- 1 teaspoon nutritional yeast
- ½ teaspoon garlic powder

1. Preheat the air fryer to 400ºF (204ºC). 2. Coat the potatoes with the rest of the ingredients. 3. Transfer to the air fryer basket and air fry for 16 minutes, shaking the basket at the halfway point. 4. Serve immediately.

Southwestern Roasted Corn

Prep time: 10 minutes | Cook time: 10 minutes | Serves 4

Corn:

- 1½ cups thawed frozen corn kernels
- 1 cup diced yellow onion
- 1 cup mixed diced bell peppers
- 1 jalapeño, diced

For Serving:

- ¼ cup queso fresco or feta cheese
- ¼ cup chopped fresh

- 1 tablespoon fresh lemon juice
- 1 teaspoon ground cumin
- ½ teaspoon ancho chile powder
- ½ teaspoon kosher salt

cilantro
- 1 tablespoon fresh lemon juice

1. For the corn: In a large bowl, stir together the corn, onion, bell peppers, jalapeño, lemon juice, cumin, chile powder, and salt until well incorporated. 2. Pour the spiced vegetables into the air fryer basket. Set the air fryer to 375ºF (191ºC) for 10 minutes, stirring halfway through the cooking time. 3. Transfer the corn mixture to a serving bowl. Add the cheese, cilantro, and lemon juice and stir well to combine. Serve immediately.

Rosemary-Roasted Red Potatoes

Prep time: 5 minutes | Cook time: 20 minutes | Serves 6

- 1 pound (454 g) red potatoes, quartered
- ¼ cup olive oil
- ½ teaspoon kosher salt
- ¼ teaspoon black pepper
- 1 garlic clove, minced
- 4 rosemary sprigs

1. Preheat the air fryer to 360ºF(182ºC). 2. In a large bowl, toss the potatoes with the olive oil, salt, pepper, and garlic until well coated. 3. Pour the potatoes into the air fryer basket and top with the sprigs of rosemary. 4. Roast for 10 minutes, then stir or toss the potatoes and roast for 10 minutes more. 5.

Remove the rosemary sprigs and serve the potatoes. Season with additional salt and pepper, if needed.

Broccoli Salad

Prep time: 5 minutes | Cook time: 7 minutes | Serves 4

- 2 cups fresh broccoli florets, chopped
- 1 tablespoon olive oil
- ¼ teaspoon salt
- ⅛ teaspoon ground black pepper
- ¼ cup lemon juice, divided
- ¼ cup shredded Parmesan cheese
- ¼ cup sliced roasted almonds

1. In a large bowl, toss broccoli and olive oil together. Sprinkle with salt and pepper, then drizzle with 2 tablespoons lemon juice. 2. Place broccoli into ungreased air fryer basket. Adjust the temperature to 350ºF (177ºC) and set the timer for 7 minutes, shaking the basket halfway through cooking. Broccoli will be golden on the edges when done. 3. Place broccoli into a large serving bowl and drizzle with remaining lemon juice. Sprinkle with Parmesan and almonds. Serve warm.

Lush Vegetable Salad

Prep time: 15 minutes | Cook time: 10 minutes | Serves 4

- 6 plum tomatoes, halved
- 2 large red onions, sliced
- 4 long red pepper, sliced
- 2 yellow pepper, sliced
- 6 cloves garlic, crushed
- 1 tablespoon extra-virgin
- olive oil
- 1 teaspoon paprika
- ½ lemon, juiced
- Salt and ground black pepper, to taste
- 1 tablespoon baby capers

1. Preheat the air fryer to 420ºF (216ºC). 2. Put the tomatoes, onions, peppers, and garlic in a large bowl and cover with the extra-virgin olive oil, paprika, and lemon juice. Sprinkle with salt and pepper as desired. 3. Line the inside of the air fryer basket with aluminum foil. Put the vegetables inside and air fry for 10 minutes, ensuring the edges turn brown. 4. Serve in a salad bowl with the baby capers.

Bacon-Wrapped Asparagus

Prep time: 10 minutes | Cook time: 10 minutes | Serves 4

- 8 slices reduced-sodium bacon, cut in half
- 16 thick (about 1 pound /
- 454 g) asparagus spears, trimmed of woody ends

1. Preheat the air fryer to 350ºF (177ºC). 2. Wrap a half piece of bacon around the center of each stalk of asparagus. 3. Working in batches, if necessary, arrange seam-side down in a single layer in the air fryer basket. Air fry for 10 minutes until the bacon is crisp and the stalks are tender.

Baked Jalapeño and Cheese Cauliflower Mash

Prep time: 10 minutes | Cook time: 15 minutes | Serves 6

- 1 (12 ounces / 340 g) steamer bag cauliflower florets, cooked according to package instructions
- 2 tablespoons salted butter, softened
- 2 ounces (57 g) cream

- cheese, softened
- ½ cup shredded sharp Cheddar cheese
- ¼ cup pickled jalapeños
- ½ teaspoon salt
- ¼ teaspoon ground black pepper

1. Place cooked cauliflower into a food processor with remaining ingredients. Pulse twenty times until cauliflower is smooth and all ingredients are combined. 2. Spoon mash into an ungreased round nonstick baking dish. Place dish into air fryer basket. Adjust the temperature to 380ºF (193ºC) and bake for 15 minutes. The top will be golden brown when done. Serve warm.

Balsamic Brussels Sprouts

Prep time: 5 minutes | Cook time: 12 minutes | Serves 4

- 2 cups trimmed and halved fresh Brussels sprouts
- 2 tablespoons olive oil
- ¼ teaspoon salt
- ¼ teaspoon ground black

- pepper
- 2 tablespoons balsamic vinegar
- 2 slices cooked sugar-free bacon, crumbled

1. In a large bowl, toss Brussels sprouts in olive oil, then sprinkle with salt and pepper. Place into ungreased air fryer basket. Adjust the temperature to 375ºF (191ºC) and set the timer for 12 minutes, shaking the basket halfway through cooking. Brussels sprouts will be tender and browned when done. 2. Place sprouts in a large serving dish and drizzle with balsamic vinegar. Sprinkle bacon over top. Serve warm.

Cheesy Loaded Broccoli

Prep time: 10 minutes | Cook time: 10 minutes | Serves 2

- 3 cups fresh broccoli florets
- 1 tablespoon coconut oil
- ¼ teaspoon salt
- ½ cup shredded sharp Cheddar cheese
- ¼ cup sour cream

- 4 slices cooked sugar-free bacon, crumbled
- 1 medium scallion, trimmed and sliced on the bias

1. Place broccoli into ungreased air fryer basket, drizzle with coconut oil, and sprinkle with salt. Adjust the temperature to 350ºF (177ºC) and roast for 8 minutes. Shake basket three times during cooking to avoid burned spots. 2. Sprinkle broccoli with Cheddar and cook for 2 additional minutes. When done, cheese will be melted and broccoli will be tender. 3. Serve warm in a large serving dish, topped with sour cream, crumbled bacon, and scallion slices.

Saltine Wax Beans

Prep time: 10 minutes | Cook time: 7 minutes | Serves 4

- ½ cup flour
- 1 teaspoon smoky chipotle powder
- ½ teaspoon ground black pepper
- 1 teaspoon sea salt flakes

- 2 eggs, beaten
- ½ cup crushed saltines
- 10 ounces (283 g) wax beans
- Cooking spray

1. Preheat the air fryer to 360ºF (182ºC). 2. Combine the flour, chipotle powder, black pepper, and salt in a bowl. Put the eggs in a second bowl. Put the crushed saltines in a third bowl. 3. Wash the beans with cold water and discard any tough strings. 4. Coat the beans with the flour mixture, before dipping them into the beaten egg. Cover them with the crushed saltines. 5. Spritz the beans with cooking spray. 6. Air fry for 4 minutes. Give the air fryer basket a good shake and continue to air fry for 3 minutes. Serve hot.

Buttery Green Beans

Prep time: 5 minutes | Cook time: 8 to 10 minutes | Serves 6

- 1 pound (454 g) green beans, trimmed
- 1 tablespoon avocado oil
- 1 teaspoon garlic powder
- Sea salt and freshly ground

- black pepper, to taste
- ¼ cup (4 tablespoons) unsalted butter, melted
- ¼ cup freshly grated Parmesan cheese

1. In a large bowl, toss together the green beans, avocado oil, and garlic powder and season with salt and pepper. 2. Set the air fryer to 400ºF (204ºC). Arrange the green beans in a single layer in the air fryer basket. Air fry for 8 to 10 minutes, tossing halfway through. 3. Transfer the beans to a large bowl and toss with the melted butter. Top with the Parmesan cheese and serve warm.

Crispy Chickpeas

Prep time: 5 minutes | Cook time: 15 minutes | Serves 4

- 1 (15 ounces / 425 g) can chickpeas, drained but not rinsed

- 2 tablespoons olive oil
- 1 teaspoon salt
- 2 tablespoons lemon juice

1. Preheat the air fryer to 400ºF (204ºC). 2. Add all the ingredients together in a bowl and mix. Transfer this mixture to the air fryer basket. 3. Air fry for 15 minutes, ensuring the chickpeas become nice and crispy. 4. Serve immediately.

Stuffed Red Peppers with Herbed Ricotta and Tomatoes

Prep time: 10 minutes | Cook time: 20 minutes | Serves 4

- 2 red bell peppers
- 1 cup cooked brown rice
- 2 Roma tomatoes, diced
- 1 garlic clove, minced
- ¼ teaspoon salt
- ¼ teaspoon black pepper
- 4 ounces (113 g) ricotta
- 3 tablespoons fresh basil, chopped
- 3 tablespoons fresh oregano, chopped
- ¼ cup shredded Parmesan, for topping

1. Preheat the air fryer to 360°F(182°C). 2. Cut the bell peppers in half and remove the seeds and stem. 3. In a medium bowl, combine the brown rice, tomatoes, garlic, salt, and pepper. 4. Distribute the rice filling evenly among the four bell pepper halves. 5. In a small bowl, combine the ricotta, basil, and oregano. Put the herbed cheese over the top of the rice mixture in each bell pepper. 6. Place the bell peppers into the air fryer and roast for 20 minutes. 7. Remove and serve with shredded Parmesan on top.

Chapter 9

Vegetarian Mains

Italian Baked Egg and Veggies

Prep time: 10 minutes | Cook time: 10 minutes | Serves 2

- 2 tablespoons salted butter
- 1 small zucchini, sliced lengthwise and quartered
- ½ medium green bell pepper, seeded and diced
- 1 cup fresh spinach, chopped
- 1 medium Roma tomato, diced
- 2 large eggs
- ¼ teaspoon onion powder
- ¼ teaspoon garlic powder
- ½ teaspoon dried basil
- ¼ teaspoon dried oregano

1. Grease two ramekins with 1 tablespoon butter each. 2. In a large bowl, toss zucchini, bell pepper, spinach, and tomatoes. Divide the mixture in two and place half in each ramekin. 3. Crack an egg on top of each ramekin and sprinkle with onion powder, garlic powder, basil, and oregano. Place into the air fryer basket. 4. Adjust the temperature to 330°F (166°C) and bake for 10 minutes. 5. Serve immediately.

Air Fryer Veggies with Halloumi

Prep time: 5 minutes | Cook time: 14 minutes | Serves 2

- 2 zucchinis, cut into even chunks
- 1 large eggplant, peeled, cut into chunks
- 1 large carrot, cut into chunks
- 6 ounces (170 g) halloumi
- cheese, cubed
- 2 teaspoons olive oil
- Salt and black pepper, to taste
- 1 teaspoon dried mixed herbs

1. Preheat the air fryer to 340°F (171°C). 2. Combine the zucchinis, eggplant, carrot, cheese, olive oil, salt, and pepper in a large bowl and toss to coat well. 3. Spread the mixture evenly in the air fryer basket and air fry for 14 minutes until crispy and golden, shaking the basket once during cooking. Serve topped with mixed herbs.

Basic Spaghetti Squash

Prep time: 10 minutes | Cook time: 45 minutes | Serves 2

- ½ large spaghetti squash
- 1 tablespoon coconut oil
- 2 tablespoons salted butter,
- melted
- ½ teaspoon garlic powder
- 1 teaspoon dried parsley

1. Brush shell of spaghetti squash with coconut oil. Place the skin side down and brush the inside with butter. Sprinkle with garlic powder and parsley. 2. Place squash with the skin side down into the air fryer basket. 3. Adjust the temperature to 350°F (177°C) and air fry for 30 minutes. 4. Flip the squash so skin side is up and cook an additional 15 minutes or until fork tender. Serve warm.

Crustless Spinach Cheese Pie

Prep time: 10 minutes | Cook time: 20 minutes | Serves 4

- 6 large eggs
- ¼ cup heavy whipping cream
- 1 cup frozen chopped
- spinach, drained
- 1 cup shredded sharp Cheddar cheese
- ¼ cup diced yellow onion

1. In a medium bowl, whisk eggs and add cream. Add remaining ingredients to bowl. 2. Pour into a round baking dish. Place into the air fryer basket. 3. Adjust the temperature to 320°F (160°C) and bake for 20 minutes. 4. Eggs will be firm and slightly browned when cooked. Serve immediately.

Cheese Stuffed Zucchini

Prep time: 20 minutes | Cook time: 8 minutes | Serves 4

- 1 large zucchini, cut into four pieces
- 2 tablespoons olive oil
- 1 cup Ricotta cheese, room temperature
- 2 tablespoons scallions, chopped
- 1 heaping tablespoon fresh parsley, roughly chopped
- 1 heaping tablespoon coriander, minced
- 2 ounces (57 g) Cheddar cheese, preferably freshly grated
- 1 teaspoon celery seeds
- ½ teaspoon salt
- ½ teaspoon garlic pepper

1. Cook your zucchini in the air fryer basket for approximately 10 minutes at 350°F (177°C). Check for doneness and cook for 2-3 minutes longer if needed. 2. Meanwhile, make the stuffing by mixing the other items. 3. When your zucchini is thoroughly cooked, open them up. Divide the stuffing among all zucchini pieces and bake an additional 5 minutes.

Air Fryer Winter Vegetables

Prep time: 5 minutes | Cook time: 16 minutes | Serves 2

- 1 parsnip, sliced
- 1 cup sliced butternut squash
- 1 small red onion, cut into wedges
- ½ chopped celery stalk
- 1 tablespoon chopped fresh thyme
- 2 teaspoons olive oil
- Salt and black pepper, to taste

1. Preheat the air fryer to 380°F (193°C). 2. Toss all the ingredients in a large bowl until the vegetables are well coated. 3. Transfer the vegetables to the air fryer basket and air fry for 16 minutes, shaking the basket halfway through, or until the vegetables are golden brown and tender. 4. Remove from the basket and serve warm.

Parmesan Artichokes

Prep time: 10 minutes | Cook time: 10 minutes | Serves 4

- 2 medium artichokes, trimmed and quartered, center removed
- 2 tablespoons coconut oil
- 1 large egg, beaten
- ½ cup grated vegetarian
- Parmesan cheese
- ¼ cup blanched finely ground almond flour
- ½ teaspoon crushed red pepper flakes

1. In a large bowl, toss artichokes in coconut oil and then dip each piece into the egg. 2. Mix the Parmesan and almond flour in a large bowl. Add artichoke pieces and toss to cover as completely as possible, sprinkle with pepper flakes. Place into the air fryer basket. 3. Adjust the temperature to 400°F (204°C) and air fry for 10 minutes. 4. Toss the basket two times during cooking. Serve warm.

Whole Roasted Lemon Cauliflower

Prep time: 5 minutes | Cook time: 15 minutes | Serves 4

- 1 medium head cauliflower
- 2 tablespoons salted butter, melted
- 1 medium lemon
- ½ teaspoon garlic powder
- 1 teaspoon dried parsley

1. Remove the leaves from the head of cauliflower and brush it with melted butter. Cut the lemon in half and zest one half onto the cauliflower. Squeeze the juice of the zested lemon half and pour it over the cauliflower. 2. Sprinkle with garlic powder and parsley. Place cauliflower head into the air fryer basket. 3. Adjust the temperature to 350°F (177°C) and air fry for 15 minutes. 4. Check cauliflower every 5 minutes to avoid overcooking. It should be fork tender. 5. To serve, squeeze juice from other lemon half over cauliflower. Serve immediately.

Broccoli with Garlic Sauce

Prep time: 19 minutes | Cook time: 15 minutes | Serves 4

- 2 tablespoons olive oil
- Kosher salt and freshly ground black pepper, to

Dipping Sauce:
- 2 teaspoons dried rosemary, crushed
- 3 garlic cloves, minced
- ⅓ teaspoon dried
- taste
- 1 pound (454 g) broccoli florets

- marjoram, crushed
- ¼ cup sour cream
- ⅓ cup mayonnaise

1. Lightly grease your broccoli with a thin layer of olive oil. Season with salt and ground black pepper. 2. Arrange the seasoned broccoli in the air fryer basket. Bake at 395°F (202°C)

for 15 minutes, shaking once or twice. In the meantime, prepare the dipping sauce by mixing all the sauce ingredients. Serve warm broccoli with the dipping sauce and enjoy!

Sweet Potatoes with Zucchini

Prep time: 20 minutes | Cook time: 20 minutes | Serves 4

- 2 large-sized sweet potatoes, peeled and quartered
- 1 medium zucchini, sliced
- 1 Serrano pepper, deseeded and thinly sliced
- 1 bell pepper, deseeded and thinly sliced
- 1 to 2 carrots, cut into matchsticks
- ¼ cup olive oil
- 1½ tablespoons maple
- syrup
- ½ teaspoon porcini powder
- ¼ teaspoon mustard powder
- ½ teaspoon fennel seeds
- 1 tablespoon garlic powder
- ½ teaspoon fine sea salt
- ¼ teaspoon ground black pepper
- Tomato ketchup, for serving

1. Put the sweet potatoes, zucchini, peppers, and the carrot into the air fryer basket. Coat with a drizzling of olive oil. 2. Preheat the air fryer to 350°F (177°C). 3. Air fry the vegetables for 15 minutes. 4. In the meantime, prepare the sauce by vigorously combining the other ingredients, except for the tomato ketchup, with a whisk. 5. Lightly grease a baking dish. 6. Transfer the cooked vegetables to the baking dish, pour over the sauce and coat the vegetables well. 7. Increase the temperature to 390°F (199°C) and air fry the vegetables for an additional 5 minutes. 8. Serve warm with a side of ketchup.

Greek Stuffed Eggplant

Prep time: 15 minutes | Cook time: 20 minutes | Serves 2

- 1 large eggplant
- 2 tablespoons unsalted butter
- ¼ medium yellow onion, diced
- ¼ cup chopped artichoke
- hearts
- 1 cup fresh spinach
- 2 tablespoons diced red bell pepper
- ½ cup crumbled feta

1. Slice eggplant in half lengthwise and scoop out flesh, leaving enough inside for shell to remain intact. Take eggplant that was scooped out, chop it, and set aside. 2. In a medium skillet over medium heat, add butter and onion. Sauté until onions begin to soften, about 3 to 5 minutes. Add chopped eggplant, artichokes, spinach, and bell pepper. Continue cooking 5 minutes until peppers soften and spinach wilts. Remove from the heat and gently fold in the feta. 3. Place filling into each eggplant shell and place into the air fryer basket. 4. Adjust the temperature to 320°F (160°C) and air fry for 20 minutes. 5. Eggplant will be tender when done. Serve warm.

Fried Root Vegetable Medley with Thyme

Prep time: 10 minutes | Cook time: 22 minutes | Serves 4

- 2 carrots, sliced
- 2 potatoes, cut into chunks
- 1 rutabaga, cut into chunks
- 1 turnip, cut into chunks
- 1 beet, cut into chunks
- 8 shallots, halved
- 2 tablespoons olive oil
- Salt and black pepper, to taste
- 2 tablespoons tomato pesto
- 2 tablespoons water
- 2 tablespoons chopped fresh thyme

1. Preheat the air fryer to 400ºF (204ºC). 2. Toss the carrots, potatoes, rutabaga, turnip, beet, shallots, olive oil, salt, and pepper in a large mixing bowl until the root vegetables are evenly coated. 3. Place the root vegetables in the air fryer basket and air fry for 12 minutes. Shake the basket and air fry for another 10 minutes until they are cooked to your preferred doneness. 4. Meanwhile, in a small bowl, whisk together the tomato pesto and water until smooth. 5. When ready, remove the root vegetables from the basket to a platter. Drizzle with the tomato pesto mixture and sprinkle with the thyme. Serve immediately.

Zucchini and Spinach Croquettes

Prep time: 9 minutes | Cook time: 7 minutes | Serves 6

- 4 eggs, slightly beaten
- ½ cup almond flour
- ½ cup goat cheese, crumbled
- 1 teaspoon fine sea salt
- 4 garlic cloves, minced
- 1 cup baby spinach
- ½ cup Parmesan cheese, grated
- ⅓ teaspoon red pepper flakes
- 1 pound (454 g) zucchini, peeled and grated
- ⅓ teaspoon dried dill weed

1. Thoroughly combine all ingredients in a bowl. Now, roll the mixture to form small croquettes. 2. Air fry at 340ºF (171ºC) for 7 minutes or until golden. Tate, adjust for seasonings and serve warm.

Herbed Broccoli with Cheese

Prep time: 5 minutes | Cook time: 18 minutes | Serves 4

- 1 large-sized head broccoli, stemmed and cut into small florets
- 2½ tablespoons canola oil
- 2 teaspoons dried basil
- 2 teaspoons dried rosemary
- Salt and ground black pepper, to taste
- ⅓ cup grated yellow cheese

1. Bring a pot of lightly salted water to a boil. Add the broccoli florets to the boiling water and let boil for about 3 minutes. 2. Drain the broccoli florets well and transfer to a large bowl. Add the canola oil, basil, rosemary, salt, and black pepper to the bowl and toss until the broccoli is fully coated. 3. Preheat the air fryer to 390ºF (199ºC). 4. Place the broccoli in the air fryer basket and air fry for about 15 minutes, shaking the basket halfway through, or until the broccoli is crisp. 5. Serve the broccoli warm with grated cheese sprinkled on top.

Broccoli-Cheese Fritters

Prep time: 5 minutes | Cook time: 20 to 25 minutes | Serves 4

- 1 cup broccoli florets
- 1 cup shredded Mozzarella cheese
- ¾ cup almond flour
- ½ cup flaxseed meal, divided
- 2 teaspoons baking powder
- 1 teaspoon garlic powder
- Salt and freshly ground black pepper, to taste
- 2 eggs, lightly beaten
- ½ cup ranch dressing

1. Preheat the air fryer to 400ºF (204ºC). 2. In a food processor fitted with a metal blade, pulse the broccoli until very finely chopped. 3. Transfer the broccoli to a large bowl and add the Mozzarella, almond flour, ¼ cup of the flaxseed meal, baking powder, and garlic powder. Stir until thoroughly combined. Season to taste with salt and black pepper. Add the eggs and stir again to form a sticky dough. Shape the dough into 1¼-inch fritters. 4. Place the remaining ¼ cup flaxseed meal in a shallow bowl and roll the fritters in the meal to form an even coating. 5. Working in batches if necessary, arrange the fritters in a single layer in the basket of the air fryer and spray generously with olive oil. Pausing halfway through the cooking time to shake the basket, air fry for 20 to 25 minutes until the fritters are golden brown and crispy. Serve with the ranch dressing for dipping.

Vegetable Burgers

Prep time: 10 minutes | Cook time: 12 minutes | Serves 4

- 8 ounces (227 g) cremini mushrooms
- 2 large egg yolks
- ½ medium zucchini, trimmed and chopped
- ¼ cup peeled and chopped
- yellow onion
- 1 clove garlic, peeled and finely minced
- ½ teaspoon salt
- ¼ teaspoon ground black pepper

1. Place all ingredients into a food processor and pulse twenty times until finely chopped and combined. 2. Separate mixture into four equal sections and press each into a burger shape. Place burgers into ungreased air fryer basket. Adjust the temperature to 375ºF (191ºC) and air fry for 12 minutes, turning burgers halfway through cooking. Burgers will be browned and firm when done. 3. Place burgers on a large plate and let cool 5 minutes before serving.

Super Veg Rolls

Prep time: 20 minutes | Cook time: 10 minutes | Serves 6

- 2 potatoes, mashed
- ¼ cup peas
- ¼ cup mashed carrots
- 1 small cabbage, sliced
- ¼ cups beans
- 2 tablespoons sweetcorn
- 1 small onion, chopped
- ½ cup bread crumbs
- 1 packet spring roll sheets
- ½ cup cornstarch slurry

1. Preheat the air fryer to 390ºF (199ºC). 2. Boil all the vegetables in water over a low heat. Rinse and allow to dry. 3. Unroll the spring roll sheets and spoon equal amounts of vegetable onto the center of each one. Fold into spring rolls and coat each one with the slurry and bread crumbs. 4. Air fry the rolls in the preheated air fryer for 10 minutes. 5. Serve warm.

Cayenne Tahini Kale

Prep time: 5 minutes | Cook time: 15 minutes | Serves 2 to 4

Dressing:
- ¼ cup tahini
- ¼ cup fresh lemon juice
- 2 tablespoons olive oil

Kale:
- 4 cups packed torn kale leaves (stems and ribs removed and leaves torn into palm-size pieces)
- 1 teaspoon sesame seeds
- ½ teaspoon garlic powder
- ¼ teaspoon cayenne pepper

- Kosher salt and freshly ground black pepper, to taste

1. Preheat the air fryer to 350ºF (177ºC). 2. Make the dressing: Whisk together the tahini, lemon juice, olive oil, sesame seeds, garlic powder, and cayenne pepper in a large bowl until well mixed. 3. Add the kale and massage the dressing thoroughly all over the leaves. Sprinkle the salt and pepper to season. 4. Place the kale in the air fryer basket in a single layer and air fry for about 15 minutes, or until the leaves are slightly wilted and crispy. 5. Remove from the basket and serve on a plate.

Stuffed Portobellos

Prep time: 10 minutes | Cook time: 8 minutes | Serves 4

- 3 ounces (85 g) cream cheese, softened
- ½ medium zucchini, trimmed and chopped
- ¼ cup seeded and chopped red bell pepper
- 1½ cups chopped fresh spinach leaves
- 4 large portobello mushrooms, stems removed
- 2 tablespoons coconut oil, melted
- ½ teaspoon salt

1. In a medium bowl, mix cream cheese, zucchini, pepper, and spinach. 2. Drizzle mushrooms with coconut oil and sprinkle with salt. Scoop ¼ zucchini mixture into each mushroom. 3. Place mushrooms into ungreased air fryer basket. Adjust the temperature to 400ºF (204ºC) and air fry for 8 minutes. Portobellos will be tender and tops will be browned when done. Serve warm.

Eggplant Parmesan

Prep time: 15 minutes | Cook time: 17 minutes | Serves 4

- 1 medium eggplant, ends trimmed, sliced into ½-inch rounds
- ¼ teaspoon salt
- 2 tablespoons coconut oil
- ½ cup grated Parmesan cheese
- 1 ounce (28 g) 100% cheese crisps, finely crushed
- ½ cup low-carb marinara sauce
- ½ cup shredded Mozzarella cheese

1. Sprinkle eggplant rounds with salt on both sides and wrap in a kitchen towel for 30 minutes. Press to remove excess water, then drizzle rounds with coconut oil on both sides. 2. In a medium bowl, mix Parmesan and cheese crisps. Press each eggplant slice into mixture to coat both sides. 3. Place rounds into ungreased air fryer basket. Adjust the temperature to 350ºF (177ºC) and air fry for 15 minutes, turning rounds halfway through cooking. They will be crispy around the edges when done. 4. Spoon marinara over rounds and sprinkle with Mozzarella. Continue cooking an additional 2 minutes at 350ºF (177ºC) until cheese is melted. Serve warm.

Chapter 10

Desserts

Baked Apples and Walnuts

Prep time: 6 minutes | Cook time: 20 minutes | Serves 4

- 4 small Granny Smith apples
- ⅓ cup chopped walnuts
- ¼ cup light brown sugar
- 2 tablespoons butter,

- melted
- 1 teaspoon ground cinnamon
- ½ teaspoon ground nutmeg
- ½ cup water, or apple juice

1. Cut off the top third of the apples. Spoon out the core and some of the flesh and discard. Place the apples in a small air fryer baking pan. 2. Insert the crisper plate into the basket and the basket into the unit. Preheat the unit by selecting BAKE, setting the temperature to 350°F (177°C), and setting the time to 3 minutes. Select START/STOP to begin. 3. In a small bowl, stir together the walnuts, brown sugar, melted butter, cinnamon, and nutmeg. Spoon this mixture into the centers of the hollowed-out apples. 4. Once the unit is preheated, pour the water into the crisper plate. Place the baking pan into the basket. 5. Select BAKE, set the temperature to 350°F (177°C), and set the time to 20 minutes. Select START/STOP to begin. 6. When the cooking is complete, the apples should be bubbly and fork-tender.

Apple Hand Pies

Prep time: 15 minutes | Cook time: 25 minutes | Serves 8

- 2 apples, cored and diced
- ¼ cup honey
- 1 teaspoon ground cinnamon
- 1 teaspoon vanilla extract

- ⅛ teaspoon ground nutmeg
- 2 teaspoons cornstarch
- 1 teaspoon water
- 4 refrigerated piecrusts
- Cooking oil spray

1. Insert the crisper plate into the basket and the basket into the unit. Preheat the unit by selecting AIR FRY, setting the temperature to 400°F (204°C), and setting the time to 3 minutes. Select START/STOP to begin. 2. In a metal bowl that fits into the basket, stir together the apples, honey, cinnamon, vanilla, and nutmeg. 3. In a small bowl, whisk the cornstarch and water until the cornstarch dissolves. 4. Once the unit is preheated, place the metal bowl with the apples into the basket. 5. Select AIR FRY, set the temperature to 400°F (204°C), and set the time to 5 minutes. Select START/STOP to begin. 6. After 2 minutes, stir the apples. Resume cooking for 2 minutes. 7. Remove the bowl and stir the cornstarch mixture into the apples. Reinsert the metal bowl into the basket and resume cooking for about 30 seconds until the sauce thickens slightly. 8. When the cooking is complete, refrigerate the apples while you prepare the piecrust. 9. Cut each piecrust into 2 (4-inch) circles. You should have 8 circles of crust. 10. Lay the piecrusts on a work surface. Divide the apple filling among the piecrusts, mounding the mixture in the center of each round. 11. Fold each piecrust over so the top layer of crust is about an inch short of the bottom layer. (The edges should not meet.) Use the back of a fork to seal the edges. 12. Insert the crisper plate into the basket and the basket into the unit. Preheat the unit by selecting AIR FRY, setting the temperature to 400°F (204°C), and setting the time to 3 minutes. Select START/STOP to begin. 13. Once the unit is preheated, spray the crisper plate with cooking oil, line the basket with parchment paper, and spray it with cooking oil. Working in batches, place the hand pies into the basket in a single layer. 14. Select AIR FRY, set the temperature to 400°F (204°C), and set the time to 10 minutes. Select START/STOP to begin. 15. When the cooking is complete, let the hand pies cool for 5 minutes before removing from the basket. 16. Repeat steps 13, 14, and 15 with the remaining pies.

Cream-Filled Sponge Cakes

Prep time: 10 minutes | Cook time: 10 minutes | Makes 4 cakes

- Oil, for spraying
- 1 (8-ounce / 227-g) can refrigerated crescent rolls

- 4 cream-filled sponge cakes
- 1 tablespoon confectioners' sugar

1. Line the air fryer basket with parchment and spray lightly with oil. 2. Unroll the dough into a single flat layer and cut it into 4 equal pieces. 3. Place 1 sponge cake in the center of each piece of dough. Wrap the dough around the cake, pinching the ends to seal. 4. Place the wrapped cakes in the prepared basket and spray lightly with oil. 5. Bake at 200°F (93°C) for 5 minutes, flip, spray with oil, and cook for another 5 minutes, or until golden brown. 6. Dust with the confectioners' sugar and serve.

Chickpea Brownies

Prep time: 10 minutes | Cook time: 20 minutes | Serves 6

- Vegetable oil
- 1 (15-ounce / 425-g) can chickpeas, drained and rinsed
- 4 large eggs
- ⅓ cup coconut oil, melted
- ⅓ cup honey

- 3 tablespoons unsweetened cocoa powder
- 1 tablespoon espresso powder (optional)
- 1 teaspoon baking powder
- 1 teaspoon baking soda
- ½ cup chocolate chips

1. Preheat the air fryer to 325°F (163°C). 2. Generously grease a baking pan with vegetable oil. 3. In a blender or food processor, combine the chickpeas, eggs, coconut oil, honey, cocoa powder, espresso powder (if using), baking powder, and baking soda. Blend or process until smooth. Transfer to the prepared pan and stir in the chocolate chips by hand. 4. Set the pan in the air fryer basket and bake for 20 minutes, or until a toothpick inserted into the center comes out clean. 5. Let cool in the pan on a wire rack for 30 minutes before cutting into squares. 6. Serve immediately.

Jelly Doughnuts

Prep time: 5 minutes | Cook time: 5 minutes | Serves 8

- 1 (16.3 ounces / 462 g) package large refrigerator biscuits
- Cooking spray
- 1¼ cups good-quality raspberry jam
- Confectioners' sugar, for dusting

1. Preheat the air fryer to 350ºF (177ºC). 2. Separate biscuits into 8 rounds. Spray both sides of rounds lightly with oil. 3. Spray the basket with oil and place 3 to 4 rounds in the basket. Air fry for 5 minutes, or until golden brown. Transfer to a wire rack; let cool. Repeat with the remaining rounds. 4. Fill a pastry bag, fitted with small plain tip, with raspberry jam; use tip to poke a small hole in the side of each doughnut, then fill the centers with the jam. Dust doughnuts with confectioners' sugar. Serve immediately.

Cardamom Custard

Prep time: 10 minutes | Cook time: 25 minutes | Serves 2

- 1 cup whole milk
- 1 large egg
- 2 tablespoons plus 1 teaspoon sugar
- ¼ teaspoon vanilla bean
- paste or pure vanilla extract
- ¼ teaspoon ground cardamom, plus more for sprinkling

1. In a medium bowl, beat together the milk, egg, sugar, vanilla, and cardamom. 2. Place two 8 ounces (227 g) ramekins in the air fryer basket. Divide the mixture between the ramekins. Sprinkle lightly with cardamom. Cover each ramekin tightly with aluminum foil. Set the air fryer to 350ºF (177ºC) for 25 minutes, or until a toothpick inserted in the center comes out clean. 3. Let the custards cool on a wire rack for 5 to 10 minutes. 4. Serve warm, or refrigerate until cold and serve chilled.

Strawberry Pecan Pie

Prep time: 15 minutes | Cook time: 10 minutes | Serves 6

- 1½ cups whole shelled pecans
- 1 tablespoon unsalted butter, softened
- 1 cup heavy whipping cream
- 12 medium fresh strawberries, hulled
- 2 tablespoons sour cream

1. Place pecans and butter into a food processor and pulse ten times until a dough forms. Press dough into the bottom of an ungreased round nonstick baking dish. 2. Place dish into air fryer basket. Adjust the temperature to 320ºF (160ºC) and set the timer for 10 minutes. Crust will be firm and golden when done. Let cool 20 minutes. 3. In a large bowl, whisk cream until fluffy and doubled in size, about 2 minutes. 4. In

a separate large bowl, mash strawberries until mostly liquid. Fold strawberries and sour cream into whipped cream. 5. Spoon mixture into cooled crust, cover, and place in refrigerator for at least 30 minutes to set. Serve chilled.

Cream Cheese Danish

Prep time: 20 minutes | Cook time: 15 minutes | Serves 6

- ¾ cup blanched finely ground almond flour
- 1 cup shredded Mozzarella cheese
- 5 ounces (142 g) full-fat cream cheese, divided
- 2 large egg yolks
- ¾ cup powdered erythritol, divided
- 2 teaspoons vanilla extract, divided

1. In a large microwave-safe bowl, add almond flour, Mozzarella, and 1 ounce (28 g) cream cheese. Mix and then microwave for 1 minute. 2. Stir and add egg yolks to the bowl. Continue stirring until soft dough forms. Add ½ cup erythritol to dough and 1 teaspoon vanilla. 3. Cut a piece of parchment to fit your air fryer basket. Wet your hands with warm water and press out the dough into a ¼-inch-thick rectangle. 4. In a medium bowl, mix remaining cream cheese, erythritol, and vanilla. Place this cream cheese mixture on the right half of the dough rectangle. Fold over the left side of the dough and press to seal. Place into the air fryer basket. 5. Adjust the temperature to 330ºF (166ºC) and bake for 15 minutes. 6. After 7 minutes, flip over the Danish. 7. When done, remove the Danish from parchment and allow to completely cool before cutting.

Peach Cobbler

Prep time: 15 minutes | Cook time: 12 to 14 minutes | Serves 4

- 16 ounces (454 g) frozen peaches, thawed, with juice (do not drain)

Crust:
- ½ cup flour
- ¼ teaspoon salt
- 3 tablespoons butter
- 6 tablespoons sugar
- 1 tablespoon cornstarch
- 1 tablespoon water
- 1½ tablespoons cold water
- ¼ teaspoon sugar

1. Place peaches, including juice, and sugar in a baking pan. Stir to mix well. 2. In a small cup, dissolve cornstarch in the water. Stir into peaches. 3. In a medium bowl, combine the flour and salt. Cut in butter using knives or a pastry blender. Stir in the cold water to make a stiff dough. 4. On a floured board or wax paper, pat dough into a square or circle slightly smaller than your baking pan. Cut diagonally into 4 pieces. 5. Place dough pieces on top of peaches, leaving a tiny bit of space between the edges. Sprinkle very lightly with sugar, no more than about ¼ teaspoon. 6. Bake at 360ºF (182ºC) for 12 to 14 minutes, until fruit bubbles and crust browns.

Pecan and Cherry Stuffed Apples

Prep time: 10 minutes | Cook time: 20 minutes | Serves 4

- 4 apples (about 1¼ pounds / 567 g)
- ¼ cup chopped pecans
- ⅓ cup dried tart cherries
- 1 tablespoon melted butter
- 3 tablespoons brown sugar
- ¼ teaspoon allspice
- Pinch salt
- Ice cream, for serving

1. Cut off top ½ inch from each apple; reserve tops. With a melon baller, core through stem ends without breaking through the bottom. (Do not trim bases.) 2. Preheat the air fryer to 350°F (177°C). Combine pecans, cherries, butter, brown sugar, allspice, and a pinch of salt. Stuff mixture into the hollow centers of the apples. Cover with apple tops. Put in the air fryer basket, using tongs. Air fry for 20 to 25 minutes, or just until tender. 3. Serve warm with ice cream.

Chocolate Soufflés

Prep time: 5 minutes | Cook time: 14 minutes | Serves 2

- Butter and sugar for greasing the ramekins
- 3 ounces (85 g) semi-sweet chocolate, chopped
- ¼ cup unsalted butter
- 2 eggs, yolks and white separated
- 3 tablespoons sugar
- ½ teaspoon pure vanilla extract
- 2 tablespoons all-purpose flour
- Powdered sugar, for dusting the finished soufflés
- Heavy cream, for serving

1. Butter and sugar two 6-ounce (170-g) ramekins. (Butter the ramekins and then coat the butter with sugar by shaking it around in the ramekin and dumping out any excess.) 2. Melt the chocolate and butter together, either in the microwave or in a double boiler. In a separate bowl, beat the egg yolks vigorously. Add the sugar and the vanilla extract and beat well again. Drizzle in the chocolate and butter, mixing well. Stir in the flour, combining until there are no lumps. 3. Preheat the air fryer to 330°F (166°C). 4. In a separate bowl, whisk the egg whites to soft peak stage (the point at which the whites can almost stand up on the end of your whisk). Fold the whipped egg whites into the chocolate mixture gently and in stages. 5. Transfer the batter carefully to the buttered ramekins, leaving about ½-inch at the top. (You may have a little extra batter, depending on how airy the batter is, so you might be able to squeeze out a third soufflé if you want to.) Place the ramekins into the air fryer basket and air fry for 14 minutes. The soufflés should have risen nicely and be brown on top. (Don't worry if the top gets a little dark, you'll be covering it with powdered sugar in the next step.) 6. Dust with powdered sugar and serve immediately with heavy cream to pour over the top at the table.

Blackberry Cobbler

Prep time: 15 minutes | Cook time: 25 to 30 minutes | Serves 6

- 3 cups fresh or frozen blackberries
- 1¾ cups sugar, divided
- 1 teaspoon vanilla extract
- 8 tablespoons (1 stick) butter, melted
- 1 cup self-rising flour
- 1 to 2 tablespoons oil

1. In a medium bowl, stir together the blackberries, 1 cup of sugar, and vanilla. 2. In another medium bowl, stir together the melted butter, remaining ¾ cup of sugar, and flour until a dough forms. 3. Spritz a baking pan with oil. Add the blackberry mixture. Crumble the flour mixture over the fruit. Cover the pan with aluminum foil. 4. Preheat the air fryer to 350°F (177°C). 5. Place the covered pan in the air fryer basket. Cook for 20 to 25 minutes until the filling is thickened. 6. Uncover the pan and cook for 5 minutes more, depending on how juicy and browned you like your cobbler. Let sit for 5 minutes before serving.

Graham Cracker Cheesecake

Prep time: 10 minutes | Cook time: 20 minutes | Serves 8

- 1 cup graham cracker crumbs
- 3 tablespoons butter, at room temperature
- 1½ (8-ounce / 227-g) packages cream cheese, at room temperature
- ⅓ cup sugar
- 2 eggs, beaten
- 1 tablespoon all-purpose flour
- 1 teaspoon vanilla extract
- ¼ cup chocolate syrup

1. In a small bowl, stir together the graham cracker crumbs and butter. Press the crust into the bottom of a 6-by-2-inch round baking pan and freeze to set while you prepare the filling. 2. In a medium bowl, stir together the cream cheese and sugar until mixed well. 3. One at a time, beat in the eggs. Add the flour and vanilla and stir to combine. 4. Transfer ⅔ cup of filling to a small bowl and stir in the chocolate syrup until combined. 5. Insert the crisper plate into the basket and the basket into the unit. Preheat the unit by selecting BAKE, setting the temperature to 325°F (163°C), and setting the time to 3 minutes. Select START/STOP to begin. 6. Pour the vanilla filling into the pan with the crust. Drop the chocolate filling over the vanilla filling by the spoonful. With a clean butter knife stir the fillings in a zigzag pattern to marbleize them. Do not let the knife touch the crust. 7. Once the unit is preheated, place the pan into the basket. 8. Select BAKE, set the temperature to 325°F (163°C), and set the time to 20 minutes. Select START/STOP to begin. 9. When the cooking is done, the cheesecake should be just set. Cool on a wire rack for 1 hour. Refrigerate the cheesecake until firm before slicing.

Dark Brownies

Prep time: 10 minutes | Cook time: 11 to 13 minutes | Serves 4

- 1 egg
- ½ cup granulated sugar
- ¼ teaspoon salt
- ½ teaspoon vanilla
- ¼ cup butter, melted
- ¼ cup flour, plus 2 tablespoons
- ¼ cup cocoa
- Cooking spray

Optional:
- Vanilla ice cream
- Caramel sauce
- Whipped cream

1. Beat together egg, sugar, salt, and vanilla until light. 2. Add melted butter and mix well. 3. Stir in flour and cocoa. 4. Spray a baking pan lightly with cooking spray. 5. Spread batter in pan and bake at 330°F (166°C) for 11 to 13 minutes. Cool and cut into 4 large squares or 16 small brownie bites.

Kentucky Chocolate Nut Pie

Prep time: 20 minutes | Cook time: 25 minutes | Serves 8

- 2 large eggs, beaten
- ⅓ cup butter, melted
- 1 cup sugar
- ½ cup all-purpose flour
- 1½ cups coarsely chopped pecans
- 1 cup milk chocolate chips
- 2 tablespoons bourbon
- 1 (9-inch) unbaked piecrust

1. In a large bowl, stir together the eggs and melted butter. Add the sugar and flour and stir until combined. Stir in the pecans, chocolate chips, and bourbon until well mixed. 2. Using a fork, prick holes in the bottom and sides of the pie crust. Pour the pie filling into the crust. 3. Preheat the air fryer to 350°F (177°C). 4. Cook for 25 minutes, or until a knife inserted into the middle of the pie comes out clean. Let set for 5 minutes before serving.

Crumbly Coconut-Pecan Cookies

Prep time: 10 minutes | Cook time: 25 minutes | Serves 10

- 1½ cups coconut flour
- 1½ cups extra-fine almond flour
- ½ teaspoon baking powder
- ⅓ teaspoon baking soda
- 3 eggs plus an egg yolk, beaten
- ¾ cup coconut oil, at room temperature
- 1 cup unsalted pecan nuts,
- roughly chopped
- ¾ cup monk fruit
- ¼ teaspoon freshly grated nutmeg
- ⅓ teaspoon ground cloves
- ½ teaspoon pure vanilla extract
- ½ teaspoon pure coconut extract
- ⅛ teaspoon fine sea salt

1. Preheat the air fryer to 370°F (188°C). Line the air fryer basket with parchment paper. 2. Mix the coconut flour, almond flour, baking powder, and baking soda in a large mixing bowl. 3. In another mixing bowl, stir together the eggs and coconut oil. Add the wet mixture to the dry mixture. 4. Mix in the remaining ingredients and stir until a soft dough forms. 5. Drop about 2 tablespoons of dough on the parchment paper for each cookie and flatten each biscuit until it's 1 inch thick. 6. Bake for about 25 minutes until the cookies are golden and firm to the touch. Remove from the basket to a plate. Let the cookies cool to room temperature and serve.

Apple Fries

Prep time: 10 minutes | Cook time: 7 minutes | Serves 8

- Oil, for spraying
- 1 cup all-purpose flour
- 3 large eggs, beaten
- 1 cup graham cracker crumbs
- ¼ cup sugar
- 1 teaspoon ground cinnamon
- 3 large Gala apples, peeled, cored, and cut into wedges
- 1 cup caramel sauce, warmed

1. Preheat the air fryer to 380°F (193°C). Line the air fryer basket with parchment and spray lightly with oil. 2. Place the flour and beaten eggs in separate bowls and set aside. In another bowl, mix together the graham cracker crumbs, sugar, and cinnamon. 3. Working one at a time, coat the apple wedges in the flour, dip in the egg, and dredge in the graham cracker mix until evenly coated. 4. Place the apples in the prepared basket, taking care not to overlap, and spray lightly with oil. You may need to work in batches, depending on the size of your air fryer. 5. Cook for 5 minutes, flip, spray with oil, and cook for another 2 minutes, or until crunchy and golden brown. 6. Drizzle the caramel sauce over the top and serve.

Old-Fashioned Fudge Pie

Prep time: 15 minutes | Cook time: 25 to 30 minutes | Serves 8

- 1½ cups sugar
- ⅓ cup unsweetened cocoa powder
- ½ cup self-rising flour
- 3 large eggs, unbeaten
- 12 tablespoons (1½ sticks)
- butter, melted
- 1½ teaspoons vanilla extract
- 1 (9-inch) unbaked piecrust
- ¼ cup confectioners' sugar (optional)

1. In a medium bowl, stir together the sugar, cocoa powder, and flour. Stir in the eggs and melted butter. Stir in the vanilla. 2. Preheat the air fryer to 350°F (177°C). 3. Pour the chocolate filing into the crust. 4. Cook for 25 to 30 minutes, stirring every 10 minutes, until a knife inserted into the middle comes out clean. Let sit for 5 minutes before dusting with confectioners' sugar (if using) to serve.

Peaches and Apple Crumble

Prep time: 10 minutes | Cook time: 10 to 12 minutes | Serves 4

- 2 peaches, peeled, pitted, and chopped
- 1 apple, peeled and chopped
- 2 tablespoons honey
- ½ cup quick-cooking oatmeal
- ⅓ cup whole-wheat pastry flour
- 2 tablespoons unsalted butter, at room temperature
- 3 tablespoons packed brown sugar
- ½ teaspoon ground cinnamon

1. Preheat the air fryer to 380°F (193°C). 2. Mix together the peaches, apple, and honey in a baking pan until well incorporated. 3. In a bowl, combine the oatmeal, pastry flour, butter, brown sugar, and cinnamon and stir to mix well. Spread this mixture evenly over the fruit. 4. Place the baking pan in the air fryer basket and bake for 10 to 12 minutes, or until the fruit is bubbling around the edges and the topping is golden brown. 5. Remove from the basket and serve warm.

Cinnamon-Sugar Almonds

Prep time: 5 minutes | Cook time: 8 minutes | Serves 4

- 1 cup whole almonds
- 2 tablespoons salted butter, melted
- 1 tablespoon sugar
- ½ teaspoon ground cinnamon

1. In a medium bowl, combine the almonds, butter, sugar, and cinnamon. Mix well to ensure all the almonds are coated with the spiced butter. 2. Transfer the almonds to the air fryer basket and shake so they are in a single layer. Set the air fryer to 300°F (149°C) for 8 minutes, stirring the almonds halfway through the cooking time. 3. Let cool completely before serving.

Appendix ❶
Air Fryer Cooking Chart

Beef

Item	Temp (°F)	Time (mins)	Item	Temp (°F)	Time (mins)
Beef Eye Round Roast (4 lbs.)	400 °F	45 to 55	Meatballs (1-inch)	370 °F	7
Burger Patty (4 oz.)	370 °F	16 to 20	Meatballs (3-inch)	380 °F	10
Filet Mignon (8 oz.)	400 °F	18	Ribeye, bone-in (1-inch, 8 oz)	400 °F	10 to 15
Flank Steak (1.5 lbs.)	400 °F	12	Sirloin steaks (1-inch, 12 oz)	400 °F	9 to 14
Flank Steak (2 lbs.)	400 °F	20 to 28			

Chicken

Item	Temp (°F)	Time (mins)	Item	Temp (°F)	Time (mins)
Breasts, bone in (1 ¼ lb.)	370 °F	25	Legs, bone-in (1 ¾ lb.)	380 °F	30
Breasts, boneless (4 oz)	380 °F	12	Thighs, boneless (1 ½ lb.)	380 °F	18 to 20
Drumsticks (2 ½ lb.)	370 °F	20	Wings (2 lb.)	400 °F	12
Game Hen (halved 2 lb.)	390 °F	20	Whole Chicken	360 °F	75
Thighs, bone-in (2 lb.)	380 °F	22	Tenders	360 °F	8 to 10

Pork & Lamb

Item	Temp (°F)	Time (mins)	Item	Temp (°F)	Time (mins)
Bacon (regular)	400 °F	5 to 7	Pork Tenderloin	370 °F	15
Bacon (thick cut)	400 °F	6 to 10	Sausages	380 °F	15
Pork Loin (2 lb.)	360 °F	55	Lamb Loin Chops (1-inch thick)	400 °F	8 to 12
Pork Chops, bone in (1-inch, 6.5 oz)	400 °F	12	Rack of Lamb (1.5 – 2 lb.)	380 °F	22

Fish & Seafood

Item	Temp (°F)	Time (mins)	Item	Temp (°F)	Time (mins)
Calamari (8 oz)	400 °F	4	Tuna Steak	400 °F	7 to 10
Fish Fillet (1-inch, 8 oz)	400 °F	10	Scallops	400 °F	5 to 7
Salmon, fillet (6 oz)	380 °F	12	Shrimp	400 °F	5
Swordfish steak	400 °F	10			

Vegetables

INGREDIENT	AMOUNT	PREPARATION	OIL	TEMP	COOK TIME
Asparagus	2 bunches	Cut in half, trim stems	2 Tbsp	420°F	12-15 mins
Beets	1½ lbs	Peel, cut in ½-inch cubes	1Tbsp	390°F	28-30 mins
Bell peppers (for roasting)	4 peppers	Cut in quarters, remove seeds	1Tbsp	400°F	15-20 mins
Broccoli	1 large head	Cut in 1-2-inch florets	1Tbsp	400°F	15-20 mins
Brussels sprouts	1lb	Cut in half, remove stems	1Tbsp	425°F	15-20 mins
Carrots	1lb	Peel, cut in ¼-inch rounds	1 Tbsp	425°F	10-15 mins
Cauliflower	1 head	Cut in 1-2-inch florets	2 Tbsp	400°F	20-22 mins
Corn on the cob	7 ears	Whole ears, remove husks	1 Tbps	400°F	14-17 mins
Green beans	1 bag (12 oz)	Trim	1 Tbps	420°F	18-20 mins
Kale (for chips)	4 oz	Tear into pieces,remove stems	None	325°F	5-8 mins
Mushrooms	16 oz	Rinse, slice thinly	1 Tbps	390°F	25-30 mins
Potatoes, russet	1½ lbs	Cut in 1-inch wedges	1 Tbps	390°F	25-30 mins
Potatoes, russet	1lb	Hand-cut fries, soak 30 mins in cold water, then pat dry	½ -3 Tbps	400°F	25-28 mins
Potatoes, sweet	1lb	Hand-cut fries, soak 30 mins in cold water, then pat dry	1 Tbps	400°F	25-28 mins
Zucchini	1lb	Cut in eighths lengthwise, then cut in half	1 Tbps	400°F	15-20 mins

Appendix ❷

index

Made in United States
Orlando, FL
11 December 2024

55381518R00057